Noam Chomsky has been described as 'arguably the most important intellectual alive'. His revolutionary work in linguistics has aroused intense scholarly interest, while his trenchant critique of United States foreign policy and his incisive analysis of the role of intellectuals in modern society have made him a prominent public figure.

Raphael Salkie's timely book introduces the two parts of Chomsky's work and explores the connections between them. He provides an accessible and up-to-date introduction to Chomsky's linguistics, laying out his basic assumptions and aims – in particular, his consistent drive to make linguistics a science – and looking at a sample of Chomsky's recent work. He examines the implications for other fields such as philosophy and psychology, as well as the main challenges to Chomsky's position.

Raphael Salkie also sets out the key themes in Chomsky's political writings and his libertarian socialist views. He contrasts the 'official line' on US foreign policy – the view that the US is a 'well-meaning, blundering giant' – with Chomsky's carefully argued alternative view. By focusing on Chomsky's conception of human nature and human freedom the author draws out the links between the two sides of Chomsky's work, in the belief that both sides raise issues which can profitably be explored. The author also provides a carefully annotated guide to further reading.

As an experienced teacher of linguistics with a commitment to political activism, Raphael Salkie is uniquely qualified to present this introduction to one of the seminal thinkers of our time.

The Chomsky Update

The Chomsky Update Linguistics and Politics

RAPHAEL SALKIE

London
UNWIN HYMAN
Boston   Sydney   Wellington

Published by the Academic Division of
Unwin Hyman Ltd
15/17 Broadwick Street, London W1V 1FP, UK

Unwin Hyman Inc.,
955 Massachusetts Avenue, Cambridge, MA 02139, USA

Allen & Unwin (Australia) Ltd,
8 Napier Street, North Sydney, NSW 2060, Australia

Allen & Unwin (New Zealand) Ltd in association with the
Port Nicholson Press Ltd,
Compusales Building, 75 Ghuznee Street, Wellington 1, New Zealand

First published in 1990

British Library Cataloguing in Publication Data

Salkie, Raphael
The Chomsky update : linguistics and politics.
1. Linguistics. Theories of Chomsky, Noam, 1928–. Political aspects
I. Title
410.92

ISBN 0-04-445589-5
ISBN 0-04-445590-9 pbk

Library of Congress Cataloging in Publication Data

Salkie, Raphael.
The Chomsky update : linguistics and politics / Raphael Salkie.
p. cm.
Includes bibliographical references (p.) and index.
ISBN 0-04-445589-5. – ISBN 0-445590-9 (pbk.)
1. Chomsky, Noam.   2. Chomsky, Noam–Political and social views.
I. Title.
P85.C47S24   1990
410′ .92–dc20   90-12690
                                                                                  CIP

Typeset in 10 on 12 point Palatino
Printed in Great Britain by Billing and Sons Ltd., Worcester

To Chana, Gabe, Joe and Ruby, with love and respect

Acknowledgements

Acknowledgement is due to the copyright holders for their kind permission to reprint the following extracts from books by Noam Chomsky: extracts from *After the Cataclysm* and *The Washington Connection and Third World Fascism* are reproduced by permission of Spokesman; extracts from James Peck (ed.), *The Chomsky Reader* are reproduced by permission of Serpents Tail; extracts from *The Culture of Terrorism* and *Turning the Tide* are reproduced by permission of Pluto Press and South End Press; extracts from *On Power and Ideology* are reproduced by permission of South End Press; extracts from *Language and Problems of Knowledge* are reproduced by permission of MIT Press; extracts from *Language and Responsibility* (originally published in French by Flammarion as *Dialogues avec Mitsou Ronat*) are reproduced by permission of Harvester Wheatsheaf; extracts from *Reflections on Language* are reproduced by permission of Gower publishing company and Pantheon Books, a division of Random House Inc.; extracts from Carlos Otero (ed.), *Radical Priorities* are reproduced by permission of Black Rose Books; extracts from *Rules and Representations* are reproduced by permission of Basil Blackwell; extracts from *Towards a New Cold War*, Copyright © 1973, 1975, 1978, 1979, 1980, 1981, 1982 by J. Leonard Schatz, Trustee of the Chomsky Children's Trust #2, are reprinted by permission of Pantheon Books, a division of Random House, Inc. Every effort has been made to contact the copyright holders of this material. The publishers would be happy to hear of any omissions.

Contents

Preface

This book aims to provide a guide to Noam Chomsky's work which is accurate, clear, responsible and deals with the crucial issues rather than the details.

Chomsky's linguistics first struck me as a worthwhile intellectual challenge when I was an undergraduate student of modern languages. For someone with an interest in language the rigour and sense of direction offered by generative grammar were a strong attraction. At the same time, Chomsky's powerful criticism of US involvement in Vietnam changed my understanding of politics in crucial ways. His elegant advocacy of libertarian socialism offered an alternative to the other flawed brands of left-wing politics.

I have now taught generative grammar for a number of years. My experience has been that students need an introduction to Chomsky's main assumptions and goals in order to appreciate the purpose of this type of linguistics. I also felt that an account of Chomsky's political work was needed, especially in view of the vicious attacks and distortions to which it has been subjected. Hence this book.

My wife Chana Moshenska has been a steadfast intellectual and political companion. Thanks to her I have been able to combine a satisfying intellectual life with active involvement as father to our three children. Barry Smerin taught me a lot about libertarian socialism and political action. From Arthur Oppenheimer I learned that there is life after capitalism. John Sloboda, Harvey Jackins, Su Edwards and Charlie Kreiner provided doses of inspiration.

Thanks to Fred Newmeyer, Tom Roeper, Carlos Otero, Philip Vellender and two anonymous Unwin Hyman readers, who supplied valuable comments on various drafts of the book. Noam Chomsky provided extensive comments and encouragement, for which I am extremely grateful. None of these are responsible for what I have done with their ideas. Sue Everson and Zamy Alibhai helped me on numerous occasions. Claire L'Enfant, Sarah Roberts-West and Alison Hobson from Unwin Hyman were helpful and encouraging from start to finish.

I would welcome any comments on the book, which should be sent to me care of the publisher.

Finally I should like to echo Hilary Putnam and wish Noam Chomsky the traditional Jewish 'biz hundert un tsvantsik' – 'May he live to be a hundred and twenty'.

Raphael Salkie
January 1990

List of Abbreviations

AC   *After the Cataclysm: Postwar Indochina and the Reconstruction of American Imperial Ideology* (with Edward Herman): Volume 2 of *Political Economy of Human Rights* (Nottingham: Spokesman, 1979).

APNM   *American Power and the New Mandarins* (Harmondsworth: Penguin, 1969).

ATS   *Aspects of the Theory of Syntax* (Cambridge, Mass.: MIT Press, 1965).

BB   *The Backroom Boys* (London: Fontana, 1973).

CR   *The Chomsky Reader*, edited by James Peck (London: Serpents Tail, 1987).

CT   *The Culture of Terrorism* (London: Pluto Press, 1988).

FT   *The Fateful Triangle: the United States, Israel and the Palestinians* (London: Pluto Press, 1983).

GE   *Noam Chomsky on the Generative Enterprise: a Discussion with Riny Huybregts and Henk van Riemsdijk* (Dordrecht: Foris, 1982).

HRAFP   *'Human rights' and American Foreign Policy* (Nottingham: Spokesman, 1978).

IC   'The ideas of Chomsky', in B. Magee, *Men of Letters* (Oxford: Oxford University Press, 1982), pp. 173–93.

KL   *Knowledge of Language: Its Nature, Origin and Use* (New York: Praeger, 1986).

LM   *Language and Mind*, enlarged edition (New York: Harcourt, Brace, Jovanovich, 1972).

LPK   *Language and Problems of Knowledge* (Cambridge, Mass.: MIT Press, 1988).

LR   *Language and Responsibility* (Hassocks, Sussex: Harvester Press, 1979).

OPI   *On Power and Ideology* (Boston: South End Press, 1987).

PKF   *Problems of Knowledge and Freedom* (London: Fontana, 1972).

QEA   'Quine's empirical assumptions', in D. Davidson and
           J. Hintikka (eds), *Words and Objections: Essays on the
           Work of W. V. Quine* (Dordrecht: D. Reidel, 1969),
           pp. 53–68.
RCTII   'Recent contributions to the theory of innate ideas',
           in *Synthese* 17 (1967), reprinted in J. Searle (ed.), *Phil-
           osophy of Language* (Oxford: Oxford University Press,
           1971), pp. 121–9.
RL   *Reflections on Language* (London: Temple Smith, 1975).
RP   *Radical Priorities*, edited by C. P. Otero (Montreal:
           Black Rose, 1983).
RR   *Rules and Representations* (Oxford: Basil Blackwell,
           1980).
RS   *For Reasons of State* (London: Fontana, 1973).
RVB   Review of *Verbal Behaviour* by B.F. Skinner, in J. Fodor
           and J. J. Katz (eds), *The Structure of Language: Readings
           in the Philosophy of Language* (Englewood Cliffs, NJ:
           Prentice Hall, 1964), pp. 547–78.
TNCW   *Towards a New Cold War: Essays on the Current Crisis
           and How We Got There* (New York: Pantheon, 1982).
TTT   *Turning the Tide: US Intervention in Central America and
           the Struggle for Peace* (London: Pluto Press, 1985).
WCTWF   *The Washington Connection and Third World Fascism*
           (with Edward Herman): Volume 1 of *Political Economy
           of Human Rights.* (Nottingham: Spokesman, 1979).

The Chomsky Update

Linguistics

'At the root of Chomsky's innovative impact on linguistics lie his philosophy of science and his epistemological approach to behaviour, both of which are revolutionary.'

Jacques Mehler

1
Basics

Introduction

Avram Noam Chomsky (the 'ch' is pronounced as in *church*) was born on 7 December 1928 in Philadelphia, Pennsylvania, USA. At the time of writing he is still very much alive and working as hard as ever. On a visit to Britain in 1989 he addressed audiences in various cities, recorded a national radio interview, and was the subject of several articles in newspapers and magazines.

Chomsky's father was a noted Hebrew scholar, and was the author of one of the most popular books about the Hebrew language.[1] The family were deeply involved in Jewish culture, the revival of Hebrew and the Zionist movement. At the same time, Chomsky was strongly influenced as a young man by the vigorous Jewish intellectual life in New York, where the dominant ideas, in contrast, were anti-Zionist and socialist. He was particularly close to an uncle in New York with whom he discussed literature, Karl Marx, and Sigmund Freud, and whose libertarian socialist views he found attractive. Chomsky experienced anti-semitism first-hand on the streets of Philadelphia as a child, and his political and intellectual development were deeply affected both by the rise of fascism and anti-semitism in Europe and by the public celebrations in his neighbourhood over early Nazi triumphs. His early interest in politics is indicated by an editorial about the Spanish civil war which he wrote for a school newspaper in 1939 (he returned to this subject at length in his first political book, *American Power and the New Mandarins*, published in 1969).

It was through a shared interest in left-libertarian Jewish politics that Chomsky met Zellig Harris, a teacher of linguistics under whom he studied at the University of Pennsylvania. After a short spell at Harvard, he moved to the Massachusetts Institute of Technology (MIT) in Boston, where he has been based ever since. In 1949 he married the linguist Carol Schatz; they have a son and two daughters. Chomsky's entire working life has been spent as a scholar in linguistics. When he entered the field in the late forties it was a small and specialized one; the high profile that linguistics has achieved since then has been largely due to him.

In the fifties and sixties, Chomsky became renowned within linguistics and in other related fields as the founder and foremost exponent of a new approach to linguistics called *Generative Grammar*. Chomsky energetically criticized some of the main assumptions in the field, proposing new ideas and new methods of research. At the same time, Chomsky also became widely known for very different reasons: his outspoken and courageous opposition to the American war in Vietnam. He spoke and wrote extensively about American foreign policy, criticizing in particular the role of intellectuals in justifying and promoting the war.

Since that time, Chomsky has written many books and articles about linguistics, and many about politics. He is in great demand as a speaker, travelling widely and often talking – separately – about linguistics and politics to two different audiences. Typically, he will speak to a prestigious academic audience one day about his latest research into language and the next to an audience of socialists and peace activists about politics.

For many people, Chomsky is puzzling. Very few academics of his distinction are willing to dirty their hands with political activity to the extent that he does. His decision to take a stand against United States involvement in Vietnam in the early sixties was made in the belief that he would end up in jail for publicly supporting resistance to the draft. Since then he has been equally outspoken about American involvement in other areas, particularly the Middle East, the Pacific region and Central America, although his writings touch on all parts of the world. Pressure of time has meant that he has been unable to devote himself to linguistics to the extent he would have wished.

It isn't just Chomsky's involvement in linguistics and politics which has made people sit up and think: the quality of his work in both areas has been outstanding. John Searle writes that 'Chomsky's work is one of the most remarkable intellectual achievements of the present era, comparable in scope and coherence to the work of Keynes or Freud.'[2] The *New York Times Book Review* once described Chomsky as 'arguably the most important intellectual alive', to which Carlos Otero, suggesting that no one else comes close, added the comment: 'it is hard not to wonder who could be a plausible candidate for third place' (RP, 11). In a recent anthology of his political writings, the editor James Peck writes: 'No one has exposed more forcefully the self-righteous beliefs on which America's imperial role is based . . . No one has focussed more compellingly on the violence of our world, or conveyed more directly the responsibility of the United States for much of it' (CR, viii). These views may be overstated, although even if they are, any thinking person will want at least a minimal knowledge of his ideas so that they can judge for themselves. In any case, Chomsky's high profile in two very different areas makes it worth asking what makes this extraordinary man tick.

In this book I shall look separately at Chomsky's linguistics and his politics, and then examine what links there may be between the two. The aim of the book is to give a basic outline of his most important ideas: readers who want to know more can then turn to more specialized books, or read Chomsky's writings for themselves (see the guide to further reading at the end of the book). We begin with linguistics: the rest of this chapter looks at the basic questions which Chomsky is concerned with in this side of his work.

What linguistics isn't

Chomsky's basic aim is to make linguistics a science. He has consistently held to this aim throughout his work, and it lies behind everything he has done.

In order to understand what this means, we shall need to look carefully at the terms *linguistics* and *science*. Even before we do this, though, one thing is clear. Chomsky didn't invent linguistics, so there must be other types of linguistics which he regards as not scientific. Let's start, then, by taking a look at linguistics, distinguishing between what Chomsky sees as the unscientific types and his own scientific linguistics.

Linguistics is the name for the field of study which deals with language[3]. That much is easy, but for a number of reasons we need to enlarge this definition. Firstly, everybody is interested in language to some extent. Apart from people with certain disabilities we all talk with others, most people in industrialized countries read and write, and many of us learn more than one language. A few people are fascinated by language – they learn lots of languages, play Scrabble, do crosswords, like looking at dictionaries, admire beautiful and elegant language, or delight in imitating a variety of speech styles. This does not mean, however, that these people are doing linguistics: linguistics is more than an informal interest in language, however strong that interest is.

Most people are only concerned with language when they have a difficulty with it. Sometimes we can't find the right words for what we want to say: we get tongue-tied or muddled. Or we can't remember how to spell a word. We often have trouble with punctuation. We may find it hard to learn a second language. Some people have hearing difficulties, or speech difficulties – perhaps a stammer, or difficulty making certain sounds – or difficulties in learning to read and write. We may find the technical words and convoluted sentences of scientists or lawyers difficult to understand. People who study difficulties like these, and try to help others to deal with them, are not necessarily engaged in linguistics: linguistics is not a collection of methods to help people with language problems.

Some people work with language all the time. Authors and journalists write articles and books. Politicians make speeches. Actors have to memorize their lines. Translators take ideas expressed in one language and recreate them in another language. Advertisers choose the best words to sell a product. Students in schools and colleges use language to write essays. This is still not linguistics: using language is not the same as studying it.

Many people study and discuss language. Literary critics analyse a writer's use of language. Lexicographers – people who produce dictionaries – look carefully at how words are used. People who are interested in the history of languages (such people are often called *philologists*) look at how languages change over time, and sometimes use old manuscripts as clues about how people lived in the past, rather like archeologists use other relics. Many philosophers have written about language and its relation to thought and knowledge. The code-breakers who 'cracked' enemy codes during the Second World War did so largely on the basis of statistical information about which letters and words occur most frequently in different languages. Yet none of these people would automatically accept that what they are doing is linguistics.

The last four paragraphs show four different negative ways to help us see what linguistics is. Firstly, linguistics is not just informal thinking about language, no matter how intensive and challenging. Linguistics is not a way to solve the problems of language users. Linguistics is the study of language, not the use of language. And linguistics is not an interest in language for some other purpose.

What linguistics is

Having seen what linguistics is *not*, you are probably wondering by now what this leaves. Let us, then, begin to look more positively at linguistics by looking at some questions about language which many of the areas we have excluded from linguistics touch on in passing. Two such questions are these: firstly, how many languages are there in the world? Secondly, what are the main differences and similarities between them?

These are not simple questions. If we want to know how many different languages there are in the world, we first have to be sure that we have covered the whole world, and we next have to agree on what counts as a language. Do northern British English, broad West Country English and New Zealand English count as three different languages or as three varieties of one language? If we count Danish and Norwegian as two distinct languages, what do we say about the fact that a Dane and a Norwegian can probably understand each other better than speakers of the three types of English just mentioned?

Looking at the similarities and differences between languages is also not straightforward. The differences are perhaps easier.

People who have learned a foreign language can usually point to one or two sounds which are very different from English sounds: the vowel in the French word *lune* 'moon', for instance, or the sound at the beginning of Welsh words like *Llandudno*. Likewise, someone who has learned German can point to the word order of German as different from that of English: *Heute habe ich das Buch gelesen*, translated word for word, comes out as 'Today have I the book read': the word order in English would be *I have read the book today*. Some languages have words which are almost impossible to translate into English, either because they have special emotional overtones (French *soixante-huitard*, or *poilu*, German *Gemüt* or *Spiessbürger*), or because they refer to things not usually found outside the area where the language is spoken (French *baguette*, German *Praktikantenausweis*). What counts as 'polite' also varies from language to language: English softens the force of commands by using *Will you . . .* or *Would you mind . . .*, while other languages do this in other ways, or rarely at all.

Suppose we wanted to investigate these matters in more depth. To get a broader picture of pronunciation differences, we would need to know how we make speech sounds, and develop a way of classifying different sounds. To study word-order differences we would need to classify words in each language and devise a way to describe different word-order patterns. To look at vocabulary differences we would need to look at how languages refer to the world, and distinguish different types of meaning that an expression can have: general, specific, emotional, scientific, and so on. To look at politeness in language we would need to classify different relationships between speakers and look at the ways in which a language reflects these relationships.

We have looked at four types of difference between languages: pronunciation, grammar, vocabulary and relationships between speakers. In each case we have highlighted the need to classify the relevant facts, so that we can distinguish between them. Now we are beginning to see what is distinctive about linguistics. All the examples we gave earlier which didn't come under the heading of linguistics were of people who want to talk about language for a particular purpose. What all these people need is agreement on the basic terminology which they can use to talk about language. Any specialized terminology presupposes that the things to which you want to give names have been classified, so that there is agreement about when to use which term. In the four areas we mentioned, we need to agree about terms like *vowel, consonant, noun, participle, meaning,* and *command.* Linguistics, then, is the field which classifies (among other things) the pronunciation, grammar, meaning and use of language and hence provides terminology to talk about these matters along with clear criteria for the correct use of each term.

This way of thinking about linguistics makes the field sound as if its role is purely to serve other fields of knowledge. If linguistics merely provides some terminology which can be used by lexicographers, speech therapists, translators , language teachers and Scrabble enthusiasts, then the field is no doubt useful but not very exciting or high-powered. While many linguists would accept their servicing role, they would argue that their subject does indeed have great depth and intellectual rigour. There are several thousand languages in the world, each one a rich and complex system which is deeply embedded in the culture and society of its speakers. Developing a terminology to encompass such a vast and diverse range of languages is an intellectual feat of the first order.

Modern linguistics emerged as a distinct field in the nineteenth and early twentieth century. This was the heyday of colonialism, when Europeans and Americans went out and seized large parts of the planet. One result of this process was a growing realization that the languages of Europe, diverse though they may be, are but a fraction of the languages of the world. At the same time, it became clear that many of the languages of Africa, Asia and the native peoples of America were under threat as their speakers were wiped out by colonialists or switched to colonial languages. The late nineteenth and early twentieth century saw a huge effort by European and American linguists to travel to where these languages were spoken, make friends with one or more native speakers, and learn enough about the language to describe it as fully as possible in a short time. The expertise, intuition, human warmth, patience and determination this work demands are enormous (especially since the tape recorder, an invaluable tool for such work, did not appear on the scene until very late on).

The picture I have painted of linguistics as a discipline ancillary to others is quite accurate for the period before Chomsky. Many of the major figures from this time studied linguistics along with other fields: some were also anthropologists, like Edward Sapir; some were teachers of foreign languages and literature, like Martin Joos; some were philosophers, like John Austin; others were psychologists, mathematicians and sociologists. There were few university departments devoted to nothing but linguistics. Journals, books and professional associations devoted to linguistics appeared, but many of the people involved also worked in other areas of study.

One further point about this type of linguistics is its relationship to language teaching. The period we are talking about – the nineteenth and the first half of the twentieth century – was one in which international travel and contacts increased enormously, as a result partly of colonialism and partly of technological advances in transport and communication. The need to learn foreign languages increased accordingly. Linguists who were experts in such languages and could describe them accurately were in a good position to help. During the Second World War, when it was important for many people to learn the basics of languages like Russian and Japanese quickly, many experts in linguistics were heavily involved in teaching them. A body of expertise in language learning and teaching grew up, once again with a clear servicing role: to help people teach and learn languages.

Differences, then similarities

Our discussion so far has concentrated on differences between languages. The kind of linguistics we have outlined does indeed emphasize differences, rather than similarities, between languages, for very understandable reasons. The main danger in writing descriptions of a wide range of languages is that the linguist will impose a classification system from one language on to the others. In the days when classical Latin and Greek were used widely by educated Europeans, the modern languages were sometimes described using concepts from the grammars of Latin and Greek, which were often hopelessly inappropriate for other languages. The silly and reactionary idea that the classical languages were superior to modern ones, which are supposedly corrupt and sloppy, led to all kinds of distortions in the description of modern languages. A further distorting factor at this time was the assumption that only written language was worth describing, spoken language being dismissed as degenerate and lacking in structure.

Linguists aimed instead to describe each language in its own terms. They rejected untenable ideas about the superiority of classical languages, and also fought against the colonialist notion that the languages of the native peoples who were enslaved, killed and plundered were just primitive grunts and gestures. Many such languages did not have a writing system, but were none the less complex and highly structured: this meant a shift in emphasis to the description of speech as opposed to writing. Each language was to be treated with complete respect, which meant not trying to force it into any particular mould.

None the less, the question of what languages had in common became increasingly important during this period, particularly in the study of speech sounds (phonetics) and how each language organizes its sounds (phonology). The sounds of an unfamiliar language are its most accessible part: you don't need to know a language's grammar, or to understand what its speakers are saying, to describe the sounds its speakers are making. Phonetics and phonology therefore developed rapidly during this period, and linguists began to be able to generalize about which sounds were common in the languages of the world and which were rare. General phonological principles, applicable to any language, could be proposed. Some linguists began to formulate the hypothesis that as children learn to make speech sounds, they do so in a sequence which is constant for all languages and does not depend on the sounds they hear around them.

In other areas of linguistics, proposals about similarities between languages were less developed, but none the less began to be put forward. Charles Hockett devised a set of criteria which distinguish human languages from animal communication systems. Some general principles of grammar were also proposed.

Joseph Greenberg began to notice regular connections between
different parts of grammar in a wide range of languages.
The French linguist Gustave Guillaume argued that the psychological mechanisms underlying our use of language were
common to all languages. A general method for analysing any
language was proposed by Zellig Harris, Chomsky's teacher,
in a book, *Methods in Structural Linguistics*,[4] which summarized
the descriptive, classificatory linguistics of this period. While
these attempts to think about similarities between languages
did take place during this period, they were exceptions to the
main emphasis on differences between languages.

Linguistics as a science

We can now try to encapsulate the different view of linguistics
that Chomsky put forward when he arrived on the scene in the
mid-fifties. Perhaps the most important differences are these:

1. Chomsky rejects the view that the best way to think of lin-
    guistics is as a field which services other fields by providing
    a classification and a terminology to talk about language.
2. He emphasizes similarities between languages, rather than
    differences.
3. Chomsky tends to focus on well-studied languages like
    English rather than languages from far afield.

The first of these points is the most important one. What
Chomsky is proposing here is a new method for studying
language. The second and third points reflect the subject-matter
to which he proposes to apply this method. In other words, the
first point involves the type of questions about language which
Chomsky thinks are worth asking. The other two points relate
to the kinds of answers he gives to these questions.

Chomsky often compares the kind of linguistics we have
just been discussing to 'natural history' or 'butterfly collecting'. Museums in Europe and America are full of weird and
wonderful plants and animals which were collected as another
by-product of European colonialism. Many of the explorers who
travelled to Asia, Africa and America were fascinated by the

wild life they found there, which they studied and collected. Naturally, one of the key issues which faced naturalists at this time was how to classify, describe and name the numerous new species which were constantly being discovered.

Not only did this activity take place at the same period, and for the same reasons, as the development of linguistics, but the methods employed were similar in many respects. When you are collecting specimens – whether of plants or of languages – obviously the more you can find, the better. The more exotic, unusual, or beautiful the specimen is, the more interesting it is. The differences between specimens are crucial for classifying them. Rigorous and reliable fieldwork techniques are vital. All this work demands great patience and attention to detail, as well as the time and money to travel and, in the case of natural history, the money to store specimens safely.

Chomsky claims that in linguistics, at least, it is possible to go further than this. No matter how diligently people collect specimens, and how painstakingly they classify them, what they are doing is not science, in his view. All they are doing is describing, with varying degrees of care and sometimes brilliantly, the way things are. The point about science, for Chomsky, is that it seeks to explain *why* things are the way they are.

It is the search for *explanations* which in Chomsky's eyes distinguishes science from other human activities. This is important, because many people think that the key thing about science is its subject-matter, the things that scientists study. For such people the essential point is that science is the study of the physical world, concentrating on what it is made of (chemistry), the forces and energy that operate in it (physics), living things (biology), stars and planets (astronomy), and so on. Things that are not physical (the mind, emotions, human behaviour, art and literature, etc.) cannot be part of science.

For Chomsky (and, in fairness, for most philosophers of science), it is the search for explanations, attempts to answer the question why, which are the essence of science. Another way of putting this is that science is more than just the collection of facts or specimens: science is about solving puzzles. A puzzle is a problem or a group of related problems which does not have an obvious solution. To solve a puzzle you have to observe the facts closely, decide which facts are relevant and which aren't, making imaginative guesses, and then check your guesses using rigorous logical reasoning. A detective trying to establish who committed a crime and why, for example, has to observe the available evidence, eliminate irrelevant information, follow his or her best hunch about the identity of the criminal, and support that hunch by a careful chain of reasoning.

The puzzles which scientists deal with tend to be more far-reaching than those which preoccupy detectives. Scientists have wanted to know, for example, why the size of the moon changes from night to night; which substances burn best and why; how to prevent and cure disease; how to navigate on the open seas; or, to take an example from linguistics, why many English words are similar to German ones (man :: Mann; father :: Vater; brother :: Bruder, etc.). The achievement of a scientist is measured by the importance and complexity of the puzzles she or he sets out to solve, and the degree of success achieved in solving them.

Along with many others, Chomsky sees physics as the science which has recorded the most outstanding achievements. He therefore takes physics as his model in attempting to make linguistics a science, referring frequently to the success of physics in his writings. Let us now, therefore, take a look at the history of this science, picking out the crucial parts which can serve as a model for other fields of study.

A brief foray into the history of physics

One of the principal periods in which physics made major advances was the seventeenth and eighteenth centuries, when people like Nicolas Copernicus, Galileo Galilei and Isaac Newton dismantled the previous orthodoxy, which was based largely on the ideas of Aristotle.[5]

Aristotle believed that the earth was the centre of the universe, and that the sun, the moon and the moving stars (what we would now call the planets) rotated round the earth. When we observe the sun and the moon, they both appear to move in a circle around us: it is thus understandable that a first attempt to describe this movement should treat the sun and the moon in the same way. Aristotelian physics also raised some deeper issues. Firstly, why do the sun and the moon move in this way? And secondly, how does this type of motion tie in with everyday motion on earth? If we drop something, it falls in a straight line, not in a circle. The Aristotelians had to say that heavenly motion and terrestrial motion were two quite different things, one circular, the other in straight lines. They included under 'terrestrial motion' such things as vision and the growth of plants, as well as the movement of objects.

Careful observation of the movement of the planets led Copernicus to believe that Aristotle's account of heavenly motion was inadequate. Galileo subsequently cast further doubt on the orthodox view when the development of telescopes enabled him to observe the moons of Jupiter. Galileo's aim was not only to replace Aristotle's account of heavenly motion, but also to unify heavenly and terrestrial motion. If the earth was the centre of the universe, different laws of motion might apply to it from those which governed the movement of minor items like the sun and the moon. But if the earth was just one of a number of planets which rotated round the sun, as the evidence now strongly suggested, there was no reason to expect motion on earth to have a special status.

In order to achieve this unified theory, Galileo had to narrow the concept of motion to mechanical motion, excluding areas like biological growth which Aristotle had tried to cover. He also had to face the fact that there were certain observations even within this narrowed domain that his new theory could not handle: as Chomsky notes, 'Galileo did not abandon his enterprise because he was unable to give a coherent explanation for the fact that objects do not fly off the earth's surface' (RR, 10). Galileo's new theory could explain certain things more successfully than Aristotle's, so he was content to assume that the problems with his theory would be solved at some point in the future. It was Newton's theory of gravity which later solved the particular problem to which Chomsky refers. Newton proposed that one force – gravity – could explain terrestrial and heavenly motion at the same time.

In some respects, the theory of Galileo and Newton had a wider scope than that of Aristotle, since it handled terrestrial and heavenly motion in the same way and could explain certain phenomena, such as the moons of Jupiter, which Aristotle's theory could not. In other respects, the new theory had a narrower scope. It excluded certain phenomena, such as biological growth, which the earlier theory had tried to cover. *Galileo and Newton were convinced that the increased insight and unity in the more limited domain outweighed the disadvantage of the narrower overall scope of the theory.*

Another feature of the new theory was its *abstractness*. As we saw, the Aristotelian theory of heavenly motion was initially plausible because the motion of the sun and that of the moon appear to the ordinary observer to be the same. Galileo's theory seemed to fly in the face of this observation, and explained the apparent circular movement of the sun in different terms. His willingness to take everyday experiences and look at them in seemingly counter-intuitive ways meant that his theory was abstract: it did not directly reflect the way we perceive reality, but started with notions, such as the rotation of the earth round its axis, which require a leap of the imagination. Of course, his theory had to explain why we have the everyday experience in question: scientific theories are not just speculative intellectual exercises, like pure mathematics, but stand or fall by the success with which they explain the real world. They do not, however, have to do this directly. Galileo's theory was complex: it started with some abstract notions and involved a chain of inferences and calculations before it made contact successfully, or at least more successfully than the older theory, with the real world.

Another successful abstraction was the idea of gravity in Newton's work. As we've seen, Newton proposed that heavenly and terrestrial motion could be unified with the idea of gravity, a force which in his theory operated in perfectly straight lines. Clearly, this theory was more abstract than Aristotle's, in which heavenly motion was circular – as it appears to the ordinary observer. It is worth emphasizing, though, that the idea of gravity is abstract even in relation to terrestrial motion. If we throw a ball, it does not move in a straight line but in an arc. An object dropped on to a flat surface does not move in a perfectly straight line if we measure it carefully. But in Newton's theory, all movement is in a perfectly straight line. His theory *idealizes* what actually happens in order to achieve a successful explanation of why things happen.

The history of physics, of which we have only given the barest outline here, is widely – and rightly – regarded as one of the greatest intellectual achievements of all time. It took painstaking observation, courage, imagination and persistence to construct the profound and complex theories which have had such a far-reaching impact. The important features of the success of physics for our purposes are these:

1. The conviction that explanation is more important than just describing and classifying a wide range of data.
2. The willingness to narrow the data which physicists attempted to explain, and to put off for the time being problems that could not be solved at the time.
3. Abstraction and idealization, using concepts and principles often remote from everyday experience.
4. The recognition that being proved wrong does not devalue a scientist's contribution. This point is worth expanding on. The fact that Aristotelian physics was overturned does not detract from Aristotle's monumental achievement. In the same way, the theory of Galileo and Newton has now been largely replaced by relativity and quantum theory, but this does not take away from their achievement. In a healthy scientific field, new observations are constantly being made and new theories continually being put forward. What is correct in the older theory can often be incorporated into the new theory. And finally, the *methods* used by successful scientists in the past can be studied and used by scientists today.

Back to linguistics as a science

We can now see what Chomsky says about the use of the scientific method in linguistics, expanding the remarks cited above about Galileo:

> The 'Galilean style' in physics is 'making abstract mathematical models of the universe to which at least the physicists give a higher degree of reality than they accord the ordinary world

of sensation' . . . We have no present alternative to pursuing the 'Galilean style' in the natural sciences at least.

Some might argue . . . that we can do still better in the 'human sciences' by pursuing a different path. I do not mean to disparage such possibilities. It is not unlikely, for example, that literature will forever give far deeper insight into what is sometimes called 'the full human person' than any mode of scientific inquiry can hope to do. But I am interested here in a different question: to what extent and in what ways can inquiry in something like the 'Galilean style' yield insight and understanding of the roots of human nature in the cognitive domain? Can we hope to move beyond superficiality by a readiness to undertake perhaps far-reaching idealisation and to construct abstract models that are accorded more significance than the ordinary world of sensation, and correspondingly, by readiness to tolerate unexplained phenomena or even as yet unexplained counterevidence to theoretical constructions that have achieved a certain degree of explanatory adequacy in some limited domain, much as Galileo did not abandon his enterprise because he was unable to give a coherent explanation for the fact that objects do not fly off the earth's surface. (RR, 8–10)

The first thing to note is that Chomsky does not mention language in this passage: what he is concerned with, he says, is 'the roots of human nature in the cognitive domain'. We shall see later why he formulates the problem in this way: for now, we can simply imagine that he is talking about language. Essentially, then, Chomsky is proposing to apply the 'Galilean style' to language. He is not saying that this is the only way to study language, merely that it is the way which interests him. He emphasizes the need for idealization and abstraction, and for narrowing the domain of inquiry, leaving aside unresolved problems for the future so long as the theory has been reasonably successful in a limited area.

In the following passages, Chomsky spells out the specific questions which he wishes to investigate in this 'Galilean' way:

A person who speaks a language has developed a certain system of knowledge, represented somehow in the mind and, ultimately, in the brain in some physical configuration. In pursuing an inquiry into these topics, then, we face a series of questions, among them:

1. What is the system of knowledge? What is in the mind/brain of the speaker of English or Spanish or Japanese?
2. How does this system of knowledge arise in the mind/brain?
3. How is this knowledge put to use in speech (or secondary systems such as writing)?
4. What are the physical mechanisms that serve as the material basis for this system of knowledge and for the use of this knowledge? (LPK, 3)

The answer to the first question is given by a particular generative grammar, a theory concerned with the state of the mind/brain of the person who knows a particular language. The answer to the second is given by a specification of Universal Grammar (UG) along with an account of the ways in which its principles interact with experience to yield a particular language; UG is a theory of the 'initial state' of the language faculty, prior to any linguistic experience. The answer to the third question would be a theory of how the knowledge of language attained enters into the expression of thought and the understanding of presented specimens of language, and derivatively, into communication and other special uses of language. (KL, 3–4)

The fourth question is a relatively new one, in fact one that is still on the horizon. The first three questions fall within the domain of linguistics and psychology, two fields that I would prefer not to distinguish, regarding linguistics (or more precisely, those areas of linguistics with which I am concerned here) as just that part of psychology that deals with the particular aspects of this discipline outlined in the first three questions. Let me stress also that I would include large areas of philosophy under the same rubric, following traditional though not modern practice. Insofar as the linguist can provide answers to questions 1, 2 and 3, the brain scientist can begin to explore the physical mechanisms that exhibit the properties revealed in the linguist's abstract theory. In the absence of answers to these questions, brain scientists do not know what they are looking for: their inquiry is in this respect blind. (LPK, 6)

Generative Grammar

We can see here how far Chomsky has moved from the descriptive, classificatory linguistics he rejects. As his first question shows, he is not interested in describing particular samples of spoken or written language, but rather in the 'system of knowledge' which a speaker of a language has in her/his head. This is still description, but of a rather different order than early descriptive linguistics, and Chomsky gives a special name to such a description: *Generative Grammar*. We shall look at some examples of generative grammar in Chapter 3. A generative grammar of a language must be completely *explicit*: if it genuinely describes exactly what is in the head of a speaker of that language, it must spell out even the things that someone reading it might take as obvious. In other words, it must not assume, implicitly or explicitly, that whoever is reading it is linguistically informed or will sympathize if it cuts corners. It should be explicit enough for a mindless automaton – for example, a computer – to use it without any help.

Some people argue that Chomsky is wrong to use the word *knowledge* to describe what is in the head of a speaker of a language. We shall return to this issue in Chapter 5. Notice, however, the way in which he uses the terms *mind* and *brain*. The human brain is a physical object, which can be studied just like any other physical object (though its extraordinary complexity means that there is much about the brain that is still poorly understood). The word *mind*, on the other hand, is a tricky one. Philosophers have disagreed strongly about what the mind is, some saying that we shouldn't use the term in science at all, others saying that mental phenomena are completely different from physical ones. In Chomsky's usage, talking about the mind is just an abstract way of talking about the brain. By studying the way people behave, we can theorize about what is going on in their mind.

For example, speakers of English normally put adjectives in front of nouns: we say *generative grammar* rather than **grammar generative* (the asterisk is used in linguistics to mark bad, ungrammatical expressions). Speakers of French normally put the adjective after the noun : *grammaire générative*. To capture these different regularities, we can say that the mind of an English speaker contains a different piece of knowledge from that of a French speaker. A generative grammar of English will include a rule saying that the adjective precedes the noun, while a generative grammar of French will contain a different rule (we are using *rule* here to mean 'a statement which captures an observed regularity about a language', not 'a piece of advice about how to talk properly, which you can choose to obey or not').

Chomsky argues that if these rules can be shown to be in the 'minds' of speakers, then they must exist in some physical form in their 'brains'. So when he uses the terms *mind* and *brain*, he is not talking about different things, but about the same thing in two different ways. When he talks about rules in the mind, he is talking abstractly, not worrying about the precise physical form these rules take. As he makes clear in his comments on question 4, the latter question is not part of linguistics but falls in the province of the brain scientist. It is rather like talking about a piece of music, say Mozart's Jupiter Symphony. A music theorist will be concerned with the score, which is an abstract set of instructions about how to play the symphony, while a conductor will be interested in a particular concrete performance of the score. The two perspectives are different, though each can enrich the other.

At the beginning of the section on linguistics as science, we noted that Chomsky prefers to concentrate on well-studied languages like English (though some of his early work was on Hebrew). The reason for this should now be clear. A generative grammar must be explicit and detailed. It is much easier to achieve this for a language which you know well than for one you are in the process of learning from scratch. Any language will do: English has no privileged status, apart from the accidental fact that it is Chomsky's native language, and indeed generative work has been done on hundreds of languages. The point is that linguists who try to learn and describe languages different from their own may produce useful descriptive material, but the kind of explicit detail to which generative grammar aspires is a different matter.

Universal Grammar

So far we have not moved from description to explanation, even if the description is of a different order from traditional linguistics. The crucial step toward explanation – the step that can make linguistics look more like physics than butterfly collecting – comes for Chomsky in his second question: How does this system of knowledge arise in the mind/brain?

A more familiar way of asking this question might be: How do people learn their native language? For Chomsky, this formulation makes the unjustified assumption that 'learning' is the only thing involved. It is in principle possible – indeed, probable – that human beings are predisposed to learn a language by our psychological make-up (ultimately, our biological make-up: recall that for him, psychology is just an abstract way of looking at biology), and that this predisposition is passed on by our genes. The simple fact that no other organism on earth has anything resembling language argues strongly that genetic factors play a part, though how important a part is an empirical question, one that we can only answer by looking at the evidence.

Linguists usually, in fact, talk of 'acquiring' our first language, to avoid the assumption that learning is the only mechanism involved. Mastering one's first language is a quite different process from learning a second language later in life. Someone who wants to learn a second language normally needs instruction in the form of a language course or classes. She or he will undertake regular exercises, and may make use of such things as dictionaries, grammars, phrase books, audio and video tapes, and language laboratories. Clearly, this is 'learning' in the normal sense of the word. An English speaker who learns Russian does it in basically the same way as someone studying mathematics or history: by mastering certain skills and absorbing new information. The process is often painstaking and difficult, and there is a need for constant instruction and practice. Only in rare cases is perfect mastery achieved.

Compare this with the way a first language is mastered. Young people receive little or no explicit instruction. They do not, in general, need to attend classes, consult grammars or dictionaries, or take special courses. Yet by the age of five or six almost every human being – severe disability aside – has mastered most of the vocabulary, pronunciation and grammar of her or his native language. The general intelligence of the person concerned apparently plays a relatively small part. All a young human needs is regular exposure to a language, and she or he will acquire it. It is because of of these striking differences between the two processes that linguists use the terms first language *acquisition* and second language *learning*.

First language acquisition is a fascinating thing to observe.[6] Parents are often delighted and amazed as their children first gurgle and babble at random, go on to form single words and sequences of words, and finally construct whole sentences. The range of things that a young person can talk about increases at the same time, of course, and new possibilities for learning, imaginative play, social interaction and taking charge of the environment open up as language develops. In recent times this process has been studied and researched intensively. There have been many studies of individuals and groups learning a wide range of languages, and a great deal of insight into the process of language acquisition has been gained.

One thing must be made clear here: Chomsky himself has not contributed directly to this research. His own work has been limited to answering question 1, and the first half of his proposed answer to question 2: 'a specification of Universal Grammar': as for the second half of question 2, 'an account of the ways in which UG interacts with experience to yield a particular language', he has been content to leave that to others. There is a logical sequence here: clearly, you have to begin to describe a system of knowledge (question 1) before you can ask how it is acquired, and you have to make some proposals about the initial state of the language faculty (first half of question 2) before looking at how the faculty develops and interacts with experience. This is not to say that you have

to know everything about the system of knowledge before
you can ask how it is acquired. And of course, research into
acquisition can influence our ideas about the nature of what
is acquired. The better the work is in Chomsky's own areas,
however, the more fruitful interaction there is likely to be
with research on actual language acquisition. Chomsky sees
himself as preparing the ground for a successful theory of
first language acquisition, even if his contribution to the field
is indirect.

Chomsky proposes that one part of our biological make-
up is specifically designed for language: he calls it *the language faculty*. To answer question 2, we need to specify what
this faculty contains at birth, and describe the contribution
that learning makes. The initial state of the language faculty is called *Universal Grammar* (UG). One point is worth
stressing here: at present we have no direct evidence about
the state of the language faculty at birth. We cannot, to put
it crudely, open a baby's head and look inside. This does not
mean that we are reduced to uninformed speculation, however: if we have an explicit, generative grammar of at least
one language, and if we can demonstrate that only parts
of that grammar were learned from experience, it follows
that whatever is left must be part of UG, that is, part of
human biology. We shall see a detailed example of this type
of reasoning in the next chapter. If some grammatical rule
or principle is part of UG, that explains why it is found in
the grammar of English (and, supposedly, every other language). UG thus enables us to move from description to explanation.

We can leave these issues for now by clarifying what we
said at the beginning of the section on linguistics as a science
about Chomsky's emphasis on what languages have in common
rather than on what distinguishes them. The point is that
'universal' means what it says. If there is a significant genetic
element in language acquisition, it must be common to all
human beings: there is no evidence that any particular people
are predisposed to learn one language rather than others. For
linguists who are interested in this genetic element, finding
features which are common to all languages may therefore be
a vital first step.

Use of language

Chomsky's third question asks how knowledge of language is put to use. What is noteworthy here is not the answers he proposes, but the assumptions which underlie the question. Chomsky makes a distinction between knowledge of language, other psychological mechanisms involved in the use of language, and physical skills which are needed to produce and understand language. An example of another psychological mechanism which plays a part in language use is memory: acquiring a particular language involves memorizing many words and their meanings, for instance. Our memory is not restricted to language, however: we memorize many other things in the course of our lives. Memory is therefore a distinct faculty from the language faculty, but one which interacts with the language faculty in important ways.

Physical skills necessary to use language include the ability to move our mouth, tongue, vocal cords, and so on to produce speech sounds, and the ability to hear and distinguish between different sounds. Like memory, these skills are crucial in our ordinary use of language, but they are not specific to language. We use the same organs for eating, whistling, and so on as we do for speaking, and our ears can distinguish many other sounds and noises than just speech sounds. These skills may deteriorate, as a result of injury or disease, while the language faculty remains intact. It is thus possible – indeed, Chomsky would argue, necessary – to distinguish the language faculty as a unique part of the mind, ultimately the brain.

Another assumption in the way Chomsky formulates question 3 is that communication is just one special use of language among others. Many people, including many linguists, would disagree with him here: they would claim that the whole point of language is to enable people to communicate with each other. Here is what Chomsky has to say on this point:

> What is the function of language? It is frequently alleged that the function of language is communication, that its 'essential purpose' is to enable people to communicate with each other. It is further alleged that only by attending to this essential purpose can we make any sense of the nature of language.

It is not easy to evaluate this contention. What does it mean to say that language has an 'essential purpose'? Suppose that in the quiet of my study I think about a problem, using language, and even write down what I think. Suppose that someone speaks honestly, merely out of a sense of integrity, fully aware that his audience will refuse to comprehend or even consider what he is saying. Consider informal conversation conducted for the sole purpose of maintaining friendly relations, with no particular concern as to its content. Are these examples of 'communication'? If so, what do we mean by 'communication' in the absence of an audience, or with an audience assumed to be completely unresponsive, or with no intention to convey information or modify belief or attitude?

It seems that either we must deprive the notion 'communication' of all significance, or else we must reject the view that the purpose of language is communication. While it is quite commonly argued that the purpose of language is communication and that it is pointless to study language apart from its communicative function, there is no formulation of this belief, to my knowledge, from which any substantive proposals follow. (RR, 229–30)

It is important to be clear about what Chomsky is doing here. He is not saying that the study of language and communication is impossible, or uninteresting. As his outlined answer to question 3 showed, the study of communication is one part of his research programme. What he is doing is defending himself against the argument that his type of linguistics is pointless or impossible because it does not make communication central. We shall see many other examples of this kind, where Chomsky defends his basic approach against often bitter attacks. He does not usually counterattack by saying that what his critics propose instead is pointless or impossible. Instead, he defends the integrity of his approach, and says that *if* you are interested in explanation rather than description, and *if* you want to achieve the kind of profound and complex theories in linguistics which have been so successful in physics, then his approach offers the best prospects. His aim is to counter those who say that their approach is the *only* correct one.

The attacks on Chomsky's work have often been bitter and angry, so Chomsky's responses have not always been models of objectivity: dismissing traditional linguistics as 'butterfly collecting', for example, is not likely to win you many friends. On the other hand, the virulence of the attacks on Chomsky has often been ludicrous. Charles Hockett described different parts of his work as 'completely bankrupt'[7] and 'unmitigated nonsense'.[8] Yorick Wilks wrote that his ideas were 'an intellectual embarrassment';[9] other writers have described his work as 'catastrophic',[10] 'an intellectual fraud',[11] and 'a rubbish-heap'.[12] In Chapter 5 we shall look at the more important – and less irrational – challenges to Chomsky's linguistics.[13] What we need first is a detailed example of how he answers the questions he sets himself. We shall look at such an example in the next chapter.

Summary

We looked in this chapter at Chomsky's starting-point: his aim of devising an approach to the study of language which can hope to achieve some of the explanatory power and depth of work in the natural sciences, particularly physics. We started with traditional linguistics, whose purpose is to provide a terminology and a classificatory system for talking about languages. Then we looked briefly at physics, highlighting those aspects of the method used there which Chomsky takes as significant and worth adopting. We then saw the questions which Chomsky proposes to ask about language, and the outlines of his answers to these questions. In particular, we saw how Chomsky wants to construct a theory of the human language faculty in the same way as Galileo and Newton constructed a theory of motion. We looked at some of the assumptions which lie behind these questions: Chomsky's view of 'mind' and 'brain', his view that there is a distinct, genetically determined 'language faculty', and his rejection of the claim that the purpose of language is communication.

2

Achievements

In this chapter we look at an example of Chomsky's approach in action. The aim is to go into enough detail to give a genuine feel of what generative grammar looks like, without going into all the complexities and technicalities which would be out of place in a book like this. We will sometimes have to cut corners in order to keep the discussion reasonably clear, so the sharp reader will find counter-examples to what is said for this reason (and also because much is still not understood). A few essential technical terms are defined as we proceed. If you are worried (or discover in the course of reading) that you cannot handle terms like *noun, verb, pronoun, subject* and *object*, take the time to look them up in a book like *Rediscover Grammar* by David Crystal.[1]

Why can't each other help the women?

We can begin by studying a small fragment of the grammar of English.[2] Look at these sentences:

(1)   The gardener looked after the flowers and shrubs
(2)   Many ordinary people adored Nye Bevan's speeches
(3)   Everyone respects a good listener
(4)   Paul's caring attitude impressed me
(5)   Rachel surprised herself
(6)   The women helped each other

There are all sorts of observations that one could make about these sentences, and many kinds of questions one could raise about them. Scrabble players might note that the letters Z, X, Q and J do not occur in any of them. Someone concerned above all with honesty might note that sentence (2) is certainly true, sentence (3) probably, but that with the others it is hard to tell without more information. One might ask whether these sentences were ever spoken or written before I wrote them in this book. One might ask instead whether they are wise, elegant, or great literature. Depending on your interests, these observations and questions might be useful or not.

For Chomsky, interested above all in scientific linguistics, the important initial observation about these sentences is that they are all perfectly acceptable English sentences. He is not concerned with who might utter these sentences and why, or any of the things in the last paragraph: simply the fact that any speaker of English who was presented with these six sentences would accept them as possible English sentences.

Chomsky's observation may seem trivial: some of the observations later in this chapter are by no means trivial, however. Remember also that some profound ideas in science have resulted from trivial observations, such as watching an apple fall from a tree . . .

Chomsky's focus on this one observation may seem bizarre, or lacking in 'common sense'. Here again, care is in order. The observations and questions which scientists home in on are often very different from those of 'common sense'. If I meet someone for the first time, I am unlikely to pay any attention to how many of their teeth have fillings, or to ask questions about the cellular structure of their left kidney. A medical scientist might well concentrate on these issues. In the same way, the concerns of a linguistic scientist may be quite different from those of common sense. Chomsky's work should be evaluated as a whole, not rejected because of its unfamiliar starting-point.

Let's make a further observation about these six sentences. One thing that you can do with the first three sentences is put them in the passive, like this:

(1′)   The flowers and shrubs were looked after by the gardener
(2′)   Nye Bevan's speeches were adored by many ordinary people
(3′)   A good listener is respected by everyone

The passive sentences are just another way of saying the same thing as the original 'active' sentences, perhaps emphasizing different words and perhaps in a more formal style. Any speaker of English could invent more pairs of active and passive sentences along these lines.

If we want to describe what happens when an English speaker forms a passive sentence from an active one, we could do it like this, using sentence (3) as an illustration:

PASSIVE RULE

1. Find the subject, the verb and the object of the active sentence. (In sentence (3), the subject is *everyone*, the verb is *respects* and the object is *a good listener*.)
2. Make the object of the active sentence the subject of the passive one. (*A good listener* becomes the subject of the passive.)
3. Put *-ed* on the end of the verb, and precede it by the appropriate form of the verb *be*. (The verb *respects* becomes *is respected*.)
4. Put the subject of the active sentence after the verb, and precede it by the word *by*. (We get *by everyone*.)

Let's now try to apply this same rule to sentences (4), (5) and (6). Each time, the result is a sentence that is not grammatical:

(4')   *Me was impressed by Paul's caring attitude
(5')   *Herself was surprised by Rachel
(6')   *Each other were helped by the women

It's not hard to see what's wrong with (4'). The pronoun *me* can't be replaced by the subject of a sentence. We can make (4') grammatical if we replace *me* by *I*:

(4")   I was impressed by Paul's caring attitude

The word *me* is called an OBJECT PRONOUN; it can only occur as the object of a sentence, not as the subject. The word *I* is the SUBJECT PRONOUN which corresponds to *me*.

It's reasonable to assume that (5') and (6') don't work for the same reason: *herself* and *each other* are object pronouns like *me*.

Unlike *me*, however, they don't have subject pronouns which correspond to them. So there is no way to improve (5') and (6') as we did with (4'). They are simply ungrammatical. (This account of (5') and (6') is based on page 164 of *A Comprehensive Grammar of the English Language*.[3] I'll refer to it from now on as 'the CGEL account'.)

There is additional evidence that this account is correct. Only object pronouns can appear after prepositions like *with*. So we say (7a), not (7b):

(7) a.   Paul was delighted with me
     b.   *Paul was delighted with I

If *herself* and *each other* are indeed object pronouns, we would expect to find them after *with* in the same way, and we do:

(8)   Rachel was delighted with herself
(9)   The women were delighted with each other

A puzzle about language

So far as it goes, then, this description accurately accounts for the ungrammaticality of sentences (4'), (5'), (6') and (7b). Now if, like Chomsky, we want to find explanations rather than just descriptions, we might ask: *why* does English behave like this – that is, why are *herself* and *each other* object pronouns? There is no point in asking this about the word *me* – it's just a fact about English that *I* is the first person subject pronoun and *me* is its corresponding object pronoun. But *herself* and *each other* are more mysterious. Why can they not occur as the subject of a sentence? The intended meaning of (5') and (6') is quite clear; it's not that they are nonsensical. So why does the grammar of English not allow them? We have here a puzzle about language just like the examples in the natural sciences that we discussed in Chapter 1.

What kind of solution could we propose to this puzzle? There are two kinds that might seem likely, a historical one or a statistical one. If we were looking for a historical solution we would look at the origins of expressions like *each other* and *herself* in Old English. We would look at the way usage has changed since the earliest written records, hoping that the development of these expressions would shed some light on their present-day behaviour. Many linguists have looked at language in this way, and many interesting facts about the ways language change have been collected. This has not, however, been an approach which has led to explanatory theories, at least, not the sort we are looking for. We want to be able to say that the phenomena we are interested in result from the nature of language, not from accidental facts about historical change.

[handwritten margin note: Do it / is assumed already that there is a nature of language.]

If we decided to seek a statistical solution, we might extend our inquiry to include equivalent constructions in other languages. Words like *herself, myself, themselves* etc. are called REFLEXIVE PRONOUNS. French has a reflexive pronoun *se* as in (10):

(10)   Rachel s'est surprise

In German, the reflexive pronoun *sich* occurs in sentences like (11):

(11)   Rachel überraschte sich

(These are direct translations of example [5].) It turns out that if we try to put the French and German sentences into the passive, the result is ungrammatical just like the English sentences:

(10')   *Se a été surprise par Rachel
(11')   *Sich wurde von Rachel überrascht

It appears, then, that it is quite common in languages for reflexive pronouns to be object pronouns. It is thus not surprising that this is the case in English. But of course, we now have a further puzzle: *why* is this so? It seems that there is no answer: that's just the way languages are.

Another reason why a statistical explanation is not satisfactory is this: suppose for the sake of argument that there are exactly three languages in the world in which reflexives are *not* object pronouns. Imagine that there was a 'limited' nuclear war in which the entire human race was wiped out except for the speakers of these three languages. The situation would then be that in all the world's existing languages – all three of them – reflexives can appear in subject position. This would be a valid statistical generalization, but it would not be an insight into human language in general, for obvious reasons. Returning to the real world, it may just be a historical accident, of no linguistic interest, that this generalization about reflexives holds true in most existing languages.

A different kind of explanation

Chomsky argues that there is another kind of explanation – a *biological* one – for puzzles like this. Let's illustrate what Chomsky has in mind by re-examining the sentences we have just looked at.

To begin with, Chomsky does not accept the description that we gave above. He would agree that example (4') is ungrammatical for the reason we suggested: *me* is an object pronoun and therefore can't appear as the subject of a sentence. But he does not agree that (5') and (6') are ungrammatical for the same reason.

Chomsky calls reflexives like *herself* and the reciprocal phrase *each other* ANAPHORS. (This is a traditional term used by grammarians; Chomsky uses it in a special way.) The defining feature of anaphors, in his theory, is that they are subject to the Binding Principle, defined as follows: An anaphor must be bound in its governing sentence.

To understand this principle, you will need to know what some of the words in it mean. Every anaphor normally has an ANTECEDENT – a word or phrase that comes before it and indicates what the anaphor refers to. In examples (5) and (6), repeated here for convenience, *Rachel* is the antecedent of *herself* and *the women* is the antecedent of *each other*:

(5) Rachel surprised herself
(6) The women helped each other

We say that the antecedent *binds* the anaphor. So to say that an anaphor is bound is simply to say that it has an appropriate antecedent.

GOVERNMENT is a highly technical term, and much current research is concerned with the correct way to define it. The following definition gives the basic idea. Let A and B be two items in a sentence. We will say that A governs B if

(a)   A is a noun, verb, adjective or preposition; and
(b)   B is to the right of A and part of the same phrase.

The instances of government which concern us here are where A is a verb or a preposition, and B is its object. So we say that in (5), the verb *surprised* governs *herself*, its object; in (6), *helped* governs *each other*; and in (8), repeated here, the preposition *with* governs *herself*:

(8)   Rachel was delighted with herself

The GOVERNING SENTENCE of an anaphor is the smallest sentence containing the anaphor and the nearest word which governs it. In simple sentences like the ones looked at so far, the 'governing sentence' will simply be 'the same sentence'. In such cases, the Binding Principle says, in effect: 'An anaphor must be governed and it must be bound.' In complex sentences like (12) and (13), which consist of more than one clause, the word 'smallest' is crucial:

(12)   Paul expected that Rachel would surprise herself
(13)   I noticed that the women helped each other

These two sentences consist of a MAIN CLAUSE *'Paul expected [something]'* or *'I noticed [something]'* and a SUBORDINATE or DEPENDENT CLAUSE, introduced by *that*. To find the governing sentence for the anaphors in (12) and (13), we first find the word or phrase that governs them. It's the verb of the subordinate clause in each case: *surprise* in (12) and *helped* in (13). The governing sentence is the smallest sentence containing both the anaphor and the word that governs it. In both cases it is the subordinate clause which is the governing sentence.

We are now in a position to see how the Binding Principle works. In sentence (5), the anaphor is *herself*. It's bound by the antecedent *Rachel,* and the antecedent is in the same sentence as the anaphor. So sentence (5) conforms to the Binding Principle and is grammatical. Consider now the passive (5'), repeated here:

(5') *Herself was surprised by Rachel

The anaphor here hasn't got an antecedent at all. An antecedent must *precede* the anaphor it binds (otherwise it wouldn't be an antecedent but a 'postcedent'). So (5') violates the Binding Principle – the anaphor isn't bound at all, hence it certainly isn't bound in its governing sentence.

The Binding Principle will also handle complex sentences like (12). The anaphor is *herself* again, and the antecedent is *Rachel.* The anaphor is governed by the verb *surprise,* so the governing sentence is the subordinate clause. By the Binding Principle, the antecedent must be in the subordinate clause as well. This is the case, so the sentence is grammatical. Similar reasoning shows that (13) also conforms to the Binding Principle.

Suppose we construct sentences like (12) and (13), except that the antecedent is not in the subordinate clause but in the main clause. The Binding Principle predicts that such sentences will be ungrammatical, and this turns out to be correct:

(14) *Rachel expected that Paul would surprise herself
(15) *The women noticed that I helped each other

In (14), *herself* requires an antecedent in the subordinate clause. The only word available is *Paul.* But that doesn't work: the antecedent of *herself* must be female. The obvious candidate for antecedent, *Rachel,* is not available because it is in the main clause. Similarly in (15), the only permitted antecedent is the word *I.* But *each other* requires a *plural* antecedent, and *I* is singular. So the Binding Principle predicts, correctly, that native speakers of English reject these sentences as ungrammatical.

Examples like (14) and (15) are important in Chomsky's view. He points out that it is possible to make sense of them, but that they simply cannot express the intended meaning. So we cannot use (14) to mean (14') or (15) to mean (15'):

(14') Rachel expected that Paul would surprise her

(15′)   The women each noticed that I helped the other

The fact that there is nothing wrong with the meaning of (14) and (15) is strong evidence in support of the Binding Principle. The CGEL account of reflexive and reciprocal constructions does not help us at all with more complex cases like (14) and (15). So examples like these indicate that the CGEL account was wrong and that Chomsky's more complex account is correct.[4]

The puzzle again

Let's now return to the question we asked before about the CGEL approach: why does English behave in this way – that is, why does the Binding Principle apply to English sentences? Chomsky argues that we can arrive at an interesting solution to this puzzle if we first ask a different question: how do speakers of English acquire the Binding Principle? He thus puts us firmly into the area of language acquisition. What we are doing here is moving from question 1 from the last chapter (What is the system of knowledge?) to question 2 (How does this system of knowledge arise in the mind/brain?).

At first sight, there may seem to be no problems of principle in answering this question. Presumably a young person acquires the Binding Principle in the same way as she acquires other grammatical rules: by listening to the sentences spoken around her, trying out sentences of her own, and so on. One might need to investigate in more detail to see exactly at what stage of development this principle is acquired, or whether some young people have special difficulties with it. But there seems to be no reason why we should be unable to give a general account of how it is acquired.

Now in certain cases, what I've said in the preceding paragraph is probably correct. As we saw in Chapter 1, it is a rule of English, for example, that adjectives generally precede the noun they modify: we say *a good cry*, not *a cry good*. A young person learning English will hear innumerable examples where the adjective comes first, and almost none where the noun comes first. It will clearly be possible for her to arrive at the rule that adjectives come first. Of course, this whole process is unconscious, just as most of language acquisition is. But there is no difficulty in reconstructing this unconscious process of acquisition.

While this account may be true of adjectives, it cannot be true of the Binding Principle. To see why, we must bear in mind a simple but important fact about language acquisition: the only information available to a young person acquiring a language is that certain sentences are acceptable. In general, young people are rarely informed that certain sentences are *not* acceptable, and more rarely still are they informed *why* certain sentences are not acceptable. Linguists say that children have access to 'positive evidence' (grammatical sentences), but not to 'negative evidence' (ungrammatical sentences).

This simple fact puts the acquisition process in a new light. A young person only hears a small sample of sentences. There are an enormous number of possible sentences that she has never heard. Of these, some are grammatical and some are not. If adult speakers uniformly agree that a sentence which they have not encountered before is ungrammatical, then whatever rule they are applying must be based solely on the evidence from grammatical sentences which they *have* encountered.

In our discussion of reflexives and reciprocals we argued that the Binding Principle worked better than the CGEL account. The evidence was examples (14) and (15): the CGEL account could not explain why these two sentences, which would be judged unacceptable by any speaker of English, were ungrammatical. It was these two *ungrammatical* sentences which were crucial evidence in favour of Chomsky's analysis.

Linguists analysing English can easily obtain judgements about examples like (14) and (15). Unlike linguists, a young person acquiring English does not have access to the information that these two sentences are not grammatical. But such sentences are the *only* evidence for choosing the Binding Principle rather than the other alternative. If young people do not have access to this evidence, how is it that they invariably choose the Binding Principle? One would expect instead variation from speaker to speaker, and hesitation in judging sentences like (14) and (15) to be unacceptable. But we do not find this: any English speaker would not hesitate to rule them out. Why is this?

This is the crux of the matter!

The solution: genetic programming

Chomsky's solution is outlined in this passage:

> It seems plain that language acquisition is based on the child's discovery of what from a formal point of view is a deep and abstract theory – a generative grammar of his language – many of the concepts and principles of which are only remotely related to experience by long and intricate chains of unconscious quasi-inferential steps. A consideration of the character of the grammar that is acquired, the degenerate quality and narrowly limited extent of the available data, the striking uniformity of the resulting grammars, and their independence of intelligence, motivation and emotional state, over wide ranges of variation, *leave little hope that much of the structure of the language can be learned by an organism initially uninformed as to its general character.* (ATS, 58; emphasis added)

one has to have the capacity already!

Essentially what Chomsky is saying here is that grammars contain the Binding Principle because it is innate: he argues that we have certain abstract properties of language like the Binding Principle genetically encoded in our brains.

We'll discuss Chomsky's idea of innate programming in more detail in a moment. First let's see how it solves the puzzle about reflexives and reciprocals. Recall that the puzzle is how a child could arrive at the Binding Principle without 'negative evidence' – evidence that is available to linguists but not to a child. The puzzle we have looked at is just one of many which have exactly the same structure: how do children come to acquire knowledge of their language for which there is insufficient evidence in the speech they hear around them?

Kripke's exact question

Taken together, these puzzles make up what has been called 'the logical problem of language acquisition'. It's a 'logical' problem in the sense that you can't solve it by studying the way constructions like reflexives and reciprocals are actually acquired. The problem is not 'how is the Binding Principle acquired?' but 'how is it *possible* for the Binding Principle to be acquired?'. The solution is one that we can reason our way to: basically, the only way someone can come to know something for which there is no evidence is if they already know it to begin with.

Chomsky asked how speakers of English acquire the Binding Principle. His answer, we now see, is that they do not acquire it because it is in their heads to begin with. This also answers the original question of why the Binding Principle applies in English. The principle is part of the grammar of English because the human brain is built in such a way that it could not be otherwise. The Binding Principle is part of what Chomsky calls UG, a theory of 'our biological endowment', and this endowment places limits on what human languages can be like. In particular, if Chomsky is right then *no* language can contain sentences which violate the Binding Principle.

Chomsky's conclusion in interesting in two ways. Firstly, to say that every human language must conform to the Binding Principle is to make a very strong claim. It's a claim which can easily be tested by looking at similar constructions in a wide range of languages. If the claim is wrong, it will be relatively easy to falsify it, that is, to prove that it is wrong. This is exactly what a scientific hypothesis should be like.

Secondly, Chomsky is saying something about the structure of the human mind. He says that pursuing explanations in this way can lead to insight into our essential human nature. If our minds are structured at birth in certain ways which generative grammarians can reconstruct, this is important and worth knowing.

Genetics and language

In the last chapter we looked briefly at the idea that language acquisition is partly genetic and partly the result of experience. While most people would accept this in principle, there has been intense controversy about the relative importance of each part. The controversy has not just been about language: throughout the biological sciences what is sometimes called the 'nature–nurture' debate has long been a bone of contention. Now that we have seen how Chomsky formulates a specific proposal about the genetic component in language acquisition, it is worth looking at this important issue in rather more depth.

It is generally accepted that many aspects of human growth and development are controlled by our genes. A new-born child's body will increase in size, develop teeth, grow hair of a particular colour, and undergo the physical changes of puberty in ways laid down by the genes the child is born with. The possibilities of variation among members of the human species are limited to the possible permutations of our genes.

In some areas it is difficult to disentangle the influence of genes and the influence of the environment. Clearly, women are genetically equipped to conceive, bear and breast-feed babies while men are not. It has often been maintained that women are also genetically prepared to do child care and housework while men are not. Thoughtful people nowadays regard this view as a crude and intellectually unfounded attempt to justify the oppression of women. The fact that women are often found in these roles is explained by early conditioning and economic pressures – environmental factors, not genetics.

To take another example, consider the development of walking. Almost every human being is able to walk by the second year of life. The regularity with which this occurs suggests that the process is genetically determined. Environmental factors play some part: adequate diet, a good supply of objects to hold, throw and retrieve, and enthusiastic encouragement by adults make the process easier. But they cannot make the development of walking take place if a child is not yet ready for it, that is, if her genetically determined physical development has not yet reached the necessary stage.

Acquiring a language is in some ways comparable with learning to walk. Almost every human being has mastered the phonology, grammar and everyday vocabulary of her native language by her fifth birthday. The stages of development seem to be broadly uniform across the languages of the world. This suggests, once again, that genetics plays a large part. Of course, social interchange and adult encouragement help, but they cannot make a child learn how to use language if her genes decide otherwise.

Our genetic endowment does not determine that a child will acquire English rather than, say, Hebrew or Vietnamese. *Which* language is acquired depends on the environment. What our genes do, according to Chomsky, is provide certain linguistic rules and principles which every language must conform to. There may be a lot of apparent differences between languages, but at an abstract level the degree of variation is severely limited. He argues that our genetic programming includes a set of abstract rules and principles like the Binding Principle, which together make up UG. If every human being is born with UG encoded in her or his brain, then every human language must conform to UG.

The information in UG is clearly of an abstract kind. Chomsky is *not* saying that every child is born knowing which anaphors English has. He is saying this: UG lays down that *if* a language has anaphors, they will be subject to the Binding Principle. All the environment has to do is present each young person acquiring English with evidence that words like *myself*, *yourselves*, *each other* etc. are anaphors. UG will do the rest, enabling each child to (unconsciously) construct a grammar of English which goes beyond the evidence available in the ways we have seen.

Notice how easy this makes it for a young person acquiring English. It is easy to see how the right sort of evidence is available, indeed plentiful. The anaphors in question behave differently from other nouns and pronouns, and their meanings also give obvious clues. With very little work, then, a young person can reach the stage where the Binding Principle comes into play and does the rest. The best sort of theory, in Chomsky's view, is one where a small amount of exposure to a language triggers principles of UG which have far-reaching consequences. In particular, the principles of UG should enable speakers of a language to make judgements about sentences they have never encountered before, ungrammatical sentences, and so on. As we shall see later in this chapter, the Binding Principle also has implications for other areas of grammar, which look on the surface quite different from the areas we have looked at so far. This again is to be expected if such principles are part of UG.

Principles like the Binding Principle are just hypotheses, intended to be modified and refined in the light of further research on English and other languages. Chomsky has said on many occasions that future work will no doubt replace current thinking by other theories. The new theories will be of the same general type, however, resting on the same set of assumptions that we outlined in Chapter 1. As proposals about UG are developed and refined, they will come closer to being a correct, albeit abstract, theory of one part of the structure of the human mind.

It is important to distinguish between general evidence for innateness and the specific linguistic arguments like the one we have looked at. For example, Chomsky has stressed how complex language is, what a 'tremendous intellectual accomplishment' it is for human beings to acquire it at such a young age, and how 'this task is entirely beyond the capacities of an otherwise intelligent ape' (RCTII, 123), the suggestion being that only innateness can account for this accomplishment. Whatever one may think of these arguments, they are not crucial to the issue because they only have a supporting role. The *only* argument for innateness which is crucial to the task of developing an explanatory theory of language is what we have called 'the logical problem of language acquisition': the claim that people come to know certain specific things about their language for which the relevant evidence was not available to them. Unless this problem can be explained away somehow, it remains a puzzle to which the theory of UG is a reasonable solution.

There are two ways in which the logical problem of language acquisition could be argued away. One would be to show that sufficient evidence in fact *is* available. The other would be to show (a) that the facts which abstract principles like the Binding Principle are designed to explain can be handled by some other principle; and (b) that this alternative principle is learnable *on the basis of positive evidence alone*. Until someone meets the challenge in one of these two ways, the puzzle that Chomsky formulates – and his attempts to solve it – must be regarded as legitimate.

Abstractness

Chomsky's emphasis on UG is intended to encourage grammarians to look for explanatory principles rather than 'straightforward' or 'common-sense' accounts. He and his colleagues in generative grammar have naturally concentrated on areas of grammar where abstract principles can be proposed, and have simply ignored areas where the prospects of finding such principles look poor, no matter how interesting the latter areas might be for other reasons. We discuss this narrowing of focus in Chapter 3.

Chomsky's suggested way of proceeding is also intended to have another effect. He wants the hypotheses which grammarians propose about UG to become steadily more and more abstract. His model here, as we saw in Chapter 1, is the development of physics. Recall how the abstract notion of gravity, allied to the further abstract idea of forces operating in perfectly straight lines, enabled Newton to construct a powerful theory of motion which solved problems with previous theories.

Chomsky's aim is to encourage the same kind of development in linguistics. The Binding Principle is in fact a good example. In earlier work, Chomsky had proposed that sentence (14), repeated here, was ungrammatical because of a principle called the *Specified Subject Condition*,

(14) *Rachel expected that Paul would surprise herself

The idea was that the word *Paul* blocked or got in the way of the rule which connected the anaphor *herself* with its antecedent *Rachel* (Compare *Rachel expected to surprise herself*, where there is nothing in the way and the sentence is fine).

In this earlier work, an entirely separate principle, the *Tensed Sentence Condition*, was needed to explain why (16) is ungrammatical:

(16) *Rachel expected that herself would surprise Paul

The thinking here was that the anaphor *herself* in (16) is inside a tensed or 'finite' subordinate clause *(that) herself would surprise Paul*, whereas the antecedent is outside the clause, and that this blocks the anaphora rule (compare *Rachel expected herself to surprise Paul*, where there is no tensed subordinate clause containing the anaphor, and hence no problem).

The Binding Principle, which replaced the two just mentioned, will account for (16) as well as (14). In (16), *herself* is not governed at all.[5] It therefore has no governing sentence, and cannot be bound within that sentence. One principle therefore does the work of two. It is a more abstract principle than the two it replaced, introducing notions like 'governing sentence' which were not previously invented. Making theories more unified thus goes hand in hand with greater abstractness.

Another thing that Chomsky wants to encourage is a steady increase in the DEDUCTIVE STRUCTURE of the hypotheses put forward: the chain of reasoning which starts with the proposed theory – in this case, Universal Grammar – and ends with a correct account of the facts. As we have seen, UG is made up of a number of rules and principles like the Binding Principle. Following normal scientific practice, Chomsky aims to make these principles as simple as the facts of language will allow. A linguist concerned with grammar, however, quickly finds many puzzles which are far from simple and straightforward. Although the principles themselves may be simple, Chomsky's hope is that they can be shown to *interact* in ways which correctly handle complex data.

The chain of reasoning, starting with some simple principles and showing how they account for complex facts, will be long and intricate. Chomsky sees this as a good thing: for one thing, it leads to deep and elegant theories. For another, it is a plausible model of how UG operates in the process of language acquisition. As we saw with the Binding Principle, only a small amount of experience is needed to 'trigger' it in the process of acquisition. If the Binding Principle can be shown to interact with other principles which require a small amount of experience, and if this interaction can account for some of the complexities of our knowledge of language, then Chomsky's approach to linguistics is clearly getting somewhere.

The Binding Principle and Move-alpha

Let's look at an example of this interaction. We've already seen how the Binding Principle accounts for the behaviour of anaphors. In this section we'll look at some different facts, and show how the rule we propose interacts with the Binding Principle.

Chomsky proposes that there is a rule in UG which could hardly be simpler: the rule says 'Move anything', and is usually called *Move-alpha*, where 'alpha' simply stands for any grammatical unit – a word, phrase, sentence or whatever. We have already seen an example of Move-alpha, the passive sentences at the beginning of this chapter:

(3)   Everyone respects a good listener
(3') A good listener is respected by everyone

Here *a good listener* has moved from after the verb to the front of the sentence. In the following examples, the italicized section likewise moves to yield a new sentence which (like the passive examples) is another way of saying the same thing:

(17)   a.   *Apparently*, the government will resign on Tuesday
       b.   The government will resign on Tuesday, *apparently*
(18)   a.   Don't give *away* any secrets
       b.   Don't give any secrets away

We'll restrict our attention now to cases like (3), where the thing that moves is a noun phrase (that is, a noun [*listener*] along with words which modify it [*a good*]). The key problem with a general rule like Move-alpha is to stop it moving things into impossible places. For instance, we clearly want to prevent it moving *a good listener* to a position after *everyone*, yielding the ungrammatical sentence:

(3")   *Everyone a good listener respects

Chomsky proposes (following work by Joseph Emonds) that UG contains a restriction on the rule Move-alpha: an item can only move to a position where an item of that type can occur anyway. So a noun phrase can only move to a noun phrase position. In English we don't normally find a noun phrase in the place where *a good listener* has landed up in (3"), between the subject and verb of a sentence. So Move-alpha can't move

We might just have always done it this way, right?

a noun phrase into that position. Emonds's restriction is called the *Structure-Preserving Principle*.[6]

Let's now look at another instance where Move-alpha has to be restricted to stop it producing bad results. Look at these two examples:

(19)   The congregation sang
(20)   The congregation sang a hymn

Example (20) shows that the position after *sang* is a noun phrase position – it is possible for the noun phrase *a hymn* to occur there. This means that if Move-alpha applies to (19) and moves *the congregation* to the right of the verb *sang*, the Structure-Preserving Principle will not be violated and the result should be grammatical. Unfortunately, this is not so: what we get is (21), which is clearly not grammatical:

(21)   *Sang the congregation

How can we restrict Move-alpha so that it does not produce sentences like (21)?

Chomsky's solution is in two parts. First, he proposes that when a noun phrase moves, it always leaves behind a 'trace' in the place it started out. Using t to mark the traces, the structure of (3') and (21) will be:

(3')   A good listener is respected t by everyone
(21') t sang the congregation

Traces cannot be pronounced or heard. They exist as part of a theory, rather like atoms and electrons, and they are justified to the extent that the theory can solve interesting puzzles. In effect, a trace is just a way of marking a position in a sentence. It turns out, though, that there are good reasons to include traces in the grammar of English.

Chomsky's second step is this: suppose that a trace is an anaphor, just like reflexives and reciprocals except that it is invisible. The noun phrase that moves will be the antecedent of the anaphor. Like all anaphors, traces will be subject to our old friend, the Binding Principle.

If we examine (3'), we can see that the trace is governed by *respected* and bound in the same sentence by its antecedent, *a good listener*. So this sentence conforms to the Binding Principle and is grammatical. In (21'), on the other hand, the trace *precedes* the noun phrase *the congregation*. (21') is therefore ungrammatical for the same reason as (5'): an anaphor must *follow* its antecedent. The Binding Principle thus interacts with Move-alpha to get the facts right.

In general, this theory predicts that it will *never* be possible for Move-alpha to shift a noun phrase to the right, as in (21): only if a noun phrase moves to the left, as in (3'), can it be an antecedent for the trace it leaves behind. So as well as explaining why (21) doesn't work, Chomsky's account also makes a strong claim about the behaviour of noun phrases – a claim which can be tested against a wide range of data.

Parameter setting

The Binding Principle runs into a problem when we try to apply it to Japanese. Japanese has a reflexive *zibun* which behaves like English reflexives in simple clauses (the verb usually comes at the end of the sentence in Japanese):

(22) John-wa   zibun-o   seme-ta
      John   self   blamed
      'John   blamed   himself'

In more complex examples, however, *zibun* can have an antecedent in the main clause, unlike English:

(23) Bill-wa John-ga zibun-o seme-ta to   omot-ta
      Bill   John   self   blamed   that   thought

The preferred meaning of (23) is 'Bill thought that John blamed Bill' , although the other sense, 'Bill thought that John blamed himself', is possible.

What are we to say about this problem? One reaction might be to reject the Binding Principle out of hand because of this Japanese evidence (at least as part of UG; it could still be part of the grammar of English). A more interesting response by Chomsky and his associates has been to suggest that UG doesn't just offer fixed rules, but a narrow range of options from which each language can choose. These options are called 'parameters', and the idea is that a young person acquiring a language should be able to fix the parameters for that language on the basis of positive evidence alone – preferably simple positive evidence.

In the case of reflexives in English and Japanese, suppose we amend the Binding Principle so that it becomes the Parameterized Binding Principle and says: Anaphors must be bound within a local domain. This keeps the idea that an anaphor must be bound, that is, have an antecedent. The idea of a 'local domain' is that the antecedent must be 'close' to the anaphor – there are limits to how far away it can be. But what counts as a 'local domain' varies from language to language. The task of the young person acquiring a language is to establish – using only positive evidence – what counts as a local domain in that particular language.

interesting problem

For English, the 'local domain' will be the governing sentence of the anaphor. For Japanese, a different definition of 'local domain' will be needed. One proposal is that the local domain in Japanese must contain a finite (tensed) main clause. Notice that this proposal makes some clear, and testable, predictions. Remember that the Binding Principle governs the movement of noun phrases as well as the relationship between anaphors and antecedents. The Parameterized Binding Principle predicts that there should be differences in noun phrase movement between Japanese and English, parallelling the differences in the behaviour of reflexives. The system of parameters is just as much a theoretical hypothesis as the system of principles like the Binding Principle. The range of variation seems to be very limited: it isn't just a question of inventing a new parameter every time some new and unexpected phenomenon is encountered. We shall not pursue the matter further here, but the direction of research should be clear.[7]

UG in action

If Chomsky is right when he says that the Binding Principle is part of UG, it should be possible to look at how young people handle anaphors and see how the principle plays a part in their acquisition of English.[8] In this section we look at some of the work that has been done to test the theory of UG in this way.

One of the first experiments involved reflexives. Lawrence Solan presented twelve five-year old and twelve six-year old children with sentences like (24):

(24)   The dog said that the horse kicked himself

Each sentence contained the names of two animals. The children were given four toy animals and a variety of props. Each child was asked to act out the sentences using the toy animals and the props. In the case of (24), for example, if the child made the horse kick the dog that would show that she or he was not applying the Binding Principle. If the horse kicked himself, that would be consistent with the claim that the Binding Principle was part of the child's grammar. If the six-year-olds did significantly better than the five-year-olds, that would suggest either that the Binding Principle is learned, not innate; or that the principle is not in the mind at birth but is 'maturational', developing in the mind only at a certain age. Notice that the second suggestion doesn't conflict with the assumption that the principle is innate – in fact, it confirms it. The fact that puberty regularly happens at a certain age is part of the evidence that it is genetically determined.

The five-year-olds got 89 per cent of the sentences correct, the six-year-olds 87 per cent. The difference is too small to be significant, so the results are consistent with the claim that the Binding Principle is innate.

In an influential study, Nina Hyams presents evidence that setting the parameters of UG plays a crucial part in language acquisition. She looks at the 'AG/PRO parameter' which accounts for a number of differences between English and Italian. For instance, in Italian a sentence does not have to have a subject:

(25)   Mangia una mela
        'Eats an apple'

This sentence is understood as 'He/she eats an apple'. In English the sentence would have to have an actual pronoun acting as subject. Another, apparently unrelated, difference between English and Italian involves auxiliary verbs. In English, the subject can appear between a tensed auxiliary like *has* and the main verb *agreed*, as in (26b); this is not possible in Italian, as (27b) shows:

(26)   a.   Mario has agreed to help us
        b.   Has Mario agreed to help us?
(27)   a.   Mario ha accettato di aiutarci
        b.   *Ha Mario accettato di aiutarci?

For reasons which are too complex to set out here, these two differences between English and Italian (and several others) fall into place in an analysis which derives them from a different value for the AG/PRO parameter. This in itself is an impressive illustration of the power of the parametric approach to grammar, but Hyams goes further. She argues that in the early stages of acquisition, the grammars of young children acquiring English appear to set the value of the AG/PRO parameter in the Italian way. This explains why the sentences produced by these young children often lack subjects (a widely reported finding in studies of English-speaking children), do not contain auxiliaries until a later stage, and have a variety of other properties which were previously seen as unrelated. When the parameter is subsequently reset, the various properties connected to it all change at the same time. Thus differences between child grammars and the adult grammar of English are not just random 'mistakes' by children, but the systematic result of a parameter which is initially set the wrong way and later has to be reset correctly.

An important implication of these results is that the parameter is set in a particular way before a child has any relevant experience of a particular language. Hyams supports this claim by looking at sentences produced by young children learning German and Italian, which behave in a similar way to English;

the data from German are particularly suggestive, as this language sets the parameter in the same way as English does, rather than in the Italian way. She goes on to suggest why the parameter should be 'preset' in favour of languages like Italian: within Chomsky's model of UG, this option is 'simpler' in the type of grammar it needs. The scare quotes round 'simpler' are important, because a different model of UG might make the English option look 'simpler'. The connection between Hyams's acquisition findings and Chomsky's model of UG is an empirical hypothesis, though one that is beginning to look well-founded. The key point here is that proposed principles of UG can be tested in real language acquisition, and that fruitful interaction between grammarians like Chomsky and child language researchers has taken place.

Summary

This chapter has looked at one example of Chomsky's approach in action. We looked at some English sentences and saw how Chomsky proposes to account for some of their properties with the Binding Principle, which he claims is innate, part of UG. The crucial evidence for innateness is the fact that the evidence needed to learn the principle is not available to children. We saw how the Binding Principle interacts with other areas of grammar, and how the principle fails for Japanese but can be rescued if we 'parameterize' it. Finally we looked at some research into language acquisition by real children to see whether the Binding Principle receives support.

3
Costs

The last two chapters showed how Chomsky underpins and elaborates his attempt to make linguistics an explanatory science. We noted that this involves abstraction and idealization, and that sometimes it is necessary to narrow the scope of the theory in order to achieve explanatory depth. We did not look in detail, though, at the particular kinds of idealization and limiting of scope which Chomsky argues are necessary to achieve interesting explanations in linguistics; although at the end of Chapter 1 we saw one example of Chomsky defending himself against the claim that a different limitation of focus – to communicative uses of language – is the only legitimate one.

In this chapter we shall look more carefully at the limits and idealizations which Chomsky says are essential if his enterprise is to succeed. Chomsky has been criticized repeatedly in this area over the years, and the elaboration of his position has become increasingly sophisticated. It is probably fair to say that many people have reacted too quickly to those parts of his work where he discusses the limits and the need to idealize. These people have found the limits too high a price to pay, and have rejected Chomsky's work out of hand without going on to look at his achievements. It is for this reason that I have concentrated first on the achievements in this book.

None the less, the limitations discussed below can be seen as Chomsky's statement of the cost that has to be paid in order to achieve an explanatory theory of language. The question is whether the cost is worth paying.

Knowledge and behaviour

Chomsky's best known statement on the limitation issue is the following one, published in 1965; he recently commented that he would not change a word if he were writing it again today:

Linguistic theory is concerned primarily with an ideal speaker-listener, in a completely homogeneous speech community, who knows its language perfectly and is unaffected by such grammatically irrelevant conditions as memory limitations, distractions, shifts of attention and interest and errors (random or characteristic) in applying his knowledge of language in actual performance . . .

We thus make a fundamental distinction between competence (the speaker-hearer's knowledge of his language) and performance (the actual use of language in concrete situations). Only under the idealisation set forth in the preceding paragraph is performance a direct reflection of competence. In actual fact, it obviously could not directly reflect competence. A record of natural speech will show numerous false starts, deviations from rules, changes of plan in mid course, and so on. The problem for the linguist, as well as for the child learning the language, is to determine from the data of performance the underlying systems of rule that has been mastered by the speaker-hearer and that he puts to use in actual performance . . .

A grammar of a language purports to be a description of the ideal speaker-hearer's intrinsic competence. (ATS, 3–4)

Let us leave the first paragraph of this passage for now and concentrate on the second one where Chomsky distinguishes between *competence* and *performance*. As we saw in Chapter 1, Chomsky has always maintained that the primary object of investigation in his type of linguistics should be the 'system of knowledge' which native speakers of a language possess, rather than what they do with that knowledge. The basic distinction here is between the knowledge that underlies or makes possible a type of behaviour, and the behaviour itself. Chomsky has made this distinction in a number of ways: at one time or another he has referred to what he now calls a system of knowledge as competence, a cognitive system, a cognitive domain or Internal Language (I-language), while behaviour has appeared under the heading of performance. More recently, he has introduced the term External Language (E-language) to refer to the infinite set of sentences potentially generated by the system of knowledge or I-language.[1]

Few other parts of Chomsky's programme have been attacked so bitterly and so repeatedly as this one. The basic point is that behaviour is something tangible, observable, measurable. You can observe how a human being behaves, whether the behaviour is recalling things from memory, breathing in different ways, walking, or using language. You can record and measure behaviour and look for regularities or repetitions of the same kind of behaviour. Knowledge, on the other hand, is not tangible or measurable. We noted in Chapter 1 that you cannot look inside a baby's head at birth to see what it knows about language (or anything else), and this is true of an adult's knowledge of language too. This is not just a matter of scientific ethics; if a totally unscrupulous scientist were to open up a human head he would find a brain, but knowledge is simply not something physical like a brain, though it presumably must have some physical instantiation.

The criticism of Chomsky has been, then, that by shifting his declared focus from observable linguistic behaviour to unobservable linguistic knowledge, he is moving from something concrete and objective to something mystical and dangerously obscure. Using knowledge supposedly to explain behaviour, it could be argued, is rather like explaining a thunderstorm in terms of Zeus battling with his enemies, or explaining illness in terms of wicked demons. These primitive ideas may make for exciting stories, but they do not advance our understanding, there is no way to test them, they are speculative and subjective: in short, they have nothing whatever to do with science.

The first response to this criticism is that Chomsky does not use knowledge to 'explain' behaviour. Let us recall here what Chomsky understands by explanation in linguistics. The puzzle for Chomsky is to explain how certain items of linguistic knowledge (such as the Binding Principle) are present in the minds of speakers of a language when the evidence for them is not available to young people learning the language. The explanation he proposes is that these items of knowledge are based on principles which are encoded in our genes and hence part of the structure of the mind/brain. The puzzle is entirely about knowledge, and the explanation is about knowledge too: behaviour is simply not mentioned.

This does not mean, of course, that Chomsky is not concerned with behaviour at all. The best way to investigate knowledge, since we cannot observe it directly, is to look at behaviour and theorize about the knowledge that lies behind it. Now, a person's behaviour may vary for a variety of reasons. It is reasonable to assume, however, that a person's knowledge of her/his language does not change radically once the important parts are acquired in early childhood; it is also plausible that speakers of the same language, whose actual behaviour may vary enormously for a variety of linguistically irrelevant reasons, none the less share a system of knowledge which is in most respects identical. I presumably share the central rules of pronunciation, grammar and usage, and most of the same vocabulary, with readers of this book, otherwise they would be unable to understand what I write!

So Chomsky is not using knowledge to 'explain' behaviour. Rather, he is using certain aspects of behaviour as evidence for knowledge. Deciding which aspects of behaviour are useful evidence and which are not (either because they are unsystematic, or because they have nothing directly to do with language) is not always easy; but all scientists have this problem. The choice of what to concentrate on is based on what your objectives are. If you achieve your objectives – in Chomsky's case, an elaborate theory of UG – then the choice was a good one. This is the only test that matters.

Chomsky's defence of his approach goes further. He argues that *any* description of a language typically focuses on knowledge rather than behaviour. I have in front of me an introductory book about Welsh, not intended to be Chomskyan in any sense. The book lists various rules which are said to be part of the grammar of that language. If I were to make a tape recording of natural Welsh speech, I would certainly find 'false starts, deviations from rules, changes of plan in mid course', and other oddities which the book says nothing about. But clearly it would be ridiculous to expect the book to say anything about such matters. The perfect Welsh described in the book is an idealization of what actually happens, but it is a useful one because it tells me what all speakers of the language have in common by virtue of being speakers of the language. The quirks and speech difficulties of individual speakers vary so much from person to person, for reasons which have little or nothing to do with language, that books about Welsh simply ignore them. The same is true of virtually any description of any language.

Not only do nearly all linguists focus on shared linguistic knowledge, but the same kind of approach is followed in other sciences:

> Consider the problem of determining the nature of the thermonuclear reactions that take place deep in the interior of the sun. Suppose that available technique permits astronomers to study only the light emitted at the outermost layers of the sun. On the basis of the information thereby attained, they construct a theory of the hidden thermonuclear reactions, postulating that light elements are fused into heavier ones, converting mass into energy, thus producing the sun's heat. Suppose that someone now were to say: 'True, you have presented a theory that explains all the available evidence, but how do you know that the constructions of your theory have physical reality – in short, how do you know that your theory is true?' The astronomer could respond only by repeating what he had already presented; here is the evidence available, and here is the theory that I offer to explain it . . . it is senseless to ask for some other kind of justification for attributing physical reality to the constructions of the theory, apart from consideration of their adequacy in explaining the evidence and their conformity to the body of natural science as currently understood. There can be no other grounds for attributing physical reality to the scientist's constructions . . .
>
> The investigation of the apparatus of the language faculty, whether in its initial or final steady state, bears some similarity to the investigation of thermonuclear reactions in the solar interior . . . We observe what people say and do, how they react and respond . . . We then try, as best we can, to devise a theory of some depth and significance with regard to these mechanisms, testing our theory by its success in providing explanations for selected phenomena. Challenged to show that the constructions postulated in that theory have 'psychological reality', we can do no more than repeat

the evidence and the proposed explanations that involve those constructions . . . needless to say, the evidence that supports the linguist's constructions is incomparably less satisfying than that available to the physicist. But in essence the problems are the same. (RR, 189–92)

In his recent work, Chomsky has gone on to the offensive on this issue by claiming that in some ways knowledge of language is *more* real than linguistic behaviour. As we saw in Chapter 1, the common-sense notion of language leads to problems: we treat Danish and Norwegian as different languages for sociopolitical reasons, whereas we treat most types of English as varieties of the same language. Such choices are quite arbitrary, and cannot be the basis of a serious definition of language. If we follow much of pre-Chomskyan linguistics and treat a language as 'a collection of actions, or utterances . . . or as a system of linguistic forms or events' (KL, 19), we run into similar problems. As we have seen, any such collection will include errors, false starts, coughs and splutters. In practice, even linguists who in theory refuse to see language as a system of knowledge have to abstract away from – that is, ignore – such irrelevant phenomena. The assumption – implicit or explicit – is that there is a system of knowledge which each speaker of a language possesses, and this is what linguists have to describe. Chomsky believes, as we have seen, that this system of knowledge has some physical existence in the brain. In this sense, knowledge of language is a real, existing thing while attempts to define language in any other way either presuppose Chomsky's definition, or degenerate into incoherence.

The ideal speaker-listener

Chomsky's reference to the 'ideal speaker-listener' is another abstraction which he has defended vigorously. The term 'speaker-listener' (or equivalently, 'speaker-hearer') was used in particular to head off misunderstanding caused by Chomsky's use of the terms *generate* and *generative*. Chomsky frequently says that a given rule of grammar 'generates' certain sentences.

Uninformed readers have taken this to mean that the rule is supposed to be a model of the way a speaker actually produces these sentences in a real situation. Chomsky was then accused of writing grammars which say lots about how people speak sentences but nothing about how they hear and understand them!

The term *generate* is a technical one from mathematics, in particular from the field of set theory. A set is a general name for any collection of distinct elements. There are two ways to specify the elements of a set: either by simply listing them, as in (1), or by giving a procedure which identifies the elements, either by stating what the elements have in common, as in (2a, b) or by giving an instruction as in (2c):

(1)   a.   {fruit tea, toast, margarine, peanut butter}
        b.   {Simches Toyra, Purim}
        c.   {21, 22, 23, 24}
(2)   a.   {What I had for breakfast this morning}
        b.   {Jewish festivals where riotous celebration is obligatory}
        c.   {Start with 21 and add 1 three times}

Mathematicians say that the statement in (2c) 'generates' the list of elements in (1c). The statements in (2) are rules, in the sense that they tell you what to look for if you want to list the elements of each set.

If a set has an infinite number of elements, it is not possible to list them, so stating a procedure to generate the set is the only method. For example, the instruction {Start with 2 and add 2 indefinitely} generates the set {2, 4, 6, 8, 10 . . .}, where the dots mean 'and so on to infinity'.

Returning to linguistics, the possible sentences of a language form an infinite set. There is no such thing as 'the longest possible sentence of English': you can always add '. . . but I don't agree' on to the end and make a longer sentence, and so on *ad infinitum*. The grammar that we have in our heads, which must be finite in size (as our heads are finite in size) can therefore be seen as a system of rules which generate – in the technical sense – this infinite set of sentences: they tell us what to look for if we want to list the sentences of

English. This has nothing to do with the actual production of these sentences by a speaker: many possible sentences of English, although conforming to the rules of grammar, will never be spoken or written down for a variety of reasons: they are boring, pointless or would take several lifetimes to say.

A generative grammar is a description of the system of knowledge which is put to use, along with other psychological and physical mechanisms, in the production and perception of language. It is not biased towards either production or perception, but is equally essential to both. So Chomsky uses the term 'speaker-listener' to emphasize this point. Linguists, including Chomsky – usually talk of 'native speakers'; in this passage, where he is being especially careful, the more accurate term 'speaker-listener' is used.

What about the term 'ideal'? Chomsky partly explains what he means by this term when he continues 'who knows its language perfectly and is unaffected by performance problems'. Here again, it is hard to object to this formulation as a basis for research in grammar, although the word *ideal* has sometimes been interpreted as meaning 'best, ultimate, most preferable', as if Chomsky has once met such a flawless individual or is hoping to do so one day. The term clearly means 'idealized' here: as usual, Chomsky is simply leaving on one side aspects of language which do not seem to cast light on the underlying system of knowledge, or the way this system is acquired.

Once again, the narrowing of focus which Chomsky defends seems to be assumed in all descriptions of languages. My book about Welsh naturally tells me about the language of an idealized, perfectly competent speaker-listener. It does not describe the language of someone who only knows a few words of Welsh, or who in some other respect does not know the language perfectly. Nor does it restrict itself to a description of how to produce well-formed Welsh sentences, or how to understand Welsh (although there are language courses which focus on one or the other): it aims to describe the system of Welsh which is put to use in production and comprehension of the language. This position is not stated explicitly in the book, but only because it is so obvious as to be taken for granted.

A completely homogeneous speech community

No two human beings speak in identical ways, and in real speech communities – groups of people who share the same language, however that can be defined – there is often wide variation in pronunciation, grammar, vocabulary and usage. The variation may be geographical, leading to regional varieties of the language; social, leading for example to class varieties, as in English where a person's accent often provides clues about their class background; occupational, different trades using specialized terminology and usage; or have to do with differences between spoken and written language. Most speakers of English, at least, are keenly aware of such variation and like to discuss it: a lot of humour is based on this awareness. The study of language variation is part of the wider field of *sociolinguistics* – the study of language in society.

Chomsky, however, proposes to ignore this area completely, and to make the simplifying assumption that the English speech community is homogeneous: that there is only one kind of English. Whether or not the layperson is interested in variation is of no concern to Chomsky: as we have seen, there is no reason to expect the interests of a layperson and those of a scientist to coincide automatically. Recall that his aim is to produce a precise and explicit description of a language so that conclusions can be drawn about UG. Variation is 'messy': not completely random and unsystematic, but difficult to specify precisely. In any case, it is not necessary for a generative grammarian to take it into account. Suppose that in my own case the reality is that I speak and understand my own variety best (educated Lancashire English), but that I also have a partial command of, say, three other varieties of English. The one I know best is obviously the one to concentrate on for research purposes. Whether or not I have a partial command of other varieties, my own variety must still conform to UG (as must each of the other varieties). If the aim is to find out about UG, then nothing is lost by ignoring variation. In addition, grammarians from time immemorial have made this simplifying assumption.

Chomsky defends this idealization in the following extract, referring to the passage we cited at the beginning of this chapter:

I once presented what I thought was an innocent and uncontroversial statement of an idealisation that seems to me of critical importance if linguistic theory is to be pursued along [Galilean] lines: namely, that 'Linguistic theory is concerned primarily with an ideal speaker-listener, in a completely homogeneous speech community . . .'. This formulation has aroused quite a storm of protest, focusing primarily on the notion 'homogeneous speech community'.

Exactly what is the source of the objection? Obviously, it cannot be that real speech communities are not homogeneous. That is as obvious as it is irrelevant . . . So we are left with what must be the crucial question: does the idealisation so falsify the real world that it will lead to no significant insight into the nature of the language faculty, or does it, on the contrary, open the possibility for discovering fundamental properties of the language faculty? In short, is the idealisation legitimate?

Suppose that someone takes the negative stand on this question. Such a person is committed to one of the following two beliefs:

1. People are so constituted that they would be incapable of learning language in a homogeneous speech community: variability or inconsistency of presented evidence is a necessary condition for language learning.
2. Though people could learn language in a homogeneous speech community, the properties of the mind that make this possible do not enter into normal language acquisition in the real world of diversity, conflict of dialects, etc.

I cannot believe that anyone who thinks the matter through would really maintain either of these beliefs. In fact, each seems hopelessly implausible. Suppose, then, that we reject them. Thus we accept that humans have some property of mind which would enable them to learn the language of a homogeneous speech community were they to be placed in one, and that this property of mind plays a role in language acquisition. But then the idealisation is legitimate: it opens the way to the study of a fundamental property of mind, namely, the one in question. (RR, 25–6)

Chomsky is not denying the right of sociolinguists to study whatever they wish. The point is that his objectives are quite different from theirs. If the objective is to discover profound things about the human language faculty, then variation is simply not a relevant consideration.

'Instantaneous' language acquisition

In order to talk about UG in the way he does, Chomsky has to pretend that language acquisition doesn't take several years but is *instantaneous*.[2] As we've seen, UG is intended to be a model of the innate knowledge of language that is put to use in language acquisition. Human beings acquire language over a period of time, modifying their speech until mastery is achieved. Chomsky says that in constructing a theory of UG we must for the time being at least leave out the time factor. In his theory, then, UG is presented with a random sample of sentences and instantly constructs a grammar of the language in question.

At first sight, this assumption may seem so unrealistic that it casts doubt on the whole enterprise. Chomsky does not accept this criticism. He argues that the assumption should more usefully be seen as an empirical hypothesis: the hypothesis that nothing in real language acquisition affects the process in such a way that the outcome is different from what it would be if the process were instantaneous. It is therefore up to opponents of the hypothesis to provide evidence that the outcome is indeed different for this reason.

Broadly speaking, there are two ways in which this evidence might be forthcoming. One is that UG changes in the course of acquisition: as Chomsky puts it, 'it might be . . . that the language faculty matures through childhood making various principles available at particular stages of the process' (KL, 53). Suppose, for instance, that the Binding Principle is not made available until around three years two months. This is certainly conceivable in principle: the various physical changes in puberty are genetically programmed to come into effect at a given time for each individual, with some variation across the species but not much. It could be that UG operates in the same way.

The alternative is that the data available to a young person acquiring a language changes in the course of acquisition. The suggestion here is not the absurd one that adults carefully select how they speak in the presence of young ones so that, for instance, no passive sentences or subordinate clauses are used near children under the age of four. It is, however, possible that because of the gradual development of memory, attention span or physical skills, 'only "simpler" parts of the evidence that leads to attainment of the [final] steady state are available to the child at early stages of language acquisition' (KL, 53). A young child may not be able to handle some of the longer examples from the last chapter, for instance, until her short-term memory has developed past a certain point.

While these two broad possibilities may well be what actually happens, they only cast doubt on the instantaneous acquisition assumption if it can be shown they affect the final outcome of acquisition – the final 'steady state' system of knowledge – in crucial ways. This does not seem likely. At worst, the two possibilities just outlined, assuming that they can be made precise and confirmed in studies of real children, simply explain why language acquisition happens at the speed it does. They give no reason to think that the final outcome would be different. Chomsky writes:

> Frankly, I doubt that the simplifying assumption, though obviously false, significantly affects the validity of the analysis based on it. If our initial assumption does indeed seriously falsify the situation, if there are substantially different stages with fundamentally different learning theories, and if furthermore the character of the learning theory at each stage depends significantly on grammars (or other cognitive structures) already attained, then we would expect to find substantial differences in the result of language [acquisition] depending on such factors as order of presentation of data, time of presentation, and so on. But we do not find this . . . Despite considerable variety in learning experience, people can communicate readily . . .
>
> These facts suggest that the initial idealisation . . . was a legitimate one . . . .At some stage in the progress of inquiry it will no doubt have to be qualified, but one may seriously

question whether this stage has been reached in the study of linguistic competence and universal grammar. (RL, 121–2)

Core Grammar

Chomsky's work has always restricted itself to the study of grammar, as opposed to other areas of linguistics; bear in mind, however, that he uses the term to include semantics and phonology, not just syntax. In recent years even this has seemed too wide to him: he has limited his attention to certain areas of grammar, which he calls *Core Grammar*. Let us look first at the restriction to grammar, then at the further limitation to core grammar.

It may look at first sight as if the exclusion of areas beyond grammar is an automatic consequence of Chomsky's concern with knowledge rather than behaviour. Remember that he insists on the need to exclude performance problems from the scope of linguistic theory, including variation within a speech community. He is concerned in the first instance with describing the system of knowledge which speakers of a language have in their minds; such a description is called a grammar of that language (if it is fully explicit, a generative grammar). So by excluding performance from his theory, he seems to be leaving no room for anything but grammar.

This is not correct, however. Focusing on knowledge rather than behaviour does not in itself mean that you have to limit yourself to a certain kind of knowledge. Ignoring performance problems (false starts, errors, coughs, splutters, and so on) does not force you to concentrate only on grammar. The question is which sorts of knowledge a scientific linguist should choose to concentrate on: there is an element of choice here, and we need to see why Chomsky makes the particular choice he does.

This point may be clearer if we consider an alternative. The sociolinguist Dell Hymes once proposed that Chomsky's notion of grammatical competence (knowledge of grammar only) was less useful than the notion of *communicative competence*.[3] This notion is wider in scope than Chomsky's, covering not only a speaker's knowledge of grammar, but also her knowledge of how to use the language for communication or social interaction.

As we saw in Chapter 1, part of being a speaker of English is knowing how to soften the force of commands by saying 'Would you mind . . .'. Being able to use language to get what you want, or to get other people to do things, or to get help when you need it, is part of communicative competence. In reality, speakers vary greatly in how well they use language for such purposes. This is because their knowledge interacts with other psychological and physical skills, and social constraints, in the same way that purely grammatical knowledge often results in ungrammatical behaviour in conditions of actual use.

Since an alternative, wider notion of competence is available, why does Chomsky stick with his narrower idea of purely grammatical competence? The answer, as so often, lies in his wish to investigate UG. He believes that the skills mentioned in the last paragraph, while no doubt important in practice, are unlikely to be part of UG: they are probably acquired entirely as the result of experience. The area of usage has its subtleties and complexities, certainly, but they are of a different order from those in the area of grammar. Remember that we do not claim that some aspect of linguistic knowledge is innate – part of UG – just because it is subtle and complex. We only make such a claim if we can show that the evidence needed to acquire the relevant bit of knowledge is not available to young people acquiring their first language. Arguments of this kind are not generally possible with knowledge of usage or communication, but are possible – as we have seen – with knowledge of grammar.

So much for the limitation to grammar. In recent work, however, Chomsky distinguishes between the *core* of a grammar, where UG plays a predominant role, and the *periphery*, where the rules and principles of UG can be violated, or are irrelevant. In part, this distinction is needed to handle the simple fact that English, like every language, has 'exceptions' to its rules: irregular verbs (*buy, bought*), strange plurals (*children, sheep*), peculiar idioms (*come what may, bold as brass*). The idea is that such constructions are in the periphery of the grammar, where they are learned perhaps entirely on the basis of experience, UG playing little or no part.

The core–periphery distinction also enables us to account for things which would otherwise cause problems for UG. In the last chapter we looked at reflexives (*myself, herself*, etc.), which

Chomsky claims are subject to a principle of UG called the Binding Principle. A broader look at reflexives in English brings to light uses which seem to violate the Binding Principle:

(3)   I wouldn't go there myself
(4)   I myself wouldn't go there
(5)   Myself, I wouldn't go there

In this last example, the reflexive precedes its antecedent, violating the Binding Principle. Other examples of reflexives which violate the principle are cited by Scheurweghs:[4]

(6)   The only reality was themselves
(7)   Nathaniel Ellis. That was myself
(8)   Myself and my own misery drum in my ears
(9)   . . . as long as no one but myself is hurt

We can say that such uses of reflexives do not come under core grammar and are therefore not subject to the Binding Principle. They are in the periphery of the grammar where the principles of UG can be relaxed.

Put like this, the notion of periphery sounds like a convenient way of avoiding problems: any time you find some examples which pose a challenge for your favourite principle of UG, you can dismiss them as part of the periphery! The claim that a given phenomenon is part of the periphery has empirical consequences, however. If UG is not involved, or is actively violated, then the construction in question should be more difficult to acquire than constructions in the core. Young people should have difficulties with constructions in the periphery, and they should appear later in their speech. For this reason, such constructions should be relatively rare, vary from speaker to speaker, and be diachronically unstable – that is, liable to change over the course of time.

In the case of reflexives, it seems correct that examples like (5–9) are rare, and vary from speaker to speaker. Some varieties of English make frequent use of reflexives in this way, others hardly at all. I do not know whether the constructions in question have changed over time, or whether they cause trouble for young people acquiring English, but it would no doubt be possible to find out. There is thus no evidence against the claim that they are in the periphery (although David Gil has put forward a different view), and some evidence that they are.[5] The point is, then, that the core–periphery distinction is a useful tool, and makes testable, empirical claims – just like the theory of parametric variation (cf. Chapter 2).

Idealization in general

We have looked at a number of idealizations and limitations which Chomsky insists are necessary for his approach to linguistics to have a chance of success. Leaving aside now the particular idealizations he makes, let us conclude this chapter by looking at the question of idealization in more general terms.

Chomsky has always argued that some idealization is inevitable in linguistics, indeed, in any domain of inquiry. Perhaps the following anecdote illustrates this. There is a type of linguistics which is at the opposite pole to Chomsky's, consisting of the collection and analysis of large collections of real data (called *corpora*), which are used as the basis for writing practical grammars or dictionaries. Linguists engaged in this type of activity see themselves as describing behaviour rather than knowledge; they look at language variation in some detail, have no interest in UG or language acquisition, and do not restrict themselves to grammar, let alone core grammar.

One of the most important projects of this type is the COBUILD project, run jointly by Collins Dictionaries and the University of Birmingham.[6] 'The research team selected 20 million words of authentic written and spoken English, entered it on to a computer, and used it to write a new dictionary of English aimed specifically at foreign learners of the language. I once heard a member of the COBUILD team say that if they only found one example of a construction in their database, they would assume that it was a personal peculiarity or an error and ignore it. Only if a construction occurred at least three times would they treat it seriously as a systematic part of English grammar. This is clearly idealization: ignoring certain facts and concentrating on others. The fact that even such a data-driven approach as the one at COBUILD has to idealize perhaps makes the idealization in Chomsky's theory-driven approach seem less suspect.

Chomsky chastises the opponents of idealization in the following passage:

> Opposition to idealisation is simply objection to rationality: it amounts to nothing more than an insistence that we shall not have meaningful intellectual work. Phenomena that are complicated enough to be worth studying generally involve the interaction of several systems. Therefore you *must* abstract some object of study, you must eliminate those factors which are not pertinent. At least if you want to conduct an investigation which is not trivial. In the natural sciences this isn't even discussed, it is self-evident. In the human sciences, people continue to question it. That is unfortunate. When you work within some idealisation, perhaps you overlook something which is terribly important. That is a contingency of rational inquiry that has always been understood. One must not be too worried about it. One has to face this problem and try to deal with it, to accommodate oneself to it. It is inevitable. (LR, 57)

The issue is not *whether* to idealize: the issue is *which* idealizations are appropriate for a particular purpose. The ones we have looked at in this chapter are those that Chomsky says are essential for his purpose, which is to develop an explanatory theory. If you accept this aim, and if you agree with Chomsky that the idealizations we have looked at do not, on the whole, distort the facts in fundamental ways, then you will not find the particular idealizations he advocates too high a price to pay for the results achieved. Of course, if you don't accept his basic aim in the first place you will be unimpressed by the limitations of Chomsky's linguistics. We return to this point in Chapter 5.

Summary

In this chapter we looked at the limitations of Chomsky's linguistics: how Chomsky has to idealize in order to build an explanatory theory of language. Chomsky is concerned with knowledge rather than behaviour. Generative grammar is not biased towards the speaker or the hearer of language, and assumes perfect knowledge of the language. Chomsky is not interested in linguistic variation, and has to pretend that language acquisition is instantaneous. He restricts himself to grammar, and in particular to core grammar. He claims that idealization is necessary in any field of study, and that none of the idealizations he proposes distorts reality in unacceptable ways.

Appendix: rules and principles

In the last two chapters I have referred in passing to 'rules' and 'principles' of grammar. For anyone who wants to study Chomsky's work in detail, the distinction between the two is important. In addition, work that draws on generative grammar often mentions notions like 'phrase-structure rule' and 'transformation', so a brief account here may be helpful. This appendix outlines the main types of rule in generative grammar, and the recent shift from 'systems of rules' to 'systems of principles'.[7]

Syntax is the study of how words combine to form sentences. If we only ever used one word at a time, like, for instance, when we say 'Hello' or 'OK', there would be no need for syntax. When we look at two- or three-word sentences, we need to describe them using syntactic rules. Here are some examples:

(1) Geoff arrived
(2) Stella won
(3) The woman won
(4) Mary likes oranges
(5) Crawley welcomes careful drivers

Most people will remember from school that words belong to different 'parts of speech' (more helpfully called 'word classes'). In sentence (1), *Geoff* is a (proper) noun and *arrived* is a verb. We can show the word classes for each sentence like this:

(1) Noun + verb

(2) Noun + verb
(3) Definite article + noun + verb
(4) Noun + verb + noun
(5) Noun + verb + adjective + noun

In general, each of these sequences of word classes can be used to form a sentence in English. If these were the only possible types of sentence, we could write a rule that said: An English sentence can consist of (article) + noun + verb + (adjective) + (noun). Brackets round an item mean that it is optional. This rule says that an English sentence has to have a noun followed by a verb (the only two items that don't have brackets round them); there may also be an article before the noun, and an adjective or a noun after the verb.

There are a few things wrong with this rule. Firstly, not just any noun can have an article in front of it: we can't say *The Stella won*, for instance. We need to distinguish between nouns which can have an article and nouns which don't. How we do this is not crucial here, though. The point is that if you choose one of the right nouns, you can put it in front of a verb and make a sentence, whereas if you pick an adjective and put it in front of a verb you will *never* make a sentence: *careful arrived* is not possible.

The second problem is that our rule allows types of sentence which go beyond the examples, some of which are not possible. For instance, if we choose every option, we can get a five-word sentence like:

(6) The team achieved brilliant successes

On the other hand, if we choose noun + verb + adjective, we get ungrammatical examples like:

(7) *Stella arrived biological

Similarly, we could choose article + verb

(8) *The won

Looking at (8), the problem is that the article 'goes with' the noun in some sense. We can capture this feeling as follows: we'll say that the article combines with the noun to form a unit, and that this unit combines with a verb to form a sentence, as in example (3), where *the woman* is the unit. Such a unit is called a NOUN PHRASE (NP): a PHRASE because it contains more than one word, and a NOUN phrase because the phrase appears in the same position in a sentence – before the verb – where a noun on its own appears: it's a phrase which functions as a noun.

We could write rules to express this idea:

article + noun = noun phrase
noun phrase + verb = sentence

These rules start with the smallest units, words, and shown how they combine to make bigger units, phrases and sentences. This is a perfectly legitimate way of doing things, but traditionally grammarians write rules the other way round, starting with the biggest units and working down to the smallest ones. So the rules would look like this:

sentence ⟶ noun phrase + verb
noun phrase ⟶ article + noun

The arrow can best be read as 'consists of', though technically it means 'rewrites as'. So the first rule here says 'A sentence consists of a noun phrase followed by a verb'. Rules like this are called PHRASE-STRUCTURE RULES: they tell us how a sentence is broken down into phrases, and these phrases into smaller units. The phrase structure of sentence (3) is shown in the 'tree diagram' in Figure 3.1.

The tree is constructed by starting with the phrase-structure rule for sentences, and then applying the rule for noun phrases. (Strictly speaking, we need more rules to put the words at the bottom of the tree, but we can ignore this complication here.)

Phrase-structure rules can tell us a lot of useful things about sentences, but they are not enough on their own. Consider these examples:

(9) Angela looked up the answer
(10) Angela looked the answer up

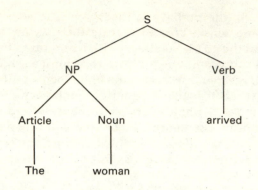

Figure 3.1

These sentences are two different ways of saying the same thing. The expression *look up* is often called a 'phrasal verb'; the word *up* in these examples is called a *particle*. The characteristic things about phrasal verbs in English is that the particle can 'move' to the end of the sentence in this way:

(11)   Reg cleared away the dishes
(12)   Reg cleared the dishes away
(13)   Brian took out the rubbish
(14)   Brian took the rubbish out

It would be possible to write phrase-structure rules for these examples – one lot of rules for (9), (11) and (13), with the particle right after the verb, and another lot for (10), (12) and (14), where the particle is at the end. This wouldn't capture the fact that each pair of sentences is related. What we need is a rule which explicitly states a relationship between the two types of sentence. In early work in generative grammar, this was done by taking one type of sentence as basic and writing a rule which tells you how to form the other type. Rules which did this were called TRANSFORMATIONS or TRANSFORMATIONAL RULES.

For the examples we are looking at, the transformation might be:

Starting sentence: NP + verb + particle + NP
Finishing sentence: NP + verb + NP + particle

An alternative way of writing the transformation (but equivalent in effect) would be to state what you have to do to the input sentence to produce the output sentence. So the second line of the rule might look like this:

Move the particle to the end of the sentence

This particular transformation is sometimes called *particle movement*. The passive rule we mentioned in the first section of Chapter 2 is another transformation, though a rather more complex one than particle movement.

We shall not go into transformations in more detail here, except to make one more point. In Chomsky's system, transformations don't change sentences into other sentences. The idea is more abstract: a sentence like (10), for example, 'starts out' having a structure like (9), which is 'subsequently' transformed into the actual structure in (10). I put 'starts out' and 'subsequently' in scare quotes here, because the aim is not to describe what speakers do when they utter or write sentence (10). The grammar aims to describe what a native speaker knows about sentence (10), and it does this by setting up an abstract level of structure, called DEEP STRUCTURE or UNDERLYING STRUCTURE, which is transformed into the actual structure of the sentence, its SURFACE STRUCTURE.

Think of it like this: we are trying to express what is the *same* about examples (9) and (10) (and the other similar pairs of sentences), and what the *difference* is between the two. If the grammar includes the transformation of particle movement, we can say that they have the same deep structure, but that a transformation has applied to (10) so that it has a different surface structure from (9). In a nutshell, we are formalizing the fact that the two sentences say the same thing in different ways.

Transformational rules played a crucial part in Chomsky's early work, so much so that his approach to grammar was sometimes called 'Transformational grammar'. In recent work, however, within what has become known as the 'Government and Binding' (GB) framework, transformations have not been treated in this way. Rather than having a different transformation for each different type of sentence – one for sentences with particles at the end, one for passives, and so on – Chomsky now suggests that there is one very general transformation, which is allowed to move anything anywhere: what we called 'Move-alpha' in Chapter 2. As we saw, this rule will produce all kinds of ungrammatical examples, so Chomsky also proposes that there are a number of general principles, such as Emonds's Structure-Preserving Principle and the Binding Principle, which prevent all but the few grammatical sentences from being generated.

There has thus been a shift of emphasis from 'systems of rules' to 'systems of principles'. Instead of a rule of 'particle movement', a number of independent principles have the effect that sentences (9) and (10) are both grammatical. The usual practice among grammarians was to set up a separate rule for each different construction in a language. Chomsky has suggested that this traditional notion of a rule of language no longer has a part to play in his theory. This is more than the normal attempt by scientists to generalize wherever possible. Principles of grammar, in Chomsky's use of the term, do not apply to specific constructions, but to every sentence.

Principles of grammar work in a similar way to officials who inspect new buildings to check whether they conform to all the safety regulations. Such officials do not build anything themselves; they merely apply a set of general tests for whether a building can be certified safe or not. A building which does not fail any test is approved by the official. In the same way, principles of grammar do not generate sentences themselves. They act as a set of tests which a sentence must pass to be part of a given language. A sentence which does not conflict with any of the principles is grammatical.

For a child acquiring a language, the task is no longer to learn a number of rules of grammar: instead, the task is to fix the parameters associated with certain (innate) principles, in the ways we outlined in Chapter 2 in the section on parameter setting. Each principle is simple in itself, and parameters can be set on the basis of straightforward evidence, easily available to a child. The interaction of the different principles, however, means that setting a parameter in one particular way has a variety of effects throughout the grammar.

The emphasis on systems of principles is a result of aiming for explanation rather than description. It is doubtful whether a linguist who simply wanted to describe English would have come up with an approach to grammar of this kind. Chomsky's insistence on explaining the acquisition of grammar is the driving force which has led to the new approach. Starting at the beginning of the 1980s, the new approach put the study of UG into a new gear, with a great deal of productive research taking place during the decade.

4
Implications

Chomsky's importance lies not just in the effect he has had on linguistics, but also in the more general impact of his ideas. This chapter looks at the implications of his linguistics for other fields of study. I have had to be selective: Chomsky's influence has been felt in fields as different as computer science, literary criticism and music theory.[1] Here it makes sense to focus on two fields where Chomsky himself has intervened – philosophy and psychology – and two practical fields where linguistic insights have an obvious potential relevance – second language teaching and learning, and speech pathology.

It may be useful at this point to distinguish between the implications of Chomsky's *assumptions* and the implications of his *results*. Another way of putting this is to make a distinction between the *questions* which Chomsky asks and the particular *answers* he proposes to those questions. Before Chomsky it was thought that the basic question for linguistics was: how can we best describe languages? Chomsky argued that this choice of question rested on the assumption that linguistics should aim to be a classificatory study, like natural history, and on the assumption that language was primarily a social phenomenon. Chomsky challenged both these assumptions: he aimed to make linguistics a science, and he adopted a primarily psychological view of language, treating each language as a system of knowledge. This led him to put forward a different basic question for linguistics: how can we best explain that children acquire knowledge of a language?

This new basic question, and the assumptions behind it, are interesting in themselves. Philosophers have taken up Chomsky's views about science, debating whether the methods of the natural sciences can indeed be applied to the mind in the way he suggests. Psychologists have been interested in what Chomsky says about knowledge of language, and have asked if other types of knowledge can be studied in the same way. Both psychologists and philosophers have discussed the proposal that some aspects of language are innate. Chomsky has intervened actively in these discussions, exploring the philosophical and psychological consequences of his work.

At the same time, Chomsky's results – the answers he proposes to his basic question –.have also attracted attention. He has proposed that certain parts of grammar such as the Binding Principle are part of UG and apply to all languages, perhaps in a parametric way. Language teachers have wanted to know how this might affect them. Similarly, speech pathologists have looked to see if they can learn anything useful from results like these in their work with speech-disabled people. Chomsky himself has rarely pursued these matters – indeed, he cautions against expecting too much from any science in a practical situation (see LPK, 180–2). None the less, language teachers and speech pathologists have taken a great interest in his ideas, and it is worth looking at what they have done with them, bearing in mind that Chomsky is not directly responsible for things he hasn't said himself.

Philosophy

My dictionary defines philosophy as 'the rational investigation of being, knowledge and right conduct'. Let's take these three areas in turn. One of the central issues in the philosophy of being, *ontology*, is the relationship between the body, or the material world, and the mind. In the philosophy of knowledge, *epistemology*, philosophers have asked what, if anything, we can know for sure and what we can only speculate about. And on the issue of right conduct, many philosophers have thought about what *ethical* principles should guide our behaviour and what a just society would be like.

It makes sense for our purposes to start with the issue of knowledge, partly because a clear idea of what we can be sure about will help with the other two areas, and partly because Chomsky's main contributions have been in this area of philosophy. We want to establish, then, what we can know for sure. There have been many answers to this question in the history of philosophy. Chomsky takes the view that we can't know anything for sure in advance. We have to do our best to understand and explain the things we see around us – in other words, we have to start with *science*. If we want to establish what we can know, it makes sense to begin with the scientific theories which have achieved the greatest explanatory scope and power. These theories do not give us certainty: any scientific theory is open to being superseded by a better one as research progresses. But scientific knowledge gives us the greatest certainty there is, and forms a more secure base than, say, common sense or prejudice.

We assume, then, that the knowledge which can lay most claim to being reliable is scientific knowledge, particularly theories in the most successful of sciences, physics; at the same time, we assume that any scientific theory is simply 'the best we can do so far', and is liable to be improved or replaced by a better one in the future. We can go on to assume that the methods used in science are the best methods available for finding out what we can know. And it is also reasonable to say that whatever science discovers about the world is the most reliable starting-point we have in the philosophy of being, ontology. This is also true for any beliefs about the world which aren't necessarily part of scientific knowledge but are presupposed by scientists in order for their theories to work.

Mind and body

With these preliminary remarks in mind, we can turn to a specific area where Chomsky has intervened in philosophy, the ontological question of the relationship between mind and body. The issue here is one that philosophers have wrestled with for centuries: are mind and matter fundamentally different or basically the same? The position that they are the same is called *monism*; the view that they are radically different is called *dualism*. The dualist position perhaps reflects our common-sense intuitions more closely: after all, physical objects do not seem to have feelings or to be able to make free choices. The monist position has often been put forward by philosophers who wanted to extend the domain of science to the mind, and to claim that the mind was amenable to the same kind of study as matter. Many monists have held their view because they were worried that leaving the mind outside the domain of scientific inquiry was a licence for superstitious and prejudiced views about the mind.

To understand Chomsky's position, we need to stress that the mind/body question is not resolvable if we are using the everyday, prescientific view of mind and body. If we take the everyday notion of 'body' as a starting-point, we will run into trouble if we try to compare it with our everyday notion of 'mind'. This simply shows that our everyday notion of body is inadequate, and that we should instead rely on whatever notion of body emerges from scientific investigation, no matter how remote this notion may be from common sense. Chomsky points out that the notion of body that physicists assume is quite different from our everyday one. Physicists since Newton have proposed that to explain the material world we need to postulate 'a variety of forces, particles that have no mass, and other entities' which seem to fly in the face of our 'common sense' notion of body (LPK, 144). What counts is the explanatory power of such hypotheses, not whether they fit in with 'common sense'.

The next step in the argument is to challenge the everyday notion of mind in a similar way. For Chomsky, the notion of mind that we should rely on is the one that emerges from scientific investigation, using the methods that have been so successful in physics. Any theories about the mind which are proposed by scientists form part of the general stock of scientific knowledge, as Chomsky says:

> Any intelligible theory that offers genuine explanations and that can be assimilated to the core notions of physics becomes part of the theory of the material world, part of our account of body. If we have such a theory in some domain, we seek to assimilate it to the core notions of physics, perhaps modifying these notions as we carry out this enterprise. (LPK, 144)

Chomsky is not saying this is what *should* happen; he is saying this is what *does* happen in science. Just as the concept of 'body' has been extended in physics to cover 'entities and processes that would have offended the common sense of earlier generations' (LM, 98), it will be extended to cover any concepts that are necessary for an explanatory account of the mind. What we are left with, then, is not the everyday distinction between mind and body, but 'the material world [which is] what we discover it to be, with whatever properties it must be assumed to have for the purposes of explanatory theory' (LPK, 144). Whatever science proposes about body or mind thus becomes part of the 'material world', in the only reliable sense of that term. There is accordingly only one material world, and Chomsky can be called a monist, though perhaps 'scientific monist' would be more accurate.

If we use the methods of natural science to investigate psychological phenomena, our results thus become part of the scientific conception of the material world. Notice how this monist ontology – the view that there is only one material world – follows from Chomsky's starting-point in epistemology – his view that we should take science as our most reliable starting-point and work from there, extending the domain of science as best we can. His belief in the unity of science lies behind his belief in the unity of being.

Individualism and collectivism

Chomsky's ideas are relevant to another issue in the philosophy of knowledge: if a phenomenon has an individual side and a social side, which is primary? Should we look for explanations in terms of individual people, or in terms of social groups? Fred D'Agostino describes the two positions as follows: *methodological individualism* is the view that 'all social phenomena, such as language, are to be explained, ultimately, in terms of the characteristics of individual human beings'; the opposing position, *methodological collectivism*, holds that 'some characteristics of social phenomena, such as language, are *sui generis* with respect to the characteristics of individual human beings, and must therefore be explained in non-psychological terms'.[2]

The issue here is whether the basic properties of language are social or psychological. Chomsky argues for psychology – indeed, he has often said that his type of linguistics is simply the sub-part of psychology which deals with language. As we saw in Chapter 1, a good reason for this view is that it is not easy to isolate language in general, or any particular human language, in social terms without being incoherent: where does 'Danish' stop and 'Norwegian' begin, for instance? Chomsky maintains, on the other hand, that the knowledge of a language which speakers of that language have in their heads is concrete and coherent, and amenable to scientific investigation. To put this point in a more general way, Chomsky is maintaining that individual brains are concrete and tangible, whereas 'society' is an elusive and difficult thing to define. This runs counter to the commonly held view that the notion of mind is a mysterious thing whereas the notion of society is obvious and untroublesome.

Chomsky is not saying that sociolinguistics, the study of the social aspects of language, is impossible or unnecessary. For many practical purposes, the everyday social approach to language is quite adequate. An explanatory theory, however, has to stand on secure foundations, and the view of language as a system of knowledge which exists in the minds of individual speakers provides such foundations.

Rationalism and empiricism

Chomsky's claim that UG is innate has led him to take sides on another enduring issue in philosophy: the dispute between *empiricism* and *rationalism*. Empiricists hold that the mind is a 'blank sheet' when we are born, and that all the knowledge we come to have arises from our experiences in the world. Rationalists argue that the mind contains certain types of knowledge even before we have any experience. Since the seventeenth century, empiricists like Hume and Locke and rationalists like René Descartes and Gottfried Leibniz have debated this issue.

Chomsky's contribution has been to provide factual evidence that rationalism is essentially correct when he argues that certain parts of UG cannot be learned from experience and must therefore be innate. It is worth emphasising at this point that Chomsky refuses to accept a clear-cut distinction between science and philosophy:

In discussing the intellectual tradition in which I believe contemporary work finds its natural place, I do not make a sharp distinction between philosophy and science. The distinction, justifiable or not, is a fairly recent one. In dealing with the topics that concern us here, traditional thinkers did not regard themselves as 'philosophers' as distinct from 'scientists'. Descartes, for example, was one of the leading scientists of his day. What we call his 'philosophical work' is not separable from his 'scientific work' but is rather a component of it concerned with the conceptual foundations of science and the outer reaches of scientific speculation. (LPK, 2)

In pursuing this approach, Chomsky goes on to describe as 'empiricist' not just philosophers but also descriptive (i.e. non-generative) linguistics, behaviourist psychology (see the section on behaviourism in this chapter) and Marxism. As well as being convinced that empiricism is misguided, he is concerned about why it has been so popular:

Attention to the facts quickly demonstrates that these [empiricist] ideas are not simply in error but entirely beyond any hope of repair. They must be abandoned, as essentially worthless. One has to turn to the domain of ideology to find comparable instances of a collection of ideas accepted so widely and with so little question, and so utterly divorced from the real world. And, in fact, that is the direction which we should turn if we are interested in finding out how and why these myths achieved the respectability accorded to them, how they came to dominate such a large part of intellectual life and discourse. (LPK, 137–8)

We return to this ideological question in Chapter 9. For now, the key thing to note is that, once again, Chomsky's determination to apply the methods of natural science to the study of the mind is what leads him to take the philosophical position he does. Suppose we wanted to study scientifically some part of the body – say, a person's hair. We can explain why a person has the hair she or he does by looking at three things: the initial state of the hair at birth, genetically induced changes, and change due to the environment. For instance, a person may be born with little hair, have a lot of hair as a child as it grows quickly, go bald in their thirties, and decide to cut her or his hair regularly. Discounting any one of these factors would lead to an inadequate explanation of why a person's hair is the way it is.

For Chomsky, language is interesting and worthy of study precisely because it enables us to study part of the mind in the same way. We can explain how this part of the mind – our linguistic competence – comes to have the form it does by looking at the same three things: its initial state, genetically induced changes, and change due to the environment (i.e. experience). Claiming in advance that one of these three things is irrelevant would be absurd when studying the body, and Chomsky says that it is equally absurd in studying the mind. Some empiricists make precisely this claim, though, when they deny that the initial state of the mind has any structure to it. Other empiricists have made certain claims about the initital state of the mind, but have treated these claims as unquestioned assumptions rather than as empirical hypotheses. Chomsky rejects both these types of empiricism as unscientific dogma: the sensible procedure, in his view, is to propose testable hypotheses about the structure the mind initially has, not to assume beforehand that it has none or that it *must* have a certain kind of structure.

Chomsky and Kant

In some ways, the philosopher to whom Chomsky is most similar is Immanuel Kant.[3] Kant argued that the mind has a rich internal structure, just as Chomsky does. Another similarity comes in Chomsky's suggestion that this structure enables us to know as much as we do, but at the same time imposes strict limits on what the mind can possibly know. Chomsky distinguishes between 'problems', which are amenable to human understanding, and 'mysteries', the solutions to which are in principle beyond the limits of what the human mind can know. Investigating the structure of the human language faculty is a 'problem' in this sense. But the question of 'the causation of behaviour' – why a given human chooses to behave in a particular way on a particular occasion – is a 'mystery', whose solution continues to elude us despite centuries of investigation and study:

Roughly, where we deal with cognitive structures, either in a mature state of knowledge and belief or in the initial state, we face problems, but not mysteries. When we ask how humans make use of these cognitive structures, how and why they make choices and behave as they do, although there is much that we can say as human beings with intuition and insight, there is little, I believe, that we can say as scientists. (RL, 138)

A key feature of Kant's philosophy was precisely the idea that there are strict limits on possible knowledge – and indeed, Chomsky cites Kant in support of this idea (RL, 156).

At a deeper level, the kinship between Chomsky and Kant lies in their starting-point. Kant said explicitly that the starting-point of his philosophy was the spectacular success of the natural sciences in his day, particularly Newtonian and Galilean physics. His aim was to lay secure conceptual foundations for the natural sciences and to extend the notions of science to the mind. Like Chomsky, Kant thought that the explanatory power of science was the best foundation on which to build a theory of knowledge. And like Chomsky, Kant's starting-point led him to conclude that the mind has a complex structure, and that there are certain things which in principle are beyond its reach.

A further similarity lies in a shared concern for morality. Kant thought that science should guide our theoretical understanding of the world, but that our actions should be guided by a 'moral law' which in his view was every bit as securely based as scientific knowledge. The two sides of his work – his theory of knowledge and his ethical theory – were separate but related. Like Kant, Chomsky proposes that the capacity for 'moral judgement' is part of our human nature and is innate (LPK, 152). In Chomsky's case, the exercise of this moral judgement is the driving force in his political work, separate from his linguistics but related, as we shall see in later chapters. Chomsky's commitment to science underlies his linguistics; his commitment to morality underlies his politics.

Psychology

Behaviourism

In 1959 Chomsky published a review of a book by B. F Skinner called *Verbal Behaviour*. In his review Chomsky strongly attacked both the book and the school of psychology – behaviourism – of which Skinner is a leading proponent.

Behaviourists argue that psychologists who want to be scientific should deal only with observable phenomena. Behaviour is observable – you can observe a person talking, for example. Knowledge is not observable: you can't examine it directly. Therefore the only data that a psychologist can legitimately take into account are a person's behaviour and the conditions in which that behaviour takes place. Even on this point, Chomsky does not entirely agree with Skinner's exclusion of other types of data. Neurology, biochemistry, even quantum physics may well provide evidence about the structure of language one day, in his view. At the moment, though, linguistic behaviour is a good starting-point. The question is where psychologists should go from this starting-point. What Skinner sets out to do is to predict what behaviour will take place under what conditions: he says that 'the ultimate aim is the prediction and control of verbal behavior'.

Chomsky makes two basic criticisms of Skinner. Firstly, Chomsky argues that trying to explain behaviour is far too ambitious. As we noted above, Chomsky regards the question of why a human being chooses to behave in a certain way on a given occasion as a 'mystery' rather than a 'problem'. He concedes that some headway has been made on the question of the causation of behaviour in rats and pigeons in laboratories, but can find no evidence of progress in explaining complex behaviour in humans, in particular, in the way humans use language.

Chomsky is scornful of Skinner's attempt to extend the terminology used to explain laboratory behaviour in animals to complex behaviour in animals or humans. Skinner calls a part of the environment a 'stimulus' if it regularly elicits a type of behaviour, called a 'response'. A stimulus is called 'reinforcing' if it increases the strength of the response. Thus when a pigeon presses a bar more frequently because it receives a food pellet each time, the food pellet is said to reinforce the response. Chomsky says that this makes perfect sense for pigeons under the special conditions of the experiment; he then lists many examples where Skinner attempts to use the notion of 'reinforcement' to account for the use of language.

'A man talks to himself because of the reinforcement he receives' (163) . . . 'the speaker engaged in verbal fantasy says what he is reinforced by hearing or writes what he is reinforced by reading' (439) . . . We can also reinforce someone by emitting verbal behaviour . . . , by not emitting verbal behaviour (keeping silent and paying attention, 199), or by acting appropriately on some future occasion (152) . . .

From this sample, it can be seen that the notion of reinforcement has totally lost whatever objective meaning it may ever have had. Running through these examples, we see that a person can be reinforced though he emits no response at all, and that the reinforcing 'stimulus' need not impinge on the 'reinforced person' or need not even exist (it is sufficient that it be imagined or hoped for). . . .The phrase 'X is reinforced by Y' . . . is being used as a cover term for 'X wants Y', 'X likes Y', 'X wishes that Y were the case', etc. Invoking the term 'reinforcement' has no explanatory force, and any idea that this paraphrase introduces any new clarity or objectivity into the description of wishing, liking, etc., is a serious delusion. (RVB, 557–8)

Thus the notions used in laboratory studies can only be extended to complex behaviour if Skinner abandons the rigour with which they were originally defined, and uses them in vague ways which do not help to explain anything. Skinner's work shows us nothing of genuine explanatory value about the causation of complex behaviour: indeed, the whole idea that behaviour is 'caused' may be incorrect.

In his second basic criticism of Skinner, Chomsky argues that the limitations imposed by behaviourism make it impossible to approach a question which *is* solvable: describing the knowledge which is put to use in linguistic behaviour. This is because Skinner proposes to explain verbal behaviour simply by reference to the external conditions in which it takes place. He rejects explanations which refer to what is taking place inside the mind:

It has generally been assumed that to explain behaviour, or any aspect of it, one must attribute it to events taking place inside the organism. In the field of verbal behaviour this practice was once represented by the doctrine of the expression of ideas. An utterance was felt to be explained by setting forth the ideas which it expressed. If the speaker had had a different idea, he would have uttered different words or words in a different arrangement. . . .

The difficulty is that the ideas for which sounds are said to stand as signs cannot be independently observed. If we ask for evidence of their existence, we are likely to be given a restatement in other words; but a restatement is no closer to the idea than the original utterance.[4]

Throughout the book, Skinner emphasizes the importance of external conditions as adequate explanations for verbal behaviour. Chomsky argues that the reluctance to appeal to the internal structure of the organism is simply dogma, with no scientific basis. If we want to account for the fact that the language of English speakers has certain regularities in it, we must look at the external environment and at the internal structure of English speakers – that is, their knowledge of the language. If we want to look at how English speakers acquire knowledge of their language, we need to take into account their innate knowledge, genetically-determined changes, and changes due to their experience. Insisting at the outset that one of these factors cannot be relevant is simply dogmatism, and has no place in science.

Chomsky's criticism of behaviourism has been very influential: the elegance and power of his review of Skinner's book did a great deal to establish his reputation. In Chapter 9 we return to this topic, looking there at the political implications of behaviourism.

Modularity

Chomsky argues that the mind is 'modular' in nature. Each 'module' is a discrete part of the mind, with its own structure and organizing principles. In actual behaviour, the different modules of the mind interact, but it is none the less possible – indeed, necessary – to distinguish them. One of the modules in the mind is the language module, and it is this one that linguistics should naturally concentrate on: the generative grammar of a language is an attempt to describe the form this module takes in the mind of an adult native speaker, while UG is an attempt to describe the shape of the module at birth.

Which other modules does the language module interact with? We touched on this question in Chapter 1. An example is memory. The mind has to be able to store large amounts of information. Some of this information is linguistic – the sound and meaning of words, for instance – while some of it has nothing to do with language – we remember faces, pieces of music, tastes, noises, and many other things. When we use language, we draw on our memory of words, and normally on other memories as well. Similarly, the part of our mind which controls the speech organs is separate from the language module: it may be that the same part of our brain is involved in chewing and swallowing food, breathing, and other activities quite distinct from language.

As well as assuming that the different modules interact, Chomsky suggests that there may be 'central systems of some kind' in the mind, the different modules being peripheral. The psychologist Jerry Fodor has suggested that the modular sections of the mind are the ones which take in information, while the central systems are those which organize and evaluate the information coming in, making it accessible to different modules.[5]

If the modularity thesis is correct, we would expect to find evidence to support it from actual studies of the brain. It should be possible to find distinct physical parts of the brain which correspond to different modules of the mind. A recent paper by David Caplan reviews the available evidence from research into the structure of the brain, and concludes:

> The picture that emerges is that core language functions are the responsibility of a relatively small area of human neocortex – association cortex located around the Sylvian fissure. As far as is known, this area subserves language regardless of the language spoken, the method of instruction, the number of languages spoken, the literacy of a subject, or any other environmental variable. The location of language in this area of cortex thus seems to be entirely determined by internal organic factors . . . Whatever the responsible organic

mechanisms, they are ultimately genetic and seem to be uninfluenced by the . . . environment.[6]

Chomsky argues that the modules of the brain which are genetically specified are those where, like language, the processing of information is fast and automatic. For example, our capacity for vision works extremely rapidly and without needing any decision on our part to use it: we can decide whether to *look at* something, but if we look at something we can't decide whether or not to *see* it. How we then *interpret* what we see may vary, though, since this presumably involves the central organizing and evaluating system.

This modular view of the mind was implicit in all Chomsky's work, but it is only quite recently that it has been clarified and emphasized. The full implications of this approach to the mind have yet to be worked out: none the less, it may be that psychologists will one day see this idea as comparable in importance for their field with Chomsky's other outstanding contribution, the critique of behaviourism.

Language teaching and learning

The connections between Chomsky's ideas and a practical area like second language (L2) learning take two forms. Firstly, research into L2 learning can be an extra way to test the hypotheses of generative grammar. Secondly, some of the results of generative grammar may be a useful help to language-learners and teachers. We will look at these two areas in turn.

In Chapter 1 we noted some of the differences between first language (L1) acquisition and L2 learning. Here we need to ask if there are any similarities. In particular, does UG play a part in L2 learning? If it does, is the process the same in the two cases?

One way to make sense of the similarities and the differences is to look at the 'interfering' effect of the L1. It has often been said that learners try to apply the rules of their L1 to the language they are learning, and can be reluctant to move away from their acquired 'habits' to the new behaviour needed for the the L2. Chomsky's critique of behaviourism in fact made this type of explanation unpopular for a while in language teaching circles, and there is evidence that many learner errors cannot be accounted for in this way. More recently, however, researchers in the field have taken the idea of parameter-setting proposed by Chomsky and looked at whether L2 learning can be seen in part as a process of resetting the parameters of UG. Suzanne Flynn looked at how speakers of Japanese compared with speakers of Spanish in their ability to handle certain anaphors in English.[7] She found that the Spanish speakers could handle them more easily, and argued that this was because Spanish is like English in terms of a parameter proposed in recent generative work, the head direction parameter which links a number of apparently unrelated differences between languages. Japanese sets this parameter differently from English, so Japanese learners of English first have to reset this parameter before they can handle anaphors. In addition, Japanese learners seem to go through stages of development which correspond to the early stages of L1 acquisition for young English-speaking children – and for the same reasons. In both cases, the values of an important parameter are being set. The Spanish learners of English do not need to go through this process. Flynn's results suggest that neither group of learners of English simply translates from their L1 – it is not a question of transferring acquired habits to a new language. Her claim is that learners analyse L2 data into abstract structures and then apply innate principles of UG – quite a different matter.

A related proposal, put forward by Wayne O'Neil, is that a person faced with a new language to acquire falls back on UG in such a way that those parameters which have a preset value are set to that value. In our discussion of the AG/PRO parameter on page 49 we noted the suggestion that languages like Italian have the preset value. O'Neil suggests that an English speaker learning Italian should not have difficulty with properties of Italian which result from this parameter – for instance, the fact that sentences in Italian do not have to have a subject. On the other hand, we would expect an Italian speaker learning English to have the same difficulties with this parameter which Hyams notes for English-speaking children, as we saw on page 50. If O'Neil's proposal is right, both types of L2 learner set the parameter to its preset Italian value, which of course works fine if you are learning Italian but not if you are learning English. In support of his proposal he presents some data from work with speakers of Standard American English and speakers of a variety of Caribbean English who encounter different kinds of difficulty with each other's language.

This research suggests that the idea of parameters in UG has important implications for L2 learning. Exactly how parameters are reset, though, remains an open question.

Further evidence in support of the idea of UG comes from studies where L2 learners were asked to judge whether certain sentences in the L2 were grammatical or not. The sentences were chosen to illustrate various quite abstract grammatical contrasts not found in the L1 and not in general taught in the classroom. The learners in these studies were generally able to make the correct judgements about the sentences. It is hard to explain this without saying that these learners were using the innate principles made available to them by UG, since there is apparently nowhere else that their grammatical knowledge could have come from.

The theory of UG makes certain types of sentence impossible in any language. Studies have been carried out to see if adult learners of English would accept such 'impossible' sentences as *That a boat had sunk was obvious that John had built* (with the intended meaning of 'it was obvious that a boat that John had built had sunk'). It was found that these sentences were generally rejected. Such results must be interpreted with caution, though. Tests where people's comprehension is at issue are generally less reliable than those where they are asked to imitate or produce sentences. Adults, in particular, can sometimes apply non-linguistic skills in comprehension. A variety of different tests, all leading to similar results, are needed before any firm conclusions can be drawn in this area.

There is, then, some evidence that UG, and the notion of parameter-setting, play a part in L2 learning. Let us now look at the practical value of these ideas for language learning and teaching. A perennial practical problem for language teachers is how much explicit grammar to teach. Should the teacher present grammatical rules to students, or should learners try to assimilate grammar unconsciously by being exposed to large samples of the L2? The first method treats L2 learning like any other subject learned in a classroom, whereas the second method sets out to make L2 learning more like L1 acquisition. This question has been intensely debated in the L2 literature in recent years: most teachers nowadays probably use a combination of the two methods, varying the mix according to the level of the learners and the aims they are trying to achieve.

Interestingly, Chomsky's ideas have been seized on by both sides in this debate. Some writers on L2 learning have taken up the specific rules and principles proposed in generative grammar and tried to base language teaching round these rules, with exercises designed to instil them into learners' minds. Others have been struck by Chomsky's emphasis on the role of innate rules and principles in L1 acquisition: they have argued that if learners are exposed to large samples of L2 material, these innate factors will do most of the work without explicit teaching. Both sides have reckoned that Chomsky's huge prestige would lend support to their views, but it is doubtful whether their use of his ideas has helped clarify the debate.

Many language teachers are familiar with Chomsky's critique of behaviourism, but otherwise have not taken his ideas on board to any great extent. Perhaps a deeper issue is at stake here. In Chapter 1 we noted that in L1 acquisition, the problem is how come young people do so well, given the difficulty of the task facing them. The question now is why L2 learners do so badly, since they have many advantages which should make their task easier. Adult L2 learners have already acquired an L1: they are not learning something totally new. Their other psychological faculties have already developed as well – they are not, for example, acquiring memory, motor and visual skills at the same time as learning a language. L2 learners often have help in the form of trained teachers, classes, and specially designed materials. Yet with all this people rarely achieve the same level of competence in an L2 as in their L1. Why is this?

One possible answer is that so many other factors are involved in learning a second language beyond the simple acquisition of grammatical knowledge. The most obvious of these are motivation, personality, memory, and the effects of previous teaching. However, if problems with these other factors are so important in L2 learning that they outweigh the advantages we have noted, serious questions arise. Firstly, why are these factors vastly *less* significant in L1 acquisition? Secondly, how much use is generative grammar likely to be for L2 learners and teachers? If motivation problems, for example, are significant in L2 learning, it may be more useful for now to think about these problems than to worry about UG.

The conclusion, then, is that UG seems to play a part in L2 learning and teaching, but how important a part is unclear.

Speech pathology

Speech pathologists try to help people whose use of language is impaired in some way. For reasons of space I shall concentrate here on two broad types of language disorder: problems in children acquiring their first language, and problems arising as a result of brain injury affecting mature speakers. As in the previous section, we can first ask whether work in this area has supported Chomsky's ideas about language, and then look at whether people working in the area can learn anything helpful from those ideas.

When we looked at L2 learning, we referred to work which involved specific principles of UG. In the area of speech pathology, work at such a level of detail is much harder. No one has yet found a child who has a problem specifically with the Binding Principle or some other identifiable principle of UG. Similarly, adults with brain damage seem to have more general problems rather than losing just one part of UG. We should not expect precise claims within generative grammar to be confirmed, then, by work in speech pathology.

On the other hand, we might reasonably expect evidence from speech pathology to cast some light on broader issues such as modularity. Susan Curtiss discusses a variety of cases where language acquisition was impaired and reports that grammar can be impaired while everything else seems to work normally; that a child can be mentally handicapped but develop grammatical ability almost normally; and that a child can have grammar and reading difficulties but be able to communicate and to use language quite successfully. She concludes that grammar is 'an autonomous knowledge system' in the mind.[8]

Studies of language disorders caused by an injury to the brain tend to support the same conclusion. The general term given to disorders of this kind is *aphasia*, and speech pathologists have traditionally distinguished two main types: Broca's aphasia, where the patient's pronunciation and grammar are the main casualties, and Wernicke's aphasia, in which comprehension is poor and the speech is often meaningless, despite being almost perfect as far as grammar and pronunciation are concerned. The fact that different abilities can be affected once again corroborates the modularity thesis. On the other hand, attempts to correlate specific language functions with particular parts of the brain have not advanced very far: very different injuries can produce rather similar linguistic effects.

The main contribution of linguistics to speech pathology has been to encourage a more precise description of how language is affected, particularly in aphasia. Relevant research inspired by Chomsky's work is in its infancy, however. A classic 1976 study by the linguists Crystal, Fletcher and Garman advocates the use of grammatical analysis in speech pathology but decides not to use Chomsky's generative model, preferring instead a more traditional grammatical description.[9] The reasons they give are interesting. Firstly, Crystal *et al.* argue that Chomsky's distinction between competence and performance is 'an unreal issue' in the case of speech disorders (p. 35). They say: 'We would want to argue that a remediation procedure in particular should make the fewest possible assumptions about the nature of the mental reality underlying speech, and concentrate instead on an exhaustive account of the characteristics of the speech actually produced by the patient and the therapist' (p. 35).

The idea that exhaustive description is incompatible with generative grammar is strange, to say the least. And surely any therapy must be based on some conception of the 'mental reality' of the patient: if there is any area where linguists should feel entitled to make psychological claims, speech pathology should be the one. Crystal *et al.* go on to bemoan the 'controversy and change' in generative grammar: there is no 'syntactic truth' which they can rely on, so they opt for 'a syntactic framework that has been fairly stable over a period of time', namely the one used in the *Grammar of Contemporary English* (p. 37).[10]

Here again, their objection is rather strange. It is as if a modern astronomer preferred to use Aristotle's theory of planetary motion because Einstein's theory keeps being modified: such an astronomer might say that Aristotle's framework was 'fairly stable over a period of time', ignoring the minor fact that it was superseded because it failed to correspond with reality.

There may be a more illuminating way to explain why Crystal *et al.* make their choice to opt for a non-generative framework. If I have an electrical problem with my car, I go to a car mechanic rather than a theoretical physicist. The physicist's information would be more scientifically correct, but for my purposes the intuitive practical knowledge of the mechanic is more useful. Crystal's adoption of a tried and tested grammatical framework is rather like my choice of a car mechanic rather than a physicist: the grammar has, so to speak been tested in the workshop rather than in the more rigorous setting of a laboratory, but that is good enough for certain purposes.

Summary

In this chapter we have looked at some of the main ways in which Chomsky's work has had an impact on other fields. We looked at two academic areas – philosophy and psychology – and two practical fields – L2 teaching and learning, and speech pathology. In the first two areas, Chomsky himself has intervened with proposals that have aroused widespread discussion and comment. His monism, individualism and rationalism all follow directly from his linguistics, with striking similarities to the views of Kant. His critique of behaviourism and his proposal that the mind is modular both stem from his view that the task of linguistics is to account for knowledge of language, rather than just describing language behaviour.

In the practical fields we saw substantial support for some of Chomsky's key ideas, but found few instances where these ideas had direct practical consequences. We suggested a possible reason for this in the distinction between technical expertise and scientific knowledge.

5
Challenges

This chapter looks at some of the most important challenges to Chomsky's work , and Chomsky's responses to these challenges. Some of the opposition has come from within linguistics, but a lot has also come from other fields concerned with language. Here it makes sense to pick out discussions which bring Chomsky's work into clearer focus by helping to clarify its assumptions and achievements.

It is useful to divide the criticisms of Chomsky's work into four kinds. The first and most fundamental criticism says that his whole undertaking is thoroughly misconceived. According to this type of critic, Chomsky's work either rests on assumptions which are incorrect, like an idol with feet of clay, or it sets itself aims which are impossible to achieve, and is therefore doomed to failure. Challenges of this kind usually revolve around the issue of scientific explanation in linguistics.

A less radical criticism accepts that generative grammar is possible, but rejects the way that Chomsky spells out the nature of the enterprise. For instance, some critics are willing to concede that Chomsky can tell us interesting things about language, but deny that by doing this he can give us insight into the mind or our 'essential human nature'. This type of challenge tends to involve the relationship between language and the mind.

A third sort of criticism accepts that generative grammar is possible but denies that it can tell us interesting things about language. Those who put forward this view tend to see Chomsky's work as too limited: using the formulation of Chapter 3, they say that the cost is too high because he leaves out the most interesting or important features of language. The challenge in this case is about the most useful way to study language – the best aims for linguistics.

The last and least radical type of criticism accepts the aims, assumptions and importance of Chomsky's work, but disagrees with some of the hypotheses he puts forward. Such critics might, for example, argue that the data which Chomsky proposes to explain with the Binding Principle is better accounted for using some other principle of UG. This sort of challenge is not in itself a threat to Chomsky at all, but is a normal part of scientific activity. There have, however, been cases where a discussion has started along these innocuous lines but has subsequently developed into a more serious challenge.

In the rest of this chapter, we shall look at some examples of each of these four types of challenge in turn.

Fundamental criticisms

Quine and indeterminacy

One of the most consistent - and most fundamental – challenges to Chomsky has come from the philosopher W. V. Quine. The debate between Chomsky and Quine has been pursued for many years now. A look at the main issues in this debate will help clarify what it means to make linguistics a science.

In his book *Word and Object* (1960),[1] Quine put forward a position that he called the 'indeterminacy of translation'. In outline, the indeterminacy thesis goes like this. Suppose we have a 'linguist who, unaided by an interpreter, is out to penetrate and translate a language hitherto unknown' (p. 28). 'A rabbit scurries by, the native says 'Gavagai', and the linguist notes down the sentence 'Rabbit' (or 'Lo, a rabbit') as tentative translation, subject to testing in further cases' (p. 29). Suppose further that the native speaker always says 'gavagai' in exactly the same circumstances that we would say 'rabbit'. It would seem reasonable to say that 'rabbit' is the translation of the word 'gavagai', and in practice there would be no further problem.

Being a philosopher, though, Quine suggests some other, apparently bizarre possibilities:

Who knows but what the objects to which [gavagai] applies are not rabbits, after all, but mere stages, or brief temporal segments, of rabbits? In either event the stimulus situations that prompt assent to 'Gavagai' would be the same as for 'Rabbit'. Or perhaps the objects to which 'gavagai' applies are all and sundry undetached parts of rabbits; again the stimulus

meaning would register no difference . . . Does it seem that
the imagined indecision between rabbits, stages of rabbits,
integral parts of rabbits [etc.] must be due merely to some
special fault in our formulation of stimulus meaning, and that
it should be resoluble by a little supplementary pointing and
questioning? Consider, then, how. Point to a rabbit and you
have pointed to a stage of a rabbit, to an integral part of a rabbit
[etc.]. (pp. 51–2)

This sounds absurd. Even if he were to consider the other
outlandish suggestions for the English equivalent of 'gavagai',
a linguist designing a translation manual would no doubt have
good, practical reasons to exclude them and note down 'rabbit'.
But Quine is not concerned with good, practical reasons – he
wants certainty. So long as the different translations have the
same 'stimulus meaning' – that is, so long as we would agree or
disagree with them in exactly the same situations – there seems
to be no way to decide which of them is the correct one.

Surely, though, the correct one is the one that the native
speaker has in his mind? Now we come to the heart of the
matter. For how do we decide which one he has in his mind?
The obvious suggestion is that we should ask him. (Actually, we
have assumed that our linguist does not speak the language well
enough to do this. Even if he can, though, the problem remains
the same.) But this leads us into what Quine, in his paper
'Methodological reflections on current linguistic theory', calls 'an
oddly warped circle'. We are not just trying to find the correct
translation: we are trying to define the term 'correct translation'.
To reword Quine's later paper, we are looking for a criterion of
what to count as the real or proper translation, as against an
equivalent counterfeit. And now the test suggested is that we
ask the native the very question which we do not understand
ourselves: the very question for which we are seeking a test.

Quine is not trying to describe the actual process of translation in the real world. Skilled translators can usually agree,
in practice, about whether a translation is correct or not. The
question is whether there is some *fact* to discover about whether
a word in another language has the same meaning as an English
word. Quine's position is that there is no 'fact of the matter'.
All we have to go on is the native speaker's behaviour. In a

situation where the different translations do not involve a difference in behaviour – where we would agree or disagree with them in exactly the same situations – there is nothing else we can appeal to. We certainly can't appeal to the 'idea' or the 'meaning' in the native speaker's mind: the only evidence for such 'ideas' or 'meanings' that Quine will allow is behavioural evidence, and in this case the behavioural evidence is inconclusive. Quine concludes: 'There can be no doubt that rival systems of analytical hypotheses can fit the totality of speech behaviour to perfection . . . and still specify mutually incompatible translations of countless sentences insusceptible of independent control' (*Word and Object*, p. 72).

What is the relevance of Quine's position to Chomsky's linguistics? Firstly, note that the problems that arise in the case of translation also turn up if we are analysing one language in isolation. If 'rabbit', 'rabbit segment' and 'undetached rabbit part' are equivalent in stimulus meaning, how can we decide what 'rabbit' means in English? Asking a native speaker – that is, ourselves – will not help us, just as it didn't in the case of translation. Quine writes:

> A conviction persists, often unacknowledged, that our sentences express ideas, and express these ideas rather than those, even when behavioral criteria can never say which. There is the stubborn notion that we can tell intuitively which idea someone's sentence expresses, our sentence anyway, even when the intuition is irreducible to behavioral criteria. ('Reply to Chomsky', p. 304)

If this is correct, it calls into question Chomsky's whole enterprise. Chomsky believes that a generative grammar purports to describe correctly part of the knowledge which a speaker of a language has. If Quine is right that we can't even rely on a simple claim that a word or a sentence means such and such, what hope is there for the kind of sophisticated claims that a generative grammar makes? The problem can be summed up like this. To decide between two translations which are equivalent in stimulus meaning, we need something to compare them with. We can't compare them with what is in the speaker's 'mind', because stimulus meaning is our only evidence for what is in the speaker's 'mind'. If we have two equivalent generative grammars, the same problem arises. We can't compare them with the speaker's 'knowledge of the language', since our only evidence for this knowledge is the linguistic behaviour we used to justify the two grammars: if the grammars are equivalent, there is no behavioural difference we can use to distinguish them. There is, then, a fundamental indeterminacy at the heart of generative grammar.

In his account of language Quine explicitly adopts a behaviourist approach: his use of the term 'stimulus meaning' recalls the terminology of Skinner, whose influence Quine acknowledges. Chomsky is quick to challenge this behaviourism as an account of how language is learned: the idea that a child's learning is based on 'reinforcement' is 'reduced to near vacuity' if one allows 'reinforcement' to include 'corroborative usage, whose resemblance to the child's effort is the sole reward'. As Chomsky notes, to say that learning needs reinforcement 'comes very close to saying that learning cannot proceed without data' (QEA, 55–6).

Quine's criticism of generative grammar does not depend on his assuming all of Skinner's views, however. As we saw in the last chapter, Chomsky accepts that a person's behaviour and the conditions in which that behaviour takes place are for now a good starting-point for scientific theorizing. The question is what kind of theories one can build on that basis, and how confident we can be that such theories correspond to reality. Chomsky argues that we can use behavioural data to construct theories about the linguistic knowledge in a speaker's mind. He sees no difference in principle between theories of this kind and theories in physics:

> there can surely be no doubt that Quine's statement about analytical hypotheses is true, though the question arises why it is important. It is, to be sure, undeniable that if a system of 'analytical hypotheses' goes beyond the evidence then it is possible to conceive alternatives compatible with the evidence . . . Thus the situation in the case of language . . . is, in this respect, no different from the case of physics. (QEA, 61)

In Chomsky's view, all Quine has shown is that theories are underdetermined by data – that scientists typically formulate strong theories which go beyond the evidence available. He does not see any special problem for linguistics in this respect which makes it different from physics (using physics, as ever, as the best example of a science which has developed strong, abstract explanatory theories).

Quine had explicitly said that linguistics is different from physics in *Word and Object* (p. 75). In his 'Reply to Chomsky' he tries to explain this difference:

> Where, then, does the parallel [between linguistics and physics] fail? Essentially in this: theory in physics is an ultimate parameter. There is no legitimate first philosophy, higher or firmer than physics, to which to appeal over physicists' heads. . . . Though linguistics is of course a part of the theory of nature, the indeterminacy of translation is not just inherited as a special case of the under-determination of our theory of nature. It is parallel but additional. Thus, adopt for now my fully realistic attitude toward electrons and muons and curved time-space, thus falling in with the current theory of the world despite knowing that it is in principle methodologically under-determined. Consider, from this realistic point of view, the totality of truths of nature, known and unknown, observable and unobservable, past and future. The point about indeterminacy of translation is that it withstands even all this truth, the whole truth about nature. (p. 303)

Chomsky is still unimpressed. He points out that Quine's remarks here are only true if the study of translation is not part of the theory of nature, but that Quine does not justify this assumption. Chomsky continues:

> One might argue that such concepts as 'meaning, idea, proposition' have no place in the study of language. Thus one might argue that relevant evidence will never exist for theoretical statements employing these concepts, or that there is a better theory that avoids them entirely but accounts for the relevant evidence. But this kind of critique, justified or not, rests on no novel notion of 'indeterminacy'. Rather, the issue is in principle just like those that arise in other branches of empirical inquiry. (RL, 185)

Notice in addition that the whole matter has nothing necessarily to do with meaning. In *Word and Object* Quine says that the same problem of indeterminacy arises in syntax when a linguist proposes that a sentence has a particular phrase-structure. The belief that meaning is the issue has been confusing, in Chomsky's view, because it is a poorly understood area which is taken to be 'deep' and 'important'. What Quine is challenging is the status of theoretical constructs in linguistics in general. The point that seems to separate Quine and Chomsky is whether a theory about knowledge is fundamentally different from a theory in physics – in other words, whether psychology is part of the natural sciences (RR, 19–20). From the remarks above about electrons and curved space-time, Quine apparently believes that a fully realistic attitude towards the concepts in theories of physics is legitimate. Even with this attitude, he says, indeterminacy of translation would still be a problem.

Chomsky's view is that physics and psychology are both part of the same body of scientific theory, which we rely on more than we rely on anything else, while recognizing that it will be improved by future research. The brain is part of the physical world, so a theory of the mind – remember that 'mind' is just an abstract way of talking about 'brain' – is for Chomsky as 'physical' as the theories of physics. This harks back to our discussion of the 'mind–body problem' in pages 78–80. To the extent that we succeed in linking psychological theories and theories in physics, the scientific notion of 'physical' will simply be extended to cover the new domain. In everyday life we distinguish mind and body, so that the truth about body does not help us understand the mind. But there is no reason, in Chomsky's view, why *as scientists* we have to accept this distinction.

Wittgenstein's sceptic

In his book *Wittgenstein on Rules and Private Language*, Saul Kripke[2] attempts to reconstruct a philosophical puzzle based on the discussion in *Philosophical Investigations*, the last book by Ludwig Wittgenstein.[3] Interpreting Wittgenstein is notoriously difficult,[4] and part of Kripke's aim is simply to establish that the problem he focuses on is indeed the central one in Wittgenstein's book; I should add that Kripke does not necessarily support the views he elucidates. The puzzle discussed in the book raises questions which touch on the ideas of Chomsky, who writes: 'Of the various general critiques that have been presented over the years concerning the program and conceptual framework of generative grammar, this seems to me the most interesting' (KL, 223).

Kripke presents Wittgenstein's puzzle by using as an example the rule of addition. We would normally say that someone who knows how to add has grasped a rule which can be applied to indefinitely many new sums in the future (in this respect, the rule of addition is like rules of grammar, which can be applied to indefinitely many new sentences). Kripke writes:

> Let me suppose, for example, that '68 + 57' is a computation that I have never performed before . . . I perform the computation, obtaining, of course, the answer '125'. I am confident, perhaps after checking my work, that '125' is the correct answer . . .
>
> Now suppose I encounter a bizarre sceptic. This sceptic questions my certainty about my answer. . . . Perhaps, he suggests, as I used the term 'plus' in the past, the answer I intended for '68 + 57' should have been '5'! Of course, the sceptic's suggestion is obviously insane. My initial response to such a suggestion might be that the challenger should go back to school and learn to add. Let the challenger, however, continue. After all, he says, if I am now so confident that, as I used the symbol '+', my intention was that '68 + 57' should turn out to denote 125, this cannot be because I explicitly gave myself instructions that 125 is the result of performing the addition in this particular instance. By hypothesis, I did no such thing. But of course, the idea is that, in this new instance, I should apply the very same function or rule that I applied so many times in the past. But who is to say what function this was? In the past I gave myself only a finite number of examples instantiating this function. All, we have supposed, involved numbers smaller than 57. So perhaps in the past I used 'plus' and '+' to denote a function which I will call 'quus' and symbolize by '@'. It is defined by :
>
> $$x @ y = x + y, \text{ if } x,y < 57$$
> $$= 5 \text{ otherwise.}$$
>
> Who is to say that this is not the function I previously meant by '+'?

> Now if the sceptic proposes his hypothesis sincerely, he is crazy; such a bizarre hypothesis as the proposal that I always meant quus is absolutely wild. Wild it indubitably is, no doubt it is false; but if it is false, there must be some fact about my past usage that can be cited to refute it. For although the hypothesis is wild, it does not seem to be *a priori* impossible. (pp. 8–9)

Kripke goes on to argue that there is no fact about my past experience which can distinguish between my meaning plus and my meaning quus. Thus 'the entire idea of meaning vanishes into thin air', a conclusion that Kripke describes as 'incredible' but apparently inescapable (p. 22). He adds that 'it would seem that the *use* of the ideas of rules and of competence in linguistics needs serious reconsideration, even if these notions are not rendered 'meaningless' (p. 31).

Kripke goes on to outline Wittgenstein's solution to this puzzle. The puzzle is insoluble, he says, if we look at a person in isolation:

> if one person is considered in isolation, the notion of a rule as guiding the person who adopts it can have *no* substantive content . . . The situation is very different if we widen our gaze from consideration of the rule follower alone and allow ourselves to consider him as interacting with a wider community. Others will then have justification conditions for attributing correct or incorrect rule following to the subject (p. 89).

This depends, of course, on the rule follower's answer to an addition problem corresponding with that of the others. Wittgenstein thus questions the whole basis for saying of a person that he tacitly follows a rule. Since this notion is central to generative grammar, it is natural that Chomsky should try to show that Wittgenstein is wrong. His approach is like his response to Quine: he argues that the problem is not specific to psychology but arises in any science. To say that a person has tacit knowledge of a rule of language (or arithmetic) is part of an empirical theory about that person, a theory which may be right or wrong and which is justified by looking at the person's behaviour. There is no relevant 'fact' beyond these observations about a person's behaviour. Similarly, theories in physics are justified by looking at the phenomena they purport to explain.

Let's pursue this similarity further. We normally believe, in line with theories of physics, that objects fall to the ground because of the law of gravity (more accurately, the theory of gravity). Suppose a bizarre sceptic proposes that the 'real' law that objects obey is a different one, for example, a law which states that objects are attracted to each other unless one of them is my son at age eight. How, do we prove the sceptic wrong? Quite simply, we wait until my son's eighth birthday and see if he floats out into space. If he does, the standard theory of gravity is refuted.

This is standard scientific practice, but it raises an odd problem. The theory of gravity is supposed to explain why certain events happen and not others, yet we would abandon the theory if the wrong events were to happen. The theory is only as reliable as the next event: it relies on the belief that the next event won't disconfirm it. How, then, can we take it as solid and dependable at all, as we do? We take the theory to be solid so long as it continues to make the right predictions. But who is to say that it will continue to do this?

Consider now Kripke's sceptic. How can we show that we add according to 'plus' rather than 'quus'? The answer must be that we shall continue to believe in 'plus' as long as this account continues to make the right predictions. In the case Kripke mentions, he did *in fact* reach the answer '125' for the sum '68 + 57'. This observation alone shows that the sceptic is wrong. There is no need to look for further evidence, or to talk about Kripke's 'intentions'. The next computation that Kripke does may show that some other bizarre alternative was in fact the correct one. We have no guarantee about future events here, any more than we do in physics. But so far the commonsense view of addition is not in jeopardy – at least, no more than any scientific hypothesis.

In his discussion of Wittgenstein's puzzle, Kripke tries to treat the rule of addition – and, by extension, rules of language – as both weaker and stronger than they actually are. He treats them as too weak when he looks for some extra reason to justify them beyond the fact that they make correct predictions and are part of a coherent explanatory theory. He treats them as too strong when he regards them as potentially true or false in their own right, unrelated to the behaviour they are supposed to explain. The point is that a proposed rule and the behaviour it is designed to explain *belong together*. Any solidity they have comes from the strength of the relationship between them. We treat the theory of gravity as solid because of the strong relationship it bears to large numbers of relevant facts. The same holds for any theory about the rules of arithmetic or language in a person's mind. Of course, any empirical theory may be proved wrong tomorrow by a new relevant fact. But this is normal inductive uncertainty, and applies to any science.

Chomsky quotes a passage from Tyler Burge that makes a pertinent point:

> questions of ontology, reduction, and causation generally, are epistemically posterior to questions about the success of explanatory and descriptive practices. One cannot reasonably criticize a purported explanatory or descriptive practice primarily by appeal to some prior conception of what a 'good entity' is, or of what individuation or reference should be like, or of what the overall structure of science (or knowledge) should turn out to look like. Questions of what exists, how things are individuated, and what reduces to what are questions that arise by reference to going explanatory and descriptive practices. By themselves, proposed answers to these questions cannot be used to judge an otherwise successful mode of explanation and description. (KL, 250–1)

What both Quine and Wittgenstein are attacking is the assumption that there is some realm of being to which a psychological theory has to relate beyond the behaviour it tries to explain. They both argue that there is no such realm of being. But Chomsky is not committed to any such assumption. All he assumes is that if a theory is related to some facts in an insightful way, it is reasonable to suppose, tentatively, that this relationship between theory and facts corresponds to reality. The theory and the facts together form a closed circle. Quine and Wittgenstein rightly warn against the dangers of stepping outside that circle. But Chomsky does not accept that he is doing so. Ultimately, he sees the arguments of Quine and Wittgenstein as correct, but irrelevant.

Language yes, human nature no

We turn now to the second type of challenge to Chomsky's work. The argument here is that generative grammar can tell us some interesting things about language, but nothing more than that: Chomsky is wrong, these critics say, to think that his work gives us insights into the workings of the mind or into our basic 'human nature'.

The fullest statement of this point of view is Charles Hockett's book *The State of the Art*.[5] Hockett was one of the leading figures in the descriptive, classificatory linguistics that preceded Chomsky in North America. Like many others in the field, he was unhappy with the criticisms of this type of linguistics put out by Chomsky and his supporters in the late fifties and sixties. The book is partly an attempt to 'put the record straight' about pre-Chomskyan linguistics. The bulk of the book, though, is a criticism of Chomsky's views, and it is this part that we need to concentrate on here.

Hockett concedes that some of the specific analyses proposed by Chomsky and other generative grammarians are interesting, and tell us things about language which were not known before. He accepts, for instance, that the idea of transformations has been useful (p. 3). He is also willing to grant that generative grammar is one way to find out universal properties of language, although detailed research on large numbers of languages is, for him, necessary here too (pp. 78–9). What Hockett does not accept are Chomsky's broader claims about the significance of his enterprise.

Hockett makes a distinction between 'well-defined' and 'ill-defined' systems. A well-defined system is one which can be described in a neat mechanical or 'algorithmic' way. The number system, for instance, is well-defined: for any whole number we know exactly how to write down the next larger one. Football is ill-defined: there are very precise rules, for example defining certain kinds of foul, but there is no automatic, algorithmic way of deciding whether a given action by one of the players definitely is or is not a foul: as Hockett notes, we depend on officials and their rulings to decide in unclear cases (p. 50).

Hockett believes that Chomsky's basic mistake is to treat language as a well-defined system. He argues that language is not subject to fixed rules but to flexible constraints, and that therefore languages are ill-defined (pp. 60–1). Once again, Hockett draws an analogy with (American) football, where the highest score on record is 227. He writes:

> Could speed and skill be increased (and strength of opposition decreased) to squeeze this up to 228? Possibly. To 229? Perhaps. The fact that we cannot easily name an integer greater than any member of Sf [the set of all possible scores] does not mean that there is a precise maximum element in Sf. (p. 47)

Hockett argues that the same kind of flexible constraints which make 1,000,000 an impossible score in football also make million-word sentences impossible in language. Chomsky's view has always been that huge sentences are 'unacceptable' for a variety of non-linguistic reasons, but that they can none the less be 'grammatical' according to the rules of a language. As we saw in Chapter 3, Chomsky excludes from consideration in his type of linguistics factors other than grammar. We saw, for instance, that he rejects the wider notion of 'communicative competence' as a starting-point because it does not offer the prospect of discovering principles of UG. Hockett is calling into question Chomsky's distinction between 'grammaticality' and 'acceptability'.

Similar objections are raised in another book that is critical of Chomsky, Terence Moore and Christine Carling's *Understanding Language: Towards a Post-Chomskyan Linguistics*.[6] They write:

> Chomsky at the outset made a number of ill-justified idealisations. Perhaps the most important of these was his decision to view native users of languages as having a highly specific ability: that of being able to distinguish the grammatical from the non-grammatical sentences of their language without reference to meaning. He did not do this because it had been established in any pre-theoretic way that such an ability existed . . . He did it in fact for rather a curious reason. He assumed that native speakers could distinguish between grammatical and non-grammatical sentences independently of meaning because the formalised theory which he was devising required this ability to exist in order to be testable. The idealisation which he imposed upon native speakers thus arose out of the requirements of the particular type of theory he was attempting to construct. (p. 5)

Moore and Carling, along with Hockett, argue that Chomsky is wrong to leave out questions of meaning in this way. Once again, though, deciding whether their criticism is right is not a simple matter. In the first place, Chomsky does not accept that he has left out questions of meaning. As we saw in Chapter 2, the arguments for the Binding Principle often involve reference to meaning. Secondly, what does it mean to 'establish' something 'in a pre-theoretic way'? Chomsky's position is that one can only establish something within a scientific, explanatory framework (and normal scientific caution applies, as we have stressed repeatedly). Any initial assumptions one adopts must be treated as empirical hypotheses, which are justified or refuted by their role in explanation.

Lurking behind Moore and Carling's criticism is the assumption that nothing, or very little, is unique to language. Indeed, many critics of Chomsky prefer the view that there are general psychological principles rather than principles and rules which only apply to language. Here the onus is on the critics to produce such general principles, for example, one which subsumes the Binding Principle. The prospects for this do not look good. The Binding Principle, for instance, does not look like a general feature of human intelligence. It is more likely to be a rule of language, and only of language. This is an empirical question, though, whereas Moore and Carling simply assume that it is settled in advance.

'Possible but uninteresting'

'Pointless and perverse'

Let us now look at the third type of challenge to Chomsky's work. The critics we shall look at in this section agree that Chomsky's enterprise is possible in the way he sets out. They argue, though, that his work is not very useful, because it leaves out some of the most interesting and important features of language. In particular, it is said, Chomsky says nothing about the use of language as a means of communication between people.

In Chapter 1 we saw how Chomsky defended himself against the claim that the 'essential purpose' of language is communication. Let's now look at the less radical criticism which says that it is possible to ignore the communicative function of language but that the result is an impoverished and uninteresting view of language. This criticism is expressed with particular clarity by John Searle in his paper 'Chomsky's revolution in linguistics':[7]

The common-sense picture of human language runs something like this. The purpose of language is communication in much the same sense that the purpose of the heart is to pump blood. In both cases it is possible to study the structure independently of the function but pointless and perverse to do so, since structure and function so obviously interact . . .

For Chomsky, language is defined by syntactical structure (not by the use of the structure in communication) and syntactical structure is determined by innate properties of the human mind (not by the needs of communication). (pp. 16–17)

Chomsky replies to Searle as follows:

Surely there are significant connections between structure and function; this is not, and has never been , in doubt . . . Study of structure, use, and acquisition may be expected to provide insight into essential features of language.

. . . consider Searle's contention that it is 'pointless and perverse' to study the structure of language 'independently of function' . . . Pursuing his analogy, there is no doubt that the physiologist, studying the heart, will pay attention to the fact that it pumps blood. But he will also study the structure of the heart and the origin of this structure in the individual and the species, making no dogmatic assumptions about the possibility of 'explaining' this structure in functional terms.

. . . Where it can be shown that structure serves a particular function, that is a valuable discovery. To account for or somehow explain the structure of UG, or of particular grammars, on the basis of functional considerations is a pretty hopeless prospect, I would think; it is, perhaps, even 'perverse' to assume otherwise. (RL, 56–7)

As we saw in Chapter 1, when Chomsky formulates the main questions facing linguistics, he includes a question about how knowledge of language is used. He rejects the view that we should begin by looking at this question, or that we should assume in advance that any (let alone all) of the structure of this knowledge can be accounted for in functional terms. One difficulty in accounting for grammar on the basis of communicative function comes from the frequent lack of a direct relationship between the two. Frederick Newmeyer, a linguist who sympathizes with Chomsky, gives a good example.[8] There are three common syntactic devices in English: putting the auxiliary verb before the subject as in example (1), leaving out an understood *you* subject as in (2), and putting a *wh*-word (*who*, *what*, *where*, etc.) at the beginning of a sentence as in (3).

(1)   Are you having a good time?
(2)   Go home now
(3)   What are you eating.

Newmeyer then asks us to consider four common functions of language in conversation: issuing a command, expressing a condition, asking a question, and making an exclamation. Each of these functions can be carried out using more than one syntactic device:

COMMAND
a.   Don't you leave
b.   Leave now!
c.   How about leaving!

CONDITION
a.   Had John left (I would have been sorry)
b.   Leave (and you'll regret it)

QUESTION
a.   Did he leave?
b.   Leaving now?
c.   What is it?

EXCLAMATION
a.   Am I thirsty!
b.   What a hot day it is!

Newmeyer suggests that this mismatch of form and function 'appears to be the general rule rather than the exception'. This is an empirical question, of course; there is no point, however, in simply assuming, as Searle appears to do, that there is always or usually going to be a close connection.

   Searle suggests that evolution may have played a role in shaping language structure: 'We don't know how language evolved in human prehistory, but it is quite reasonable to suppose that the needs of communication influenced the structure.' (p. 16) Once again, Chomsky is not impressed. Human beings have various higher-order cognitive systems, such as the capacity to do science or the capacity to deal with abstract mathematics. It is not clear that these capacities have any selectional value, though, since for most of evolution there was no opportunity to use them. General suggestions about evolution do not help us, he argues (RL, 58–9).

Artificial Intelligence

Similar criticisms of Chomsky's approach to language have been put forward by some workers in the field of *Artificial Intelligence* (AI).[9] The aim of AI is to construct computer programs which will enable computers to perform intelligent tasks. Using language is clearly one such task, and people like Roger Schank, Terry Winograd and Yorick Wilks have for many years been trying to design systems which can use language in ways which resemble the ways in which human beings use language. The term 'intelligence' is crucial here: it is relatively easy to program a computer to perform low-level operations on language. For instance, the word-processing software I am using now includes a 'thesaurus' which will suggest synonyms for most English words. The computer cannot 'understand' any of the synonyms, or suggest which one is closest to the idea I am trying to express. It simply makes available, much more quickly than a human being could, certain pieces of information which someone has typed into it. Computers are very good at doing simple (but useful) things like this quickly and reliably. They are not very good at making intelligent choices, and anyone who succeeds in designing one which can will have made a major breakthrough. This is the task which AI has set itself.

One might expect that AI and generative grammar would have a lot in common, and would work closely together. Some workers in AI have indeed interacted fruitfully with generative grammar. To a large extent, though, the relationship between the two fields has been marked by indifference at best, and outright hostility at worst. Criticisms of AI by generative grammarians are not directly relevant for our purposes here, but criticisms in the other direction are. Terry Winograd (who, it should be said, has tried harder than some in recent times to bring the two fields together constructively) expresses one of the main disagreements:[10]

> The most obvious difference between the two approaches is in the amount of attention paid to issues of the mental processes that go on when language is used . . . As has been pointed out many times, generative grammar 'generates' only in the most abstract sense and the formalism has little or nothing to say about what goes on when a person produces or comprehends an utterance.
>
> The computational approach takes the opposite starting-point. The information processing that goes on in the mind of a person using language is taken as fundamental. It is assumed that this process makes use of stored structures (such as a grammar) that are not themselves procedural, but whose form is constrained by the way they are used in procedures of production and comprehension. From this viewpoint, it seems that a characterization of abstract competence will inevitably fail to capture the appropriate generalities about language since it does not deal with what is 'really going on'.

A natural reply to this would be to ask for evidence that these 'procedures of production and comprehension' do in fact constrain the form of grammar. This is not as straightforward as it sounds. It may be possible to show that production and comprehension procedures influence what happens when language is used – in fact, it would be surprising if this did not happen. No one doubts that knowledge of language interacts with such procedures in actual use. The question is whether knowledge of language is itself shaped by such procedures irrespective of how it is put to use. If we assume that the language faculty is part of human biology, then it is hard to see how such shaping could happen.

To see the problem here more clearly, let's look at a different biological system, say, an acorn. Because of its internal structure, an acorn will grow into an oak tree given the right environmental conditions (soil, water, light, etc.). The environment may play a part in shaping the way the tree grows – it may become a healthy tree, a damaged tree, a tall tree, and so on. But what makes it an oak tree, as opposed to some other biological system, is the genetic structure of the acorn: if we want a clear picture of what an oak tree is like, this structure, unique to oak trees, is obviously the place to start.

None the less, Chomsky accepts that even if the 'procedures of production and comprehension' do not constrain the form of grammar, they are worth knowing. The problem for him is that AI as pursued by Winograd and those with similar views has not taught us anything significant about 'the information processing that goes on in the mind of a person using language'. One important reason for this is that efficient processing by a computer may be quite different from what human beings do. Per-Kristian Halvorsen spells out the problem in a recent survey of computer applications of linguistics:[11]

> Duplication of a narrow range of human behaviour in a machine does not imply that the machine, or the program that the machine is running, encodes the knowledge that underlies the behaviour in humans . . . In fact, deceptively clever language programs often do not have any grounding in linguistic theory . . .
>
> Programs of the complexity of natural language understanding systems, while based on linguistic technology derived from linguistic theory, involve shortcuts mandated by efficiency considerations . . . Thus, linguistic theory is only piecemeal reflected in such systems.

Halvorsen gives as an example a famous program called ELIZA, which fooled many people into thinking that there was a real person sending messages to the user. ELIZA was in fact based on a trivial idea: the program would pick out a key word in what the user said and insert it into one of a number of ready-made templates. A very successful commercial system called SYSTRAN translates from English into a variety of languages. The software is based on some simple devices and a lot of *ad hoc* patches to cope with particular recurrent problems. Neither of these programs tells us anything important about language.

Language as poetry

One of the most impassioned pleas that Chomsky's linguistics is too limited comes from Ian Robinson's book *The New*

Grammarians' Funeral.[12] Robinson starts by describing what he thinks is the right general attitude to language:

> The study of language is one mode of contemplating a mystery, and a proper awe is a measure of the sense and depth of what goes on in the study of language . . . awe at language should be present in linguistics and inform it. (p. xi)

He goes on to give many examples of uses of language which are ungrammatical, or where generative grammar does not say anything illuminating, for instance this extract from Shakespeare's *Othello*:

> When Othello cries, 'Lie with her? lie on her? We say lie on her, when they belie her. Lie with her: 'zounds, that's fulsome: Handkerchief: Confessions: Handkerchief . . .' he is not speaking well-formed sentences. But not only is what he says English, it has been found by generations of hearers to be quite unusually clear and expressive English. (37–8)

Robinson concludes by arguing that the idea of a 'science' of language is an illusion:

> 'Language is a fitting object of study because there are things like *King Lear*. But this means that the important judgements in linguistics, the judgements about the high level of meaning, must always be challengeable . . . there is no escape in the study of language from judgements essentially of the kind we make when thinking about poetry, about what matters in language. Linguistics, that is to say, cannot be a science, and if an academic discipline at all it must be a humane one.
> . . . Poets have the deepest working knowledge of language (which is to say that poets are, for better or worse, the people most humanly alive) . . . Poets show us language at full: critics are the people who try to follow poets through the fullness of language . . .
> That is why it is not strange to me, though it will seem strange to Chomsky . . . that I have learned far more about language both from the philosophy of Collingwood and of Wittgenstein and Rhees, and from the literary criticism of Leavis, than from the whole corpus of established linguistics. (pp. 181–4)

I have not quoted any of Robinson's objections to specific parts of Chomsky's framework: most of his criticisms either cover ground we have already looked at, or are based on misunderstanding. His general remarks, however, express a reaction to Chomsky's work – and to linguistics in general – which is not uncommon. Perhaps a good reply would be this. We expect sciences like physics and chemistry to tell us basic, reliable things about the structure of the physical world. We don't expect them to explain why certain sounds, shapes and structures are generally regarded as great art. People have attempted to explain what great art is, but mostly in terms which are suggestive and indirect rather than in any objective way. Sometimes reliable knowledge is possible; in other fields, oblique hints are the best we can do. Some people prefer maximum reliability, while others are willing to make do with much less certainty because of the intrinsic importance of the subject matter. Chomsky belongs with the first group, Robinson with the second. Given this difference of temperament, there is little point in either one trying to persuade the other that one approach is better. Both of them are legitimate.

Challenges within generative grammar

On several occasions, linguists working in generative grammar have put forward analyses which disagree radically with those proposed by Chomsky. In principle this is all to the good: a field where there is controversy and debate is living and developing. This book is not a history of generative grammar, so we won't go into these debates in any detail. Some of the internal debates have raised more fundamental issues, however, which illustrate aspects of Chomsky's ideas that we have not explored yet. We shall concentrate on two topics: Generative Semantics and Generalized Phrase Structure Grammar.

Generative Semantics

In the late sixties many of Chomsky's former students formed a breakaway trend which tried to extend the scope of generative grammar away from a narrow concern with grammar and into other areas of language study. The name 'Generative Semantics' suggests a desire to focus on questions of meaning more than on grammar.[13] Indeed, one of the starting-points of Generative Semantics was a series of arguments that meaning influenced grammatical form, and that a generative grammar therefore had to include references to meaning in the syntax.

For example, John Ross discussed sentences like these:[14]

(1) Max lurked near your house last night
(2) ?*I lurked near your house last night

(The ?* in front of [2] is intended to mean that the sentence is bad but not totally ungrammatical.) Ross used the difference between (1) and (2) to argue for certain grammatical rules. The problem is that the data in question presumably have a lot to do with the *meaning* of the word *lurk*. Once grammarians try to make the meanings of individual words part of the grammar (rather than dealing with facts like this in a dictionary), the way is open to including an ever wider set of facts within grammar.

Indeed, these arguments were subsequently broadened out to cover other factors which supposedly influenced grammar. George Lakoff argued, for instance, that a grammatical rule of '*will*-deletion' related pairs of sentences like these:[15]

(3) I will leave tomorrow
(4) I leave tomorrow

He noted, however, that there are certain circumstances where the type of sentence without *will* cannot be used. For example, you can say (5), but not (6):

(5) The Red Sox play the Yankees at baseball tomorrow
(6) *The Red Sox beat the Yankees at baseball tomorrow

If *will* is not 'deleted', sentence (6) is fine:

(7) The Red Sox will beat the Yankees at baseball tomorrow

Lakoff proposed that the rule of *will*-deletion can only apply 'if it is presupposed that the speaker is sure that the event will happen'.

Other examples where the grammaticality of a sentence was connected to the beliefs of the speaker are illustrated by examples like:

(8)   John called Mary a Republican and then *she* insulted *him*

Here the speaker believes that calling someone a Republican is an insult. If the stress is varied, this belief isn't necessary:

(9)   John called Mary a Republican and then she in*sult*ed him

Arguments of this kind were attractive to many linguists who did not like Chomsky's insistence on separating grammar from other features of language.[16] Disillusion spread in, however, when it became clear that opening up the scope of generative grammar in this way made it impossible to propose interesting explanatory theories. In order to handle the increasingly wide range of phenomena said to impinge on grammar, new types of rule were needed: in fact, supporters of Generative Semantics allowed so many different rules that it looked as if 'anything was possible' in their approach. Science can't be this general. A scientific theory has to be narrow: it has to say that certain things are possible and others are impossible. If a theory allows for all possibilities then it will always be right, and it isn't a scientific theory at all. Generative Semantics made a big stir but soon collapsed, in part for these reasons.

The 'power' of a linguistic theory has always been one of Chomsky's central concerns. A theory of UG has to state what conditions something must meet in order to be a possible human language. The tighter the conditions, the more interesting the theory is. A theory which says, for example, that any system of sounds is a language is so loose that almost anything goes. A theory which says that only a system of sounds which obeys the Binding Principle is a language is making a strong claim – one which can easily be tested on real languages, and refined or rejected as necessary. The aim has always been, then, to *reduce* the power of linguistic theory while at the same time being able to cover all the relevant facts.

From this point of view, Generative Semantics went in exactly the wrong direction in *increasing* the power of the theory. By introducing powerful new rule-types, Generative Semantics made it harder to formulate a tight theory of UG. Thus Chomsky regarded this breakaway tendency as a return to description and a move away from explanation. Proposing a lot of new descriptive devices to handle hitherto unnoticed or unsystematized data does not help if your aim is to propose a general, restrictive account of what a possible human language must be like.

Generalized Phrase Structure Grammar

The question of restricting the power of linguistic theory has also been a key point of conflict between Chomsky and another more recent breakaway trend known as Generalized Phrase Structure Grammar (GPSG).[17] Supporters of GPSG have presented empirical arguments that their model of grammar is superior to Chomsky's, along with claims that their theory was more restrictive and hence to be preferred, other things being equal. Chomsky maintains that their theory is in fact much more powerful than his, and that GPSG is flawed in its empirical claims.

Advocates of GPSG say that one grammar is more powerful than another if it will generate more languages. It has long been known that a grammar with transformations is more powerful in this sense than one which only has phrase-structure rules. One supposed reason why this is important comes from outside linguistics. Most computer languages can be described using phrase-structure grammars, and a great deal is known about their mathematical properties. If natural languages can be described in a similar way, as GPSG claims, then firstly we can draw on what is known about computer languages and apply this information to natural languages; and secondly, results from linguistics can be applied to computers, an exciting prospect.

Chomsky's reply is that the kind of 'power' which GPSG supporters invoke has to do with what is called 'weak generative capacity' and with E-language, neither of which have any empirical significance. The notion of E-language – an infinite set of expressions said to be generated by a grammar – is not even well-defined, for reasons discussed at length in KL. Here is one reason:

> when we speak of a person as knowing a language, we do not mean that he or she knows an infinite set of sentences . . . or a set of acts or behaviours; rather, what we mean is that the person knows what makes sound and meaning relate to one another in a specific way . . . The person has 'a notion of

structure' and knows an I-language as characterized by the linguist's grammar. (KL, 27)

Weak generative capacity is the capacity of a grammar to generate sentences. What counts for Chomsky is strong generative capacity, the ability of a grammar to describe the structure of sentences. In this respect, he argues, the class of phrase structure grammars is far too powerful, whereas transformational grammars and grammars within GB theory are more restrictive. Even more important, in Chomsky's view, is not how many languages a grammar generates, but how many grammars of a particular language UG allows in relation to the data that a child encounters. The ideal situation, Chomsky argues, is one where only a small number of grammars are possible, and where there are sharp differences between them. Given that situation, a relatively small amount of data will be enough to enable a child to select the right grammar (see ATS, 60–2). The kind of theory of UG that Chomsky has proposed recently seems to be on the right lines in this respect: parametric variation in the way the Binding Principle is set for different languages, for example, has huge consequences throughout the grammar. A small number of simple choices, each of them having important consequences: this is the kind of 'restriction' that makes sense in language acquisition.

Chomsky also argues that nothing that is known about computer languages has any relevance to natural language, so far as is known, and that the supposed usefulness in the other direction, that of GPSG to computing, is also illusory. Much has been written about these issues in recent years, and the debate continues. What is crucial here, as we leave Chomsky's linguistics and move on to the politics, are the basic questions about language which we looked at in Chapter 1. GPSG has chosen to concentrate on generating sentences, rather than on the underlying system of knowledge in the mind of speaker-hearers. For Chomsky, on the other hand, a theory of grammar has to be judged on the results it achieves in answering questions about the system of knowledge and how it is acquired, and on these alone. The central issue for him is to reduce the power of UG so that it becomes part of a plausible model of language acquisition. The consistent way he has held on to this issue is right at the heart of Chomsky's linguistics.

Politics

'Chomsky said simply that intellectuals should not lie, and more than that, [he] exposed some of the lies and liars.'

Dell Hymes

6

The 'Free World'

Finding the problem

Imagine you are a friendly extra-terrestrial who wants to make life better for the inhabitants of planet earth. As you look down at the earth from your spaceship, what would you say were our biggest problems?

You might start with the tens of thousands of nuclear weapons that threaten to destroy all higher life on the planet. You would notice too the conventional wars being fought in different parts of the world: as I write, there are people killing each other in Lebanon, Somalia, El Salvador, Northern Ireland, Mozambique, Afghanistan and Cambodia. Or you might home in on the shocking damage to the environment from deforestation, acid rain, and pollution, along with the increasing threat of global warming.

A very strong contender for the biggest problem facing the earth would be poverty. Large numbers of human beings face hunger, insufficient or unclean water, disease and squalor, along with grim despair from the knowledge that they have little prospect of earning enough to achieve a minimal decent life. If you were a well-informed extra-terrestrial, you would know that there is enough food in the world so that no one needs to go hungry. The problem is one of inequality: there are rich countries where most people have enough and some have untold wealth, while in the poor countries desperate poverty is widespread.

Most people would agree that this state of affairs is wrong, and that something should be done about it. Our extra-terrestrial might well decide that if this problem was solved, humans would have more energy and goodwill to devote to the other problems. Suppose, then, that our visitor from outer space identified poverty as our number one problem and began to look at its causes and ways to remedy them. She or he would begin by looking at the extent of the problem. Which are the poor parts of the earth, and which are the rich parts? Where does this division into rich and poor come from, and why does it persist?

Let's start at the top. Without a doubt, the richest and most powerful country in the world is the United States of America. The United States has about 5 per cent of the world's population but a quarter of the world's wealth. There are a number of reasons for this, among them the fact that the United States has large oil and mineral reserves, and plenty of arable land. The most important reasons are rather different, though. The other rich countries of the world were heavily damaged during this century by two world wars. The United States fought in both wars, of course, but at a relatively late stage, bearing a small share of the casualties and an even smaller share of the destruction. Even before this the United States was the largest industrial power in the world, but by 1945 it was pre-eminent. The previous economic superpower, Britain, had been declining for some time. Much of Europe, Japan and the Soviet Union lay in ruins.

There are two conflicting accounts of what has happened since then. The official line, put out by successive US governments, is that the United States has used its power primarily for good, in an unselfish attempt to share its freedom and prosperity with the rest of the world. The country has given huge amounts of aid and assistance to poorer countries, firstly to rebuild their economies after the war and then to expand and grow. Believing that political freedom and prosperity go together, the United States has promoted both of these throughout the world. Since nobody is perfect, US leaders have naturally made mistakes occasionally, but their intentions have always been generous and benevolent.

Unfortunately, the official picture continues, there are wicked people who are opposed to freedom, and to the free market economic system which has been the basis of US prosperity. These people are called 'communists', and they have a fanatical hatred of the United States. They will stop at nothing to attack the United States, using brutal and ruthless tactics of deceit, intimidation and murder. Spearheaded by the Soviet Union, communists throughout the world are a dangerous threat to freedom. Their state-run economic system is disastrously inefficient and wasteful compared to the free-market system. In defending itself against such people, the United States merely wishes to defend itself and its allies against attack, and has no aggressive intentions, only resorting to violence as a last resort, and generally adhering to moral principles which the fanatical enemy rejects.

The alternative account goes like this. For a rich country to share its wealth willingly with others would be unique in history, if true. It is more realistic to start with the assumption that the United States, like every other rich and powerful country in history, will use every means at its disposal to defend its privileged position. Since the end of the Second World War – and in fact going back long before that – the United States has ruthlessly used its economic and military might to enrich itself at the expense of other countries: by plundering their natural resources, treating their people as cheap labour, and ensuring that the markets of these countries remained open for the goods and services of US companies.

When the people of a country try to free themselves from the US grip, the US response ranges from diplomatic pressure and economic boycotts to subversion, political interference, assassination, terrorism, backing for military coups, or direct invasion by the most powerful military force in history. If a country none the less succeeds in gaining some measure of control over its own resources, the USA will continue to isolate and attack it. The aim is to force the regime in such countries to adopt repressive measures and seek help from the Soviet Union. When this happens, the leaders of these countries are denounced as Kremlin stooges, and their problems – for the most part, deliberate results of US policy – are held up as evidence of the wickedness and incompetence of communism.

Chomsky is one of the most forceful and convincing supporters of the alternative account. His political writings and lectures have concentrated almost exclusively on the actions of the United States and its allies throughout the world. His aim has not simply been to denounce the brutal measures used by the United States to maintain its power. The point is not just that horrific things happen, but that the official version of events tries to keep people ignorant and confused, so that they find it hard to understand what is going on and change things. The first job, in his view, is to get rid of this ignorance and confusion. For instance, in the official view anyone who denounces US-backed aggression in Nicaragua is immediately labelled a wicked communist, and people are unlikely to listen to them. If Chomsky can undo the effect of this labelling, the alternative view is more likely to get a fair hearing.

If the alternative view is correct, then the actions of the United States around the world are a key obstacle to solving the problem of poverty, the problem which we identified as the most urgent one facing the world. The importance of Chomsky's political writings, then, is that he tries to unravel the misleading propaganda of the official line, which prevents people from understanding and dealing with the main cause of the world's number one problem.

In this chapter and the next we will look at some of the evidence which Chomsky brings forward in support of his view of US foreign policy. We will see how the real state of affairs is concealed and distorted by the official line. This chapter focuses on those areas of the world which are under US control; the next chapter deals with cases where countries succeed in freeing themselves from this control.

The fifth freedom

Chomsky sums up his disagreement with the official line by talking of 'the fifth freedom':

> President Roosevelt announced in January 1941 that the Allies were fighting for freedom of speech, freedom of worship, freedom from want, and freedom from fear . . . Roosevelt spoke of Four Freedoms, but not of the Fifth and most important: the freedom to rob and to exploit . . . A careful look at history and the internal record of planning reveals a guiding geopolitical conception: preservation of the Fifth Freedom, by whatever means are feasible. Much of what US Governments do in the world can be readily understood in terms of this principle, while if it remains obscured, acts and

events will appear incomprehensible, a maze of confusion, random error and accident. Many other factors also operate – fortunately, or there would be no hope of modifying state policies and actions short of social revolution. But this principle is an invariant core, deeply rooted in the basic institutions of American society. (TTT, 45–7)

But why is this so? The basic reasons have to do with the kind of society the USA is. As Chomsky notes:

If we hope to understand anything about the foreign policy of any state, it is a good idea to begin by investigating the domestic social structure. Who sets foreign policy? What interests do these people represent? What is the domestic source of their power? It is a reasonable surmise that the policy that evolves will reflect the special interests of those who design it. An honest study of history will reveal that this natural expectation is quite generally fulfilled. (TNCW, 86)

We must begin, therefore, with a brief look at the history of the USA. As everyone knows, Columbus sailed to the 'New World' in 1492. It is estimated that when he 'discovered' the continent there were about 10 million native people in North America. 'By the time the continental borders of the United States had been established, some 200,000 were left' (CR, 122), a clear case of genocide. The United States was built by European colonists on the blood of the native people, who were moved from their homelands, starved, hunted, deliberately exposed to deadly diseases, and finally left on pitifully inadequate 'reservations'. One indication of the results is given by medical researcher Thomas Brewer:[1]

The state of health of the American Indian is a particularly shocking public disgrace. In some areas one-third of the Indian children suffer from trachoma, a preventable and treatable virus disease which causes blindness. Almost one-fourth of all American Indians are judged mentally ill by health authorities working with them. The life expectancy of an American Indian is only 43 years. About 90 per cent of all American Indians live in houses virtually unfit for human occupancy. Sixty-six per cent of them haul water from unsanitary sources in unsanitary vessels, many from a distance of over a mile from their homes.

The United States was founded on violence, and violence continues to be an important feature of US society today. Millions of ordinary Americans jealously defend their right to own and use guns. Violent crime is far more prevalent than in other advanced countries: there are more murders in Washington DC each year than in the whole of the United Kingdom. Chomsky notes that a Chicago Museum in 1968 featured an exhibit where children could fire simulated machine guns from a helicopter at Vietnamese huts, with a light flashing when a hit was scored; he asks what one can say about a country where such things happen (APNM, 17). He further notes that the Hiroshima and Nagasaki bombings are re-enacted in a stadium each year 'before an admiring audience of 20,000' (AC, 39).

The US economy is based on the same mixture of ruthlessness, greed and aggression. The history of the slave trade which brought millions of Africans across the Atlantic in appalling conditions is well known, as is the history of organized racism, particularly in the southern states, with official segregation, as well as intimidation and lynching by groups like the Ku Klux Klan. The power of organized crime in the United States is also a familiar story. American businessmen have frequently used the methods of Al Capone against workers campaigning for better wages and working conditions. To take one example among many, miners in Pennsylvania went on strike in 1875 against wage cuts and unsafe working conditions (conditions which had led to 112 deaths and 339 serious injuries in one county alone in 1871). Several union leaders were shot and killed by groups of armed thugs hired by the mine owners. In 1876 five remaining trade unionists were tried and hanged on trumped-up murder charges, with Franklin B. Gowen, a leading mine owner, acting as the prosecutor in court.[2] Few countries have glorified success in business more than the United States, and worried less about the means by which it is achieved. The result is that today a few Americans are fabulously wealthy, while according to a Harvard study 20 million are hungry (TTT, 237).

The American political scene is dominated by wealthy businessmen:

> The major decision-making positions in the Executive branch
> of the government are typically filled by representatives of
> major corporations, banks and investment firms, a few
> law firms that cater primarily to corporate interests and
> thus represent the broad interests of owners and managers
> rather than some parochial interest, and selected intel-
> lectuals . . . Furthermore, the external conditions of policy
> formation are set by the same narrow elite of privileged
> groups. They carry out the planning studies, finance the
> political parties, dominate Washington lobbying, and in a
> variety of other ways, determine the conditions within which
> the political system functions.' (OPI, 117).

How the official line works

'There is no official line'

I have spoken so far of the 'official line', but this may appear to
many readers as dishonest. One of the key differences between
western democracies like the United States and communist
states like the Soviet Union is precisely freedom of speech.
Anyone in the United States has the right to criticize the government. Journalists and academics frequently do so fiercely, in one
celebrated case – the Watergate affair – bringing about the resig-
nation of a US President and the imprisonment of several of his
advisers. To talk of an 'official line' in the Soviet Union is fair, but
to do so in the United States looks like a deliberate distortion.

One of Chomsky's main themes is that the appearance of
fierce and open debate in the United States is largely illusion,
and that in the mainstream of the media and scholarship there
is remarkable uniformity about the underlying assumptions
of US foreign policy. There is open debate, but only about
certain issues within very narrow boundaries. Debate which
goes beyond these boundaries and questions some of the fundamental assumptions is marginalized and suppressed.

A very good example of this was the Vietnam war. Chomsky
writes:

Consider the following facts. In 1962 the United States attacked
South Vietnam. In that year, President Kennedy sent the
United States Air Force to attack rural South Vietnam, where
more than 80 percent of the population lived, as part of a
program intended to drive several million people to concen-
tration camps (called 'strategic hamlets'), where they would be
surrounded by barbed wire and armed guards and 'protected'
from the guerrillas who, we conceded, they were willingly
supporting. . . . The direct U.S invasion of South Vietnam
followed our support for the French attempt to reconquer
their former colony, our disruption of the 1954 'peace process',
and a terrorist war against the South Vietnamese population
that had already left some seventy-five thousand dead while
evoking domestic resistance, supported from the northern half
of the country after 1959, which threatened to bring down the
terrorist regime that the United States had established. In the
following years, the United States continued to resist every
attempt at peaceful settlement and in 1964 began to plan
the ground invasion of South Vietnam which took place in
early 1965, accompanied by bombing of North Vietnam and
an intensification of the bombing of the South, at triple the
level of the more publicized bombing of the North. The United
States also extended the war to Laos, then Cambodia.

The United States [did not] regard [the client regime it
established in South Vietnam] as having any legitimacy: in
fact, it was regularly overthrown and replaced when its
leaders appeared to be insufficiently enthusiastic about U.S.
plans to escalate the terror, or when they were feared to
be considering a peaceful settlement. . . . The United States
openly recognized throughout that a political settlement was
impossible, for the simple reason that the 'enemy' would
win handily in a political competition, which was therefore
unacceptable.

For the past twenty-two years, I have been searching to
find some reference in mainstream journalism or scholarship
to an American invasion of South Vietnam in 1962 (or ever),
or an American attack against South Vietnam, or American
aggression in Indochina – without success. There is no such
event in history. Rather, there is an American *defense* of South
Vietnam against terrorists supported from outside (namely

from Vietnam), a defense that was unwise, the doves maintain. (CR, 224–5)

As the Vietnam war dragged on, the US establishment divided into the 'hawks', who wanted to pursue the war and believed that a conclusive US victory was possible, and the 'doves', who did not believe that victory was possible and felt that the enormous cost of the war, in money and lives, outweighed any gains to be had from it. There was a great deal of public argument between the hawks and the doves. But Chomsky points out that the well-publicized disagreements concealed a common assumption that was not challenged at all: that the United States had the right to invade in the first place. The mainstream hawks and doves both assumed that the United States had the right to use armed force to keep Vietnam and other countries safe for US business interests (not that they would have put it like this – they spoke instead of protecting the 'free world'). The establishment doves opposed the war on the grounds of expediency – they didn't think the United States could win – rather than out of principle.

The grassroots movement against the war, which grew especially among students and young people, did challenge the assumption that the United States had the right to intervene abroad wherever it chose in defence of the fifth freedom. The issue they raised was not 'Can the US win in Indochina?' but the more basic one: 'Does the US have the right to invade Indochina?' Mainstream politicians and media in the United States consistently did their best to avoid raising this question. As an example of how this was done, Chomsky cites an editorial published in the *New York Times* shortly after the liberation of Saigon in 1975:

There are those Americans who believe that the war to preserve a non-Communist, independent South Vietnam could have been waged differently. There are other Americans who believe that a viable, non-Communist South Vietnam was always a myth . . . A decade of fierce polemics has failed to resolve this quarrel.

Chomsky comments:

You see, they don't even mention the logical possibility of a third position: namely, that the United States did not have the right, either the legal or the moral right, to intervene by force in the internal affairs of Vietnam . . .

Note that as the *Times* sets the spectrum of debate, the position of much of the peace movement is simply excluded from consideration. Not that it is wrong, but rather unthinkable, inexpressible. As the *Times* sets the ground rules, the basic premises of the state propaganda system are presupposed by all participants in the debate: the American goal was to preserve an 'independent' South Vietnam – perfect nonsense, as is easy to demonstrate – and the only question that arises is whether this worthy goal was within our grasp or not. Even the more audacious propaganda systems rarely go so far as to put forth state doctrine as unquestionable dogma, so that criticism of it need not even be rejected, but may simply be ignored. (LR, 36–8)

Chomsky accepts that his freedom to criticize and question is genuine. As he notes, the United States is in many ways a remarkably open society, with information available to those who have the time, money, energy and expertise to track it down. It is important that a few individuals like Chomsky have the ability to raise fundamental questions about US foreign policy; but it is more important that, *in practice*, the mainstream channels of communication do not do so. The vast majority of the population, dependent on the mainstream media for information and debate, are prevented from thinking about these fundamental questions. Chomsky points out that this system of indoctrination is much more effective than the authoritarian system used in other countries: brute force can be identified and resisted, whereas narrowing the boundaries of thinkable thoughts is less easy to recognize.

The 'nation'

Within the narrow framework of the official line, policy-makers like to claim that they are acting in the interests of 'the nation' or 'the people', rather than in the interests of the small business elite who in fact dominate the political system in the United

States. In his book about Vietnam, former President Richard Nixon, who masterminded the later stages of the US intervention, uses this device repeatedly:[3]

> Where freedom is destroyed anywhere, it is threatened in America . . . I believe the American people are ready to accept this challenge. Defeatism, indifference, and malaise are not American characteristics. Optimism, compassion and high-spiritedness are . . . Americans are always striving for something better. We must put these qualities to work beyond our borders.

Note in passing the vague language that Nixon uses here. Characteristics like defeatism or high-spiritedness are difficult enough to pinpoint clearly in individuals, but when they are used of the American people as a whole, any concrete meaning they may once have had virtually disappears. Abstract language of this kind is typical of the official line: we shall see other examples. Here we are concerned in particular with the misleading idea that US foreign policy reflects the American people as a whole. Chomsky argues that the policy is shaped by the US business elite, not in a haphazard way but as a result of deliberate planning.

During the early 1940s it became clear to the US elite that the country would emerge from the Second World War with 'unquestioned power', in the words of a memorandum drawn up by the Council on Foreign Relations – a planning forum which includes key people from government and business – cited by Chomsky (TNCW, 96). Recognizing that the main threat to US hegemony would come from whichever side won the war in Europe, the planners recognized the need 'to secure the limitation of any exercise of sovereignty by foreign nations that constitutes a threat to the world area essential for the security and economic prosperity of the United States and the Western Hemisphere'. They wanted to organize this area 'as an integrated economic system that would offer the American economy 'the "elbow room" . . . needed to survive without major readjustment'. As Chomsky points out, the planners were aware that these aims should be kept quiet. The memorandum continues:

> If war aims are stated which seem to be concerned solely
> with Anglo-American imperialism, they will offer little to
> people in the rest of the world, and will be vulnerable to
> Nazi counter-promises . . . the interests of other peoples
> should be stressed, not only those of Europe, but also of
> Asia, Africa and Latin America. This would have a better
> propaganda effect. (TNCW, 99–100)

Given the importance of these documents, which were written
by those who actually carried out US foreign policy, Chomsky
asks how academic scholars deal with the material in them:

> The answer is simple: It is ignored. The book by Shoup and
> Minter [*Imperial Brain Trust*, New York, Monthly Review
> Press, 1977] seems to be the first to examine these records.
> American scholars justly complain that the Russians refuse
> to release documentary materials . . . Another just complaint
> is that American scholars avoid documentary materials that
> might yield much insight into the formation of American
> policy, a fact easily explained in this instance, I believe: The
> documentary record is no more consistent with the doctrines
> of the state religion, in this case, than is the historical record
> itself. (TNCW, 100–1)

One area of the world whose importance was very clear to
US policy-makers was the Middle East, particularly the key oil-
producer Saudi Arabia, which a State Department analysis of
1945 described as 'a stupendous source of strategic power, and
one of the greatest material prizes in world history' (FT, 17).
A State Department memorandum about petroleum policy had
previously described the much-vaunted 'Open Door' principle
as follows: 'vigilant protection of existing concessions in United
States hands, coupled with insistence upon the Open Door
principle of equal opportunity for United States companies in
new areas' (TNCW, 97).

Much of US policy in the Middle East springs from this
determination to keep the area's energy reserves under US
control. When in the early 1950s the Iranian government led
by Mossadegh tried to take control of the country's own oil.

A successful CIA-backed coup put an end to that, installing the regime of the Shah, which became a powerful United States client state purchasing vast quantities of American arms, conducting counterinsurgency in the Arabian peninsula, and, of course, subjecting the Iranian people to the Shah's pleasant whims'. (TNCW, 98)

In 1978 the Shah's brutal regime faced a serious crisis, leading to its eventual downfall. President Carter, who talked repeatedly of human rights while he was in office, sent a message of support to the Shah, praising his 'progressive administration' – this followed the machine-gunning of unarmed demonstrators by the Shah's military forces, at the cost of thousands of lives. (WCTWF, 292–3)

Another feature of US policy in the East has been solid support for Israel. Chomsky notes that the exact level of military and economic aid is concealed in various ways, and goes on:

> Even the public figures are astounding. For fiscal years 1978 through 1982, Israel received 48% of all U.S. military aid and 35% of U.S. economic aid, worldwide . . . In addition there is a regular pattern of forgiving loans, offering weapons at special discount prices, and a variety of other devices. (FT, 10)

Chomsky argues that the reason for this strong support is the role of Israel in counteracting the rise of radical nationalism in the Arab countries, which would endanger US control of the region's oil reserves. He quotes a National Security Council memorandum of 1958 which notes that a 'logical corollary' of opposition to radical Arab nationalism 'would be to support Israel as the only strong pro-West power left in the near East' (FT, 21). Along with aid has gone political support from US intellectuals, who have put forward what Chomsky calls 'the image of an Israeli David confronting a brutal Arab Goliath' (FT, 28). He suggests that the pragmatists who opposed the war in Vietnam because the United States did so badly found the military success of Israel an inspiration. Brutalities committed by Israel are excused, misrepresented or

ignored by US journalists and scholars, while those carried out
by Arabs, particularly Palestinians, are – rightly – highlighted
and condemned. In any case, the idea that American foreign
policy in the Middle East is an expression of the desire of the
American people to defend freedom simply does not stand up
to scrutiny.

The United States as a well-meaning, blundering giant

In 1973, the CIA masterminded a military coup in Chile which
brought down the democratically elected government of Salvador
Allende and led to a vicious dictatorship which is still in power
as I write. The record of torture, murder, and imprisonment
without trial is horrific even by Latin American standards, and
led to a huge number of Chileans fleeing the country. I note
in passing that Chile is the world's third largest producer
of copper, a metal of great industrial importance, and that
'in . . . Chile, the early client fascist years [i.e. after 1973]
have been characterized by a massive displacement of smaller
domestic firms by larger local and, more importantly, foreign
multinationals' (WCTWF, 55).

These facts are not in dispute, and clearly support Chomsky's
view of US foreign policy as guided by the 'fifth freedom'. The
official line deals with this problem by claiming that the United
States is basically trying to do good in the world, that events
like those in Chile are well-meaning mistakes, exceptions to
the general record of generosity, and that things are always
getting better. Chomsky quotes a liberal commentator in the
New York Times:

> For a quarter century, the United States has been trying to do
> good, encourage political liberty, and promote social justice in
> the Third World. . . . But benevolence, intelligence and hard
> work have proved not to be enough. Chile demonstrates the
> problem [where with the best of motives] by intervening in
> this complicated situation, the C.I.A. implicated the United
> State in the unexpected sequel of a grim military dictatorship
> that employs torture and has destroyed the very freedom
> and liberal institutions we were trying to protect. (TNCW,
> 87)

These words, which Chomsky describes as 'not untypical', have little relation to reality; but ideas of this kind rarely get challenged in the mainstream media and scholarship in the United States. In his books and articles about the Indochina war, Chomsky cites many similar examples. In the late 1960s the United States instituted the 'Phoenix Programme', a co-ordinated security operation in which South Vietnamese were given a reward for each National Liberation Front activist they denounced. Groups of criminals and thugs were recruited to torture and assassinate the people denounced. In three years, nearly 41,000 suspects were killed, according to the South Vietnamese government (WCTWF, 324). The scope for corruption and abuse was obviously huge. One US intelligence officer attached to the Phoenix programme commented: 'When I arrived in the district I was given a list of 200 names of people who had to be killed. When I left after six months, we still hadn't killed anyone on the list. But we'd killed 260 other people.'[4]

A major study of the war by Guenter Lewy paints the usual picture of generous motives by 'intelligent and reasonable men', saying 'the fact that some of their judgments in retrospect can be shown to have been flawed and that the outcome has been a fiasco does not make them villains or fools'.[5] On the Phoenix Programme, Lewy admits that there were 'shortcomings', but rejects the view that Phoenix was 'a programme of planned assassinations' because 'so few of those killed were on the Phoenix target list'. He claims that many of these 'weaknesses' were corrected, but concludes that Phoenix was 'a poorly managed and largely ineffective effort'.

Lewy's use of terms like 'weaknesses' and 'ineffective' neatly sidesteps the question of right and wrong. As Chomsky points out on many occasions, 'error' is a socially neutral category. Anyone can make mistakes – to err is human, as we all know. By focusing on the question of whether Phoenix was carried out effectively, and whether it achieved its aims, Lewy avoids the fundamental moral issue. Chomsky and Herman comment in their review of Lewy's book: 'Lewy concedes that the programme had "weaknesses" and claims that it was of limited effectiveness for US purposes, but this spokesman for Western humanism never suggests that the massacre

of large numbers of ordinary civilians is troublesome in itself'
(TNCW, 163).

We noted above that indications of brutality by the United
States and its allies are often presented in the official line as
'exceptions'. Chomsky cites Hans Morgenthau, who describes
the US invasions of Central American countries as 'isolated
forays, primarily for defensive purposes', or the bloody US
invasion of the Philippines at the turn of the century as 'a
temporary aberration' (HRAFP, 65). Similarly, Sidney Hook
describes the carpet bombing of Vietnam as 'the unfortunate
accidental loss of life incurred by the efforts of American military forces to help the South Vietnamese' (BB, 86). In 1979,
the Pentagon claimed that the Indonesian invasion of East
Timor – supported politically and with arms supplies from the
United States, and backed by Britain too – was an 'exception'
to the general improvement in Indonesia's human rights record
(TNCW, 340). During this invasion 200,000 people were killed
out of a population of under 700,000, according to Amnesty
International and church sources. The official line tries to present abuses by official enemies of the United States – communist
countries or nationalist movements – as typical and representative of the real nature of these enemies, while the incomparably
greater crimes of the United States are presented as isolated
exceptions, unfortunate errors by well-meaning people in a
complex world.

How many exceptions do you need before they become the
rule? In this century, the United States has sent military forces to
attack or invade, among others, the Philippines (1900), the Soviet
Union (1918–20) Nicaragua (1909), Guatemala (1954), Korea
(1950–3), Cuba (1906, 1916–21, and 1961), the Dominican Republic (1916 and 1965), Vietnam, Laos and Cambodia (1961–75),
Grenada (1983), Mexico (1914 and 1916), Haiti (1915), Libya
(1986), the Persian Gulf (1987) and Panama (1989). The United
States has apparently backed military coups in Chile (1973), Brazil
(1964), Argentina (1976), Iran (1953), Indonesia (1965), Laos (1958)
Vietnam (1964–5), Cambodia (1970), and Zaire (1960), though the
facts are murky in some of these cases. Are these all unfortunate
aberrations, or is there a consistent pattern?

In the official picture, the situation in US-backed dictatorships
is always 'improving'. We saw this device used in the Pentagon

statement on Indonesia. There may have been unfortunate mistakes in the past, but the human rights situation is now getting better. The US media like to use public relations material provided by repressive regimes or US multinational companies active in such countries. Shortly after the coup in Guatemala, the *New York Times* reported that 'American-controlled undertakings in Guatemala have greatly liberalized and humanized their policies' (TTT, 165). A 1977 article in the same paper spoke of improvements by the military junta in Argentina, saying that 'Unions . . . are about to be granted organizational rights' (WCTWF, 264). Any worsening of the situation is justified by appealing to the war against 'communism', or is ignored or played down in importance.

The appeal to 'expertise'

An important feature of the official line is the claim that international affairs are too complex and mysterious for ordinary people to understand. Special knowledge, skill and expertise are needed to get a genuine insight into the social, political and economic forces which shape the world. This device was used extensively during the Vietnam war. For instance, the political scientist, Ithiel de Sola Pool, wrote in 1967 that a return to 'passivity and defeatism' was needed in the Congo, Vietnam and the Dominican Republic to help 'the maintenance of order'. This was not mere dogma but what 'we have learned in the past thirty years of intensive empirical study of contemporary societies' (TNCW, 68). Chomsky cites work by analysts from the Rand Corporation and the Harvard Center for International Affairs who use the terminology of the 'behavioural sciences' in their theoretical discussion of 'counter-insurgency' in Vietnam. The aim, they say, should not be to win 'popular allegiance' to US-backed regimes but to 'influence *behaviour* rather than attitudes'. When dealing with Vietnamese villagers, 'the primary consideration should be whether the proposed measure is likely to increase the cost and difficulties of insurgent operations and help to disrupt the insurgent organisation, rather than whether it wins popular loyalty or support'. Chomsky comments wryly that this is 'extremely sane advice. It would, for example, be absurd to try to control the behaviour of a rat by winning its loyalty rather than by the proper scheduling of reinforcement' (APNM, 47–9).

Chomsky has always maintained that his kind of political analysis requires nothing more than ordinary common sense:

> it does not require very far-reaching, specialized knowledge to perceive that the United States was invading South Vietnam. And, in fact, to take apart the system of illusions and deception which functions to prevent understanding of contemporary reality, that's not a task that requires extraordinary skill or understanding. It requires the kind of normal skepticism and willingness to apply one's analytical skills that almost all people have and that they can exercise. (CR, 35)

He is scathing about the supposed expertise which establishment intellectuals claim to draw on when they justify the official line:

> I would simply like to emphasize that, as is no doubt obvious, the cult of the expert is both self-serving, for those who propound it, and fraudulent. Obviously, one must learn from social and behavioural science whatever one can . . . But it will be quite unfortunate, and highly dangerous, if they are not accepted and judged on their merits and according to their actual, not pretended accomplishments. In particular, if there is a body of theory, well-tested and verified, that applies to the conduct of foreign affairs . . . its existence has been kept a well-guarded secret . . . To anyone who has any familiarity with the social and behavioural sciences . . . the claim that there are certain considerations and principles too deep for the outsider too comprehend is simply an absurdity, unworthy of comment. (APNM, 271)

'Forces outside our control'

Advocates of the official line like to maintain that countries allied to the United States are not under US control but often take an independent line. The United States is therefore not to blame for human rights problems or economic problems in these countries.

Richard Nixon takes this tack in his book about Vietnam. When the US was negotiating a peace agreement with North Vietnam in Paris in 1973, he writes, President Thieu of South Vietnam protested strongly.

> Antiwar critics always portrayed [Thieu] as a puppet of the United States. That was never the case. Whenever he perceived a threat to the South Vietnamese national interest in our actions, he became obdurate. This was the situation with the Paris peace accords. He called it a 'surrender agreement' and categorically refused to sign it. Even after we exerted enormous pressure on him, Thieu would not budge. Only when we declared that we would sign the agreement without him if necessary did he reluctantly consent to it.[6]

Note that Thieu did agree in the end, of course: if the United States said one thing and he said the opposite, it was Thieu who had to give way. It is clear from Nixon's book that all Thieu's objections to the peace agreement were ignored by his paymaster. Naturally, there are occasionally disagreements between the United States and the local elites which it installs in other countries to act in its interests. What typically happens is that the United States makes threats to withdraw support from the local elite – as in the case of Thieu here – and if this doesn't work, the United States gets rid of the people concerned and installs a new elite – witness the various CIA-masterminded military coups in Vietnam in 1964–5. Incidentally, where Nixon says 'the South Vietnamese national interest', read 'the survival of Thieu and his cronies'.

Another instance in which bad deeds are attributed to forces outside US control happens one step further down the chain of authority: butchery by the so-called 'death squads', groups of thugs and criminals in United States client-states who kidnap, torture, rape and murder people opposed to the dictatorships installed by the United States. The claim in the US media is typically that these are independent groups, not under the control of the local government. Take the case of El Salvador, where between eight and ten thousand people were killed by 'the Army Security Forces and paramilitary organizations coordinated by the High Command of the Armed Forces' in 1980, according to the

Human Rights office of the Archdiocese of San Salvador (TTT, 15). The Carter administration stated that 'the government has been unable to end such abuses', and Jeane Kirkpatrick, who later became the US representative at the United Nations under President Reagan, said 'I think it's a terrible injustice to the government and the military when you suggest that they were somehow responsible for terrorism and assassination'.

The assumption that the death squads were independent of the government was echoed in the *Washington Post* and the *New York Times*, despite 'the detailed accounting of the Church Human Rights office and what the press was being told by US officials, but chose to conceal' (TTT, 15). Chomsky notes that the US government was privately aware of the truth about the death squads, citing a 1984 report by the Senate Select Committee on Intelligence, which concedes that 'Death Squad activities . . . have originated in the Salvadoran security services, including the National Police, National Guard and Treasury Police' and that 'numerous Salvadoran officials in the military and security forces as well as other official organizations have been involved in encouraging or conducting death squad activities or other violent human rights abuses' (TTT, 16). Once again, the gap between the official line and the private views of those who plan and execute US foreign policy is blatant, as is the subservience of the mainstream US media to the official line.

Moral catharsis

Since 1945 there have been two major 'scandals' in the United States: Watergate, in which the Nixon administration resorted to illegal tactics to ensure its re-election in 1972, and more recently Irangate, when President Reagan's officials violated the professed US opposition to 'terrorism' by secretly dealing with Iran, a country the official line presented as 'the most terrorist government in the World' (CT, 63). Both scandals led to extensive investigations in Congress, and to the trial and conviction of some of the officials involved. In both cases, the picture that mainstream US intellectuals presented was that the misdeeds were aberrations, unusual departures from the high moral standards of US political life, and that these high standards were now being restored. After Watergate, in what

Chomsky ironically describes as 'rebirth', the new President, Jimmy Carter presented himself as a man of high ideals, especially in his commitment to human rights. Kennedy Intellectual Arthur Schlesinger wrote in the *Wall Street Journal* that 'in effect, human rights is replacing self-determination as the guiding value in American foreign policy' (TNCW, 82). After Irangate a *New York Times* writer wrote that 'There is no other country so involved in talking about fundamental law, its limits and flexibility' (CT, 69).

Chomsky's discussion of these scandals is scathing. Note firstly the usual tactic that we noted above of treating misdeeds as 'exceptions' from the rule. Chomsky's main point, however, is that in both cases the press and the courts focused on extraordinarily narrow issues, ignoring far worse crimes committed by those in power. In the Watergate affair, members of the government organized a burglary and other dirty tricks aimed at the Democrat party. Chomsky notes that these same people were responsible for unspeakable atrocities in Cambodia, Laos and Vietnam, including carpet bombing of civilians, large-scale defoliation of the countryside, widespread use of napalm, 40,000 murders under the Phoenix Programme, and so on. He comments: 'If we try to keep a sense of balance, the exposures of the past several months are analogous to the discovery that the directors of Murder, Inc. were also cheating on their income tax. Reprehensible, to be be sure, but hardly the main point' (RP, 177).

The standard line in the West was that at least the Watergate conspirators and those who controlled them were found out and punished, thanks to the free press and the democratic system, and that this couldn't have happened in the Soviet Union. Chomsky agrees, but plays down the importance of the affair. Even if we just look at the dirty tricks, he notes that far worse methods have been used against the left and the labour movement in the United States for decades. The mistake of the Nixon administration was to use these methods against sections of the US establishment, instead of against marginal groups.

In the Irangate affair, official investigations were once again concerned to narrow the focus of inquiry. As Chomsky notes, even the limited investigation gave cause for concern, revealing 'contempt for democratic processes' and a belief in 'executive power immune from any requirement of accountability to the public or its elected representatives' (CT, 63). One of the key figures in the affair, Colonel Oliver North, appears to have lied repeatedly to the congressional inquiry into the affair (CT, 65), while maintaining the self-righteous attitude that he was right to deal with criminals and terrorists in conscious violation of the law. Crucially, however, the investigation drew away from questions about the extent of CIA involvement and the role of Israel in the affair, let alone topics of far greater importance such as the US support for Pol Pot-style atrocities in the 'fledgling democracies' of Central America during the same period.

One aspect of the Irangate affair was undercover support by North and his ilk for the Contra rebels in Nicaragua. We shall look at Nicaragua in more detail in the next chapter. However, as Chomsky notes, the International Court of Justice ruled in 1986 that the US attack on Nicaragua was illegal. This ruling was flouted in the United States, where 'the Senate expressed its commitment to international law by voting in favor of Reagan's $100 million military aid package two weeks after the Court had called upon the US to terminate its unlawful use of force' (CT, 68).

Chomsky sums up his view of the two scandals as follows:

> The lesson taught by the Watergate affair is stark and sim-
> ple: people with power will defend themselves, not surpris-
> ingly. Domestic repression and murderous aggression are
> legitimate, but not violation of the prerogatives of domestic
> power. Much the same is true in [the Irangate affair]. We
> learn a good deal about ourselves from the fact that these
> two incidents of submissiveness to power are regarded as
> a brilliant demonstration of the courage and integrity of the
> media and the fundamental soundness of our institutions
> and their exceptional performance under stress. (CT, 70)

Poverty in the 'Free World'

We began this chapter with the claim that poverty was perhaps the number one problem in the world. We have examined the official line, which presents the United States as generously trying to make the world a better place, and contrasted it with Chomsky's picture of US foreign policy as a ruthless and unprincipled defence of the fifth freedom, the freedom to rob and exploit. Chomsky frequently refers to the 'Free World', a phrase often used in the official line to refer to non-communist countries which the United States is defending and helping. In Chomsky's view, the 'Free World' is best seen as that part of the world which the United States is free to plunder for its own gain. (He uses the term 'free press' with similar irony, given his view that the mass-media in the United States sometimes appear to criticize the establishment, but in fact do not really challenge the key components of the official line).

In WCTWF, Chomsky and Herman cite a study of forty-three of the poorest countries in the world. The study found that the poorest people in each country have typically got poorer as a small elite has enriched itself with outside help. They conclude:

> In brief, then, income distribution has tended to worsen in the poor countries of the Free world because growth has generated wealth that has been used not to improve the condition of the masses but to serve the growing consumption needs of a neo-colonial elite and the demands of foreign business and finance. The preservation of their position has required a costly diversion of resources into the military . . . and a subordination of development and welfare needs to the consumption-oriented demands of U.S. open-door entrants and affluent domestic consumers. (WCTWF, 60)

This chapter has concentrated on the effects of US foreign policy in the 'Free World'. In the next chapter we look at what happens when countries escape from the clutches of the well-meaning, blundering giant.

7

Outside the 'Free World'

The last chapter took apart some of the key elements of the official line on US foreign policy, concentrating on how the United States exercises its power in countries which to a greater or lesser extent are under its control. This chapter looks at countries outside US control, continuing to contrast the official picture as presented to the public with Chomsky's alternative analysis and the record of internal planning by policy-makers.

'Communism'

As we noted in the last chapter, one of the key ingredients of the official line has been opposition to 'communism'. Communism is presented as an evil political and military force which endangers freedom, and an incompetent economic force which threatens prosperity. Extreme right-wingers like Richard Nixon believe that any means are justified in fighting such a vicious enemy. His book on Vietnam is peppered with charges of 'Communist atrocities' and 'totalitarian Communism' . In his view, the aim of the war was 'to resist Communist aggression in South Vietnam'.[1] US intellectuals who are more liberally-minded concede that things are far from perfect in the US-led 'Free World', but argue that things are just as bad or even worse under communism. The Soviet invasions of Hungary in 1956, Czechoslovakia in 1968, and Afghanistan in 1980 are examples of how the ruthless men in the Kremlin control their 'Evil Empire'. Freedom of speech is absent in communist countries, we are often reminded, and 'dissidents' are imprisoned, mistreated in mental hospitals, or exiled. Liberals agree with the assumption that communism is evil and should be fought, though they would prefer to use less horrific means than those employed by Nixon in Vietnam and Reagan in Nicaragua.

To present Chomsky's views on the matter, we need firstly to distinguish between communism in reality and 'communism' as the term is used in the official line. In the real world, the obvious place to start is the Soviet Union and the countries of Eastern Europe which have been under Soviet control since 1945. Chomsky makes clear his opposition to the Soviet political system in many places. For instance, he refers to the Soviet government with 'its brutal suppression of national independence in Eastern Europe and its refusal to grant elementary rights to Soviet citizens' (RP, 212). On Soviet foreign policy, he has this to say:

> Discussing the Soviet Union, no reasonable person hesitates to entertain the possibility that its foreign policy is designed to enhance the power and privilege of the ruling military-bureaucratic elite, that the system of propaganda is committed to denying and concealing this fact, and that the pattern of repression and coercion that results from Soviet intervention reflects the perceived needs of this ruling group. Indeed, this is generally taken to be the obvious truth, as it is, to a very good first approximation. (TNCW, 5)

Chomsky argues that the Soviet Union has gathered together a set of client-states, just as the United States has done. He refers to 'the second superpower', much less wealthy and powerful than number one, and 'not a major factor in the exploitation and robbery of the Third World', but essentially involved in defending its interests in the countries it controls, by force when it so decides (OPI, 11). Each superpower plays up the military strength of the other one, arguing that its own actions are simply a well-intentioned and highly moral defence against the ruthless aggression of the other.

There are, however, some important differences. As we noted in the last chapter, the United States was not invaded, or threatened with invasion, during either world war. It emerged in 1945 far and away the most powerful country on earth, militarily and economically. The Soviet Union, in contrast, was invaded twice by Germany, with 20 million killed, much of its industrial base destroyed or devoted to war needs, and all the horrors of partial Nazi occupation for several years. After the war, the Soviet

Union held on to several countries of Eastern Europe, largely to act as a buffer against future German invasion. The Western Allies (the US, Britain and France) formed NATO in 1949 with the Federal Republic of Germany as a member and later rejected the idea of a neutral, united Germany put forward – no one can say how genuinely, because the Western Allies dismissed the offer out of hand - by Stalin in 1952. Chomsky points out: '[in the case of the USSR] the defensive rhetoric has some substance; no government in Russia, whatever its composition, would relax controls over Eastern Europe as long as a rearmed Germany is part of a hostile Western military alliance, for historical and strategic reasons that are all too obvious' (OPI, 109).

After the War, the United States continued to build up its military power round the world, with a peak of 3,000 foreign military bases 'virtually surrounding both the Soviet Union and China', as a Senate Report put it in 1970 (WCTWF, 67). The USSR built up its military power too, but largely for defensive reasons. Chomsky writes:

> In Soviet propaganda, the United States is led by warmongers deterred from their limitless drive for expansion only by Russian power. In the West, it is now an article of faith that the Soviet Union is outspending its rivals in a race towards military domination of the planet. There is some basis of truth in these competing claims, as is usually the case even in the most vulgar propaganda exercises, but it is revealing to disentangle the element of truth from the web of distortion. The claim that the USSR is unrivaled in its commitment of resources to military production is based largely on CIA analyses which estimate the dollar equivalent of the USSR military effort; thus the question asked is what it would cost the United States, in dollars, to duplicate the military force deployed by the USSR. As a number of commentators have observed, these calculations have a built-in bias. The Soviet military force is labor-intensive, in contrast to the military system of the West with its superior technological level and higher cost of labor relative to capital. It would be highly inefficient, and extremely costly, for the United States to duplicate a technologically less advanced Soviet military machine that relies heavily on manpower. Hence calculations of dollar

equivalents considerably exaggerate Russian power. For the United States to duplicate the Russian agricultural system, with its intensive use of human labor power and low level of technology, would also be extremely expensive. But we do not therefore conclude that the Russians are outmatching us in the field of agricultural production. For similar reasons, calculations of dollar equivalents give a highly misleading picture of relative military strength. (TNCW, 193)

We can add that estimates of Soviet military strength in the West normally include support staff, including catering staff, medical personnel, military hairdressers and dentists, while accounts of NATO forces tend to include only combat troops. Much of Soviet military hardware in Europe is out of date, some of it unchanged since the Second World War. This is not to deny that Soviet tanks and missiles exist. The point is, as Chomsky points out in the passage above, that each superpower exaggerates the strength and evil intentions of the other one, and that these exaggerations should be treated with considerable suspicion.

It is interesting to examine one occasion when the Soviet Union posed a direct threat to the territory of the United States: the Cuban missile crisis of 1962. Chomsky's account of the affair goes like this:

Khruschev, in a move so foolhardy as to defy description, secretly installed missiles in Cuba, probably in reaction to the substantial American lead in offensive weaponry. The U.S. government response was most remarkable. Reflecting on this crisis, Robert Kennedy observed that the fourteen people involved in determining the American response were:

bright, able, dedicated people, all of whom had the greatest affection for the United States – probably the brightest kind of group you could get together under those circumstances. If six of them had been President of the United States, I think that the world might have been blown up.

These fourteen people refused to respond officially to an offer by Khruschev to withdraw the missiles from Cuba, thus terminating the crisis, because this offer was coupled with the demand that American missiles be withdrawn from

Turkey and Italy (these were obsolete missiles, for which a withdrawal order had already been given by the President) . . . fourteen bright and able people were willing to accept a high probability of nuclear war in defence of the principle that the United States alone has the right to keep missiles on the border of a potential enemy. (PKF, 80–1)

Given the existence of two superpowers, each responsible for a great deal of injustice, someone like Chomsky has to make difficult choices. His discussion is worth citing at length:

What is important? Reasonable people may differ about some cases, but others are clear, and suggest some useful guidelines. Consider, for example, two studies of human rights violations in the United States, one, a pamphlet put out in East Germany, the other, a petition submitted to the United Nations by church and civil rights groups in the United States [note omitted]. Assuming the reports in each to be true, we know at once which document is important. We are little impressed by the DDR pamphlet . . . What they say may be true, but it is not important for their domestic and international audience; what is important for this audience is a discussion of the treatment of dissidents in the Soviet zone or Soviet terror bombing in Afghanistan. Their protests about human rights violations in or by the United States, apart from the evident hypocrisy, have a mixed effect. In part, the effect may be beneficial. International protest apparently played some part in mitigating the treatment of the Wilmington Ten, for example . . . but the effects of even valid criticism of U.S. human rights practices from such sources may be harmful as well: namely, in buttressing domestic propaganda systems and thus laying the basis for oppression and atrocities – a comment which, though obvious and valid, will be ridiculed by conformist intellectuals of the state to which it is addressed.
    The conclusion from such examples is evident. One index of importance is how information leads to action. What are its likely consequences for victims of oppression? *The proper focus of concern for us lies in areas where we have a responsibility for what is happening and the opportunity to mitigate or terminate suffering*

and violence [my emphasis – RMS]. This is particularly true in a democratic society, where policies can be influenced, often significantly so, by public opinion and action. Analysis and condemnation of the practices of official enemies is legitimate, provided it is honest, and is sometimes worth undertaking, but it is often of little or no importance, by this reasonable standard.

To ask serious questions about the nature and behaviour of one's own society is often difficult and unpleasant: difficult because the answers are generally concealed, and unpleasant because the answers are often not only ugly – in foreign affairs, roughly in proportion to the power of the state – but also painful. To understand the truth about these matters is to be led to actions that may not be easy to undertake and that may even carry a significant personal cost. In contrast, the easy way is to succumb to the demands of the powerful, to avoid searching questions, and to accept the doctrine that is hammered home incessantly by the propaganda system. (TNCW, 8–9)

Chomsky is surely right to say that if your concern is to relieve suffering (as opposed to scoring propaganda points), then it makes sense to concentrate on instances where your protest is likely to have a positive effect. A clear example of how the media get things the wrong way round occurred on May Day 1989. The front pages of British newspapers, and broadcast news, reported how Czech protesters were attacked by security police. Violence at least equal in extent took place in Turkey against trade unionists on the same day: this was relegated to the inside pages, and was not mentioned on the radio or TV news. Czechoslovakia is part of the Soviet bloc, an official enemy, so abuses in that country get headline treatment. Turkey, on the other hand, currently has a pro-Western regime, so terror there gets played down. The Turkish government is desperate to join the EEC, and is anxious to project a positive image in the West (even engaging Saatchi & Saatchi, the largest advertising and public relations firm in the world, to help it). If Turkish atrocities were headlined, this might have a positive result and lead to constructive change. Bad news about communist countries may be true, but highlighting it often does little to relieve injustice, or even makes it worse.

We now turn to what 'communism' means in the official line. Here is what Chomsky has to say:

> Who are the Communists? 'Communists' is a term regularly used in American political theology to refer to people who are committed to the belief that 'the government has direct responsibility for the welfare of the people'. I'm quoting the words of a 1949 State Department intelligence report which warned about the spread of this grim and evil doctrine, which does, of course, threaten 'our raw materials' if we can't abort it somehow . . .
>
> In the mid 1950's these ideas were developed further. For example, one interesting case was an important study by a prestigious study group headed by William Yandell Eliot, who was Williams Professor of Government at Harvard. They were also concerned with what communism is and how it spreads. They concluded accurately that the primary threat of communism is the economic transformation of the Communist powers 'in ways which reduce their willingness and ability to complement the industrial economies of the West.' That is essentially correct and is a good operational definition of 'communism' in American political discourse. Our government is committed to that view.
>
> If a government is so evil or unwise as to undertake a course of action of this sort, it immediately becomes an enemy. It becomes a part of the 'monolithic and ruthless conspiracy' to take over the world, as John F. Kennedy put it. It is postulated that it has been taken over by the Russians if that's the policy that it appears to be committed to. (CR, 319–20)

Thus any country which tries to gain control over its own resources, rather than fitting in economically with the needs of the US business/political elite, gets labelled as 'communist' in the official line. Any radical nationalist movement in the 'Free World' which is opposed to the poverty, injustice, dictatorship, torture and killing that are the usual results of rule by a US-backed elite gets labelled as 'communist'. The official line plays down the economic threat to US business, of course, since intervention in other countries looks bad if it comes from naked greed. The claim is that the United States is acting unselfishly in the interests of the people of other countries, so that they shouldn't suffer the miseries of communist rule; or that the 'communists' in such countries are a threat to the security of the United States.

We have already cast doubt on the first of these claims, for example in the case of Vietnam. Let us look at the security question, taking the example of Cuba where in 1959 a nationalist movement headed by Fidel Castro ousted the US-backed regime of Fulgencio Batista.[2] Cuba is the largest island in the Caribbean, an area that the United States has long regarded as its own backyard. The reaction of the US government was to suspend trade with Cuba, a serious blow to a country heavily dependent on the United States to buy sugar, its principal export, and to supply Cuba with industrial and consumer goods. The United States put pressure on other Western countries to stop trade with Cuba, and to cut off economic aid. At the same time, the United States began a campaign of terrorism against Cuba, which we shall look at in the next section. The justification offered was that this island country of 10 million people was a threat to the security of the United States. Cuba had no choice but to turn for economic and military help to the Soviet Union. Chomsky comments:

> the Kennedy terrorism did not succeed in overthrowing the regime, but it did cause substantial damage to the Cuban economy and was a major factor – perhaps the major factor – impelling Cuba to a permanent state of military mobiliza-tion . . . Even the dependence on the Soviet Union is a net plus for the United States, for two reasons: It provides a propaganda cover for the regular U.S assaults against Latin America (in 'defense against Soviet-inspired Cuban threats', as in El Salvador); it is an *independent* Cuba that would threaten U.S. dominance in Latin America because of the potential domino effect. (TNCW, 50)

Like many nationalist leaders, Castro was initially reluctant to forge a close alliance with the Soviet Union. His political programme was initially designed to win the support of the Cuban business community, and he dealt harshly in the early years of power with pro-Moscow communists in Cuba. US

policy, having failed to overthrow him, was to make sure that
Castro had nowhere else to turn. Castro was then presented as
part of the monolithic Soviet-controlled international communist
conspiracy to take over the world. This strategy of forcing
nationalist movements to rely on the Soviet Union for help in
the face of economic and military attacks by the United States
or its proxies is one that has occurred in several countries.

Despite US hostility, Cuba has made substantial progress
since 1959:

> the Quality of Life Index of the Overseas Development
> Council . . . places Cuba well above any other Latin American
> country and approximately equal to the United States –
> actually better than the United States if we consider its
> more egalitarian character, thus with lower infant mortality
> rates than Chicago and far lower rates than the Navajo
> reservation. Tom Farer . . . former State Department assistant
> for inter-American affairs writes that
>
> > there is a consensus among scholars of a wide variety of
> > ideological positions that, on the level of life expectancy,
> > education and health, Cuban achievement is considerably
> > greater than one would expect from its level of per capita
> > income . . . What has changed remarkably is not so much
> > the gross indicators as those that reflect the changed con-
> > ditions of the poor, particularly the rural poor . . .
>
> Furthermore, polio and malaria have been eliminated, and
> the causes of death have shifted from those associated with
> underdevelopment (diseases of early infancy, etc.) to those
> of the developed world (congenital abnormalities, diabetes,
> etc.). These are the crimes for which Cuba must pay dearly;
> the real ones are of little interest to policy-makers, except for
> their propaganda effect. (CR, 360–1)

'Terrorism'

A key part of the official line is the claim that 'terrorists', either
part of the communist conspiracy or just crazy fanatics, are

engaged in a deadly campaign against civilized countries like the United States. The key feature of terrorists is their total disregard for the lives of innocent civilians, including women and children, unlike Western armies, which adhere strictly to moral standards of behaviour when they reluctantly confront the enemy in combat (when this does not happen, as in the famous My Lai massacre of Vietnamese civilians by US troops, this is an 'exception' of course, and the Free Press congratulates itself for exposing it. In any case, these things unfortunately happen in war.)

Chomsky and Herman argue that the term 'terrorism' is used selectively by Western intellectuals to refer to what he calls 'retail violence'; the wholesale violence, on a far larger scale, carried out by the United States and its client states is presented differently:

> The words 'terror' and 'terrorism' have become semantic tools of the powerful in the Western World. In their dictionary meaning, these words refer to 'intimidation' by the 'systematic use of violence' as a means of both governing and opposing existing governments. But current Western usage has restricted the sense, on purely ideological grounds, to the retail violence of those who oppose the established order . . . [From the US perspective] killings associated with revolution represent a resort to violence which is both reprehensible, and improper as a means for bringing about social change. Such atrocities are carried out by 'terrorists' . . .
>
> Bloodbaths carried out by counterrevolutionary forces are regarded in a more favorable light, as they are in the interest of a return of Third World populations to the desirable 'measure of passivity and defeatism' that prevailed before World War II, also commonly referred to as 'stability' or 'political equilibrium'. Killings undertaken to return these populations to passivity are rarely described as bloodbaths or as involving 'terror' or the use of violence – they are 'readjustments' or 'dramatic changes' tolerated or applauded as necessary and desirable . . .
>
> The victims of 'terrorism' in this restricted sense have been far fewer throughout the world than those killed by

any number of individual states; Laqueur gives an aggregate figure of 6,000–8,000, more than half in Ulster and Argentina, between 1966–1976 . . . Nevertheless, his study of 'terrorism' is limited to retail terror. This terminological decision affords endless possibilities for dredging up incidents of anti-establishment violence and for demonstrating its frequent senselessness and lack of specific connection with any injustice, while enhancing the general disregard for the wholesale terror of the established states. (WCTWF, 85–7)

A good illustration of how the term 'terrorism' is reserved for official enemies, while the far greater violence of US allies is disregarded, comes from the Israeli/Palestinian conflict. There have been numerous instances of terrorism by Palestinians against civilians in Israel, one of the most appalling being at Ma'alot in 1974. Chomsky writes:

two days before the PLO terrorist attack in Ma'alot in May 1974, where 20 teen-age Israeli hostages from a paramilitary youth group (Gadna) were killed during an attempt to rescue the hostages after Israel had rejected negotiation efforts (the terrorist unit, from Hawatmeh's Democratic Front, had previously killed five other Israelis, including 2 Arabs), an Israeli air attack on the village of El-Kfeir in Lebanon killed four civilians. The PLO raid is (properly) described here as terrorism, but not the Israeli air attack . . . According to Edward Said, the Ma'alot attack was 'preceded by weeks of sustained Israeli napalm bombing of Palestinian refugee camps in southern Lebanon', with over 200 killed. (FT, 189)

A total of 106 Israelis were killed by PLO terrorists in crossborder actions up to 1982. Meanwhile, Southern Lebanon was repeatedly bombed by the Israeli air force during the 1970s, with enormous loss of civilian life, and creating hundreds of thousands of refugees (FT, 191). On 3 June 1982, 'a terrorist group that had been engaged in a running battle with the PLO for a decade and whose head (Abu Nidal) had been condemned to death by the PLO attempted to assassinate Israeli ambassador Shlomo Argov in London' (FT, 196). In June 1982 Israeli planes bombed the Palestinian refugee camps at Sabra and Shatila for four hours, followed by ten-hour non-stop raids on Shatila and Bourj-el-brajneh, the third major Palestinian camp in Lebanon. The Palestinians retaliated by shelling northern settlements in Israel, and the Israelis then launched a full-scale invasion of Lebanon. Many thousands of Lebanese and Palestinians were killed by aerial bombing and artillery fire. In September 1982 Israeli forces surrounded Sabra and Shatila and sent in several hundred right-wing Lebanese militia troops who massacred between 800 and 2,000 Palestinian women and children. The massacre shocked the world, though, as Chomsky points out, the earlier bombing of the refugee camps had in fact caused far more casualties (FT, 371), and the earlier bombing was part of the assault on Beirut and other heavily populated centres, supported vigorously by the US government.

We cannot go into the broader issues of the Israeli/Palestinian conflict here. The point is that 'terrorism' has to be put in perspective. Anyone really concerned to end violence will condemn Palestinian terrorism, as Chomsky does, but devote more attention to the wholesale violence of the Israelis. A further point is that even if we adopt the distorted picture of terrorism in the official line, the United States comes out as the worst offender:

> The major target of terrorist attacks for the past twenty years has undoubtedly been Cuba. The bombing of the Cubana airliner in October 1976 is only one example. In April of that year, two Cuban fishing vessels were attacked by boats coming from Miami, the main centre of anti-Cuban terrorism, in which the CIA is heavily involved. A few weeks later, two persons were killed in the bombing of the Cuban embassy in Portugal. In July, the Cuban mission to the UN was bombed ... In August, two officials of the Cuban embassy in Argentina were kidnapped and Cubana airline offices in Panama were bombed. In October, the Cuban embassy in Venezuela was fired upon ... In November, the Cuban embassy in Madrid was bombed.
>
> This is only a small piece of the story. The Kennedy administration launched a major terrorist campaign against Cuba ... Apart from the attempts to assassinate Castro,

which are well known, these terrorist actions included attacks
on fishing boats and Cuban civilian installations, and poison-
ing of crops and livestock . . .

Another favourite device was economic sabotage. The CIA
contaminated sugar cargoes sent out from Cuba . . . sabo-
taged buses from England, and so on. (TNCW, 49–50)

This is quite apart from the unsuccessful invasion of Cuba by
US-backed mercenaries at the Bay of Pigs in 1961. The claim
that the United States is a victim of 'terrorism' must therefore
be treated with great suspicion: there is some truth in it, as in
all propaganda, but the broader picture lends no support to the
official line.

Refugees

The official line likes to highlight refugees from 'communist
tyranny'. In the late 1970s, after the US defeat in Indochina,
the 'boat people' who took to the sea to flee from Vietnam
were given prominent coverage in the Western press. When the
Vietnamese invaded Cambodia in 1978, the fate of Cambodians
who took refuge in Thailand was also in the headlines for a
long time. Similarly, the many refugees from Afghanistan in
the 1980s have been a key part of the reports on the war there
by Western journalists.

As with terrorism, the official line is highly selective on the
refugee problem. Hundreds of thousands of Kurds have left
for other countries to escape repression by Turkey, Iraq and
Iran. Similar numbers of people have left South Africa for the
same reason, most of them going to the front-line states. Two
million Palestinian Arabs are unable to return to their homes.
These people are not, however, fleeing from official enemies,
so they rarely make the headlines. Chomsky and Herman cite
a report in the *Economist* in mid-1978 that 16,000 boat people
from Vietnam had landed in other South-East Asian countries
so far that year. They comment:

What is unusual about the *Economist* report is that it is not
limited to refugees from postwar Communism, as is the

general practice. The *Economist* observes that 'nearly 400,000 people have walked or sailed away from their home countries since the beginning of the year in Asia' (far less than Africa, where the same report estimates the number of refugees at 2 million). 'The biggest single group', the report continues, are the Muslim Bengali people who have been fleeing from Burma to Bangladesh at the rate of about 2,000 a day . . .

The *Economist* does not mention the refugees who fled from the Philippines to Sabah at an estimated rate of 400 a day, some 140,000 by mid-1977 . . . A fuller account of refugees in Asia by mid-1978 would include the quarter of a million driven from their homes in West Asia by Israeli troops in march 1978 . . .the refugees in Asia and Africa by no means exhaust the grim story . . . in Latin America: an estimated half million from Uruguay, perhaps 700,000 from Bolivia, many more from the other subfascist states. Keeping just to 1978, in September more than 16,000 refugees fled Somoza terror to neighbouring Honduras and Costa Rica, joining the 100,000 Nicaraguan exiles already living in Costa Rica, earlier victims of oppression in a country long favoured with the benign attention of the United States. These refugees have evoked no more interest in the United States than the hundreds of thousands fleeing Burma, the Philippines, Zaire, or other non-communist states. Attention is reserved for refugees from Indochina. (AC, 50–3)

In addition to the selective nature of Western concern for the refugee problem, Chomsky notes that the responsibility of the United States for the refugee problem from 'communist' countries is routinely played down or ignored. After 1975, supporters of the official line placed the blame for the refugee problem in Indochina - and other problems in the area – on the iniquity of the 'communist' regimes which were now in power in Vietnam, Laos and Cambodia. The aim was to restore the damage to the official ideology which was brought about by the anti-war movement and the US defeat. Thus Richard Nixon writes: 'today, after Communist governments have killed over a half million Vietnamese and over 2 million Cambodians, the conclusive moral judgment has been rendered on our effort to save Cambodia and Vietnam: We have never fought in a more moral cause.'[3] News and opinions of this kind were in the headlines throughout the late 1970s. Chomsky and Herman comment:

> all problems are attributed to the evils of Communism. The propaganda barrage has not only been highly selective, but has also involved substantial fabrication . . .
>
> While all of the countries of Indochina have been subjected to endless denunciations in the West for their 'loathsome' qualities and unaccountable failure to find humane solutions to their problems, Cambodia was a particular target of abuse. In fact, it became virtually a matter of dogma in the West that the regime was the very incarnation of evil with no redeeming qualities, and that the handful of demonic creatures who had somehow taken over the country were systematically massacring and starving the population . . . Evidence suggesting popular support for the regime among certain strata – particularly among the poorer peasants – was ignored or dismissed with revulsion and contempt. The fact that peasants in co-operatives were reported to work a 9-hour day, sometimes more, evoked outrage and horror on the part of commentators who seem to find no difficulty in coming to terms with the far more onerous conditions of labor, often near-slavery, that are common within the U.S. sphere of influence, such as those of Iranian slum-dwellers or Latin American Indians . . . At the same time, any scrap of evidence that would contribute to the desired image was eagerly seized (and regularly amplified), no matter how unreliable the source. Ordinary critical examination of sources, indeed, any effort to discover the truth, was regarded as a serious moral lapse. Furthermore, there was substantial fabrication of evidence. (AC, x-xi)

To take one example, it was widely reported in the West that the 'communist' regime in Cambodia had proudly boasted that to rebuild a new, pure country 1 or 2 million people would be enough, with the implication that the regime were deliberately slaughtering the remaining 5–7 million. The primary sources of this boast were an article in *Le Monde*, and a subsequent book called *Cambodia: Year Zero*, both by François Ponchaud. Chomsky and Herman looked carefully at how Ponchaud changed the words of the alleged boast in his writings, the figure sometimes appearing as 20,000 people. Other writers went on to distort the figures even more. Ponchaud subsequently explained that 'the original *Le Monde* reference was not based on any text but rather on a report by a refugee who said that he had heard this remark from the chief of the Northwest region of Cambodia at a meeting' (AC, 181). In the American edition of the book the alleged boast disappears, though it is present in the British version (AC, 182). Chomsky and Herman describe the history of this famous boast as 'a curious comedy of errors'. They comment:

> these 'quotes', which have a curious habit of disappearing on analysis, form the most substantial part of the evidence behind one crucial element in the thesis to which the propaganda machine is committed: that the Khmer Rouge leadership was committed to systematic massacre and starvation of the population it held in its grip, that is, to 'autogenocide'. It would be of little use to contemporary Western ideology if it were to be shown that peasant revenge, undisciplined troops and similar factors (still worse, the legacy of U.S. attack) were responsible for the deaths and killings in Cambodia. It is crucial to establish in the public consciousness, whatever the facts may be, that a centralized and carefully planned programme lay behind the atrocities ... It is therefore interesting to see how flimsy is the basis on which such elaborate constructions are founded, a useful insight into the mechanism and goals of current Western propaganda. (AC, 185–6)

Chomsky and Herman do not deny that atrocities took place in post-1975 Cambodia, still less do they condone them. In a 1985 article reviewing scholarly work on the topic, Chomsky notes that the best and most comprehensive study estimates that half a million to a million people died in the US assault on Cambodia, and about 750,000 from 1975 to 1978, including '200,000 to 300,000 outright executions' (CR, 291). In their earlier book Chomsky and Herman gave no estimates, saying that there was no doubt that there was a horrible record of atrocities and that it might turn out, when the facts are available, that the most extreme estimates are correct. Their purpose was to scrutinize the concern of Western journalists and intellectuals about the alleged atrocities, pointing out how selective the concern was, how flimsy the evidence often was, and how protests about atrocities *within* the US sphere of influence would have been much more productive, in particular, the US-backed Indonesian invasion of East Timor during the same period, which led to the death of at least a quarter of the Timorese population. It is important to emphasize that Chomsky and Herman were not discussing Cambodia in a vacuum in AC: they presented Cambodia and Timor as paired cases in which history kindly ran a controlled experiment to determine just how serious Western intellectuals and governments are in their alleged concerns about human rights and truth. The Timor side of the comparision has often been ignored, being unacceptable to Western intellectuals because it reveals their tacit commitment to massive atrocities of the Pol Pot style as long as Western privilege is not harmed. The subtitle of their book *After the Cataclysm* is 'Postwar Indochina and the reconstruction of imperial ideology', an apt comment on the actual effect of all the news and discussion of Indochina in the West.

The enormous left propaganda machine

Supporters of the official line like to pretend that they are a tiny, courageous and beleaguered minority of genuine seekers after truth, while the great majority of intellectuals are either politically motivated radicals or innocent victims of a powerful socialist propaganda apparatus. This is nonsense, but it is a useful way of discrediting dissenting views. Thus Guenter Lewy, in his book on Vietnam mentioned in the last chapter, claims that the US government had 'limited leverage . . . on public opinion', whereas the Vietnamese communists were 'relentless' in 'carrying the propaganda effort to the enemy'. The outcome of this 'uneven contest' was a conviction among the 'larger educated public' of the 'gross immorality of America's conduct in the war' (note in passing that the word 'relentless' is normally reserved by people like Lewy for official enemies).[4]

Richard Nixon repeatedly complains in his book that the news media were against him: many journalists were 'viciously biased critics of the American war effort', he writes, ready to give 'equal credibility . . . to enemy propaganda and United States government statements'. Reporters 'considered it their duty to try to oppose government policy by whatever means were available'.[5]

Never was the huge left propaganda machine invoked more than in relation to post-1975 Indochina. Chomsky and Herman cite a 1977 *New York Times* article by Walter Kaufmann who bemoans 'the lack of international outrage, protests and pressure in the face of what has been going on in Cambodia' (WCTWF, 20). Similarly, an article in *Time* Magazine in 1978 complained that 'somehow the enormity of the Cambodian tragedy . . . has failed to evoke an appropriate response of outrage in the West' – even worse, some intellectuals 'are so committed to 'liberation' and 'revolution' that they can actually defend what has happened in Cambodia' (AC, 164). Chomsky and Herman comment: 'In fact, the Western Press since 1975 has poured forth reams of denunciations of Cambodia in the most strident tones, repeating the most extreme denunciations often on flimsy evidence' (AC, 164).

Chomsky argues that supporters of the official line were worried from the late sixties onward that their stranglehold on the public mind was becoming less than total as a result, in part, of the anti-war movement:

To my knowledge, in the American mass media you cannot find a single socialist journalist, not a single syndicated political commentator who is a socialist. From the ideological point of view the mass media are almost one hundred per cent 'state capitalist' . . .

In 1965 you would have had great difficulty in finding a Marxist professor, or a socialist, in an economics department at a major university . . . Some changes did take place at the end of the sixties in the universities, largely due to the student movement, which demanded and achieved some broadening of the tolerated range of thinking. The reactions have been interesting. Now that the pressure of the student movement has been reduced, there is a substantial effort to reconstruct the orthodoxy that had been slightly disturbed. And constantly, in the discussions and literature dealing with that period – often called 'the time of troubles' or something of that sort – the student left is depicted as a menace threatening freedom of research and teaching; the student movement is said to have placed the freedom of the universities in jeopardy by seeking to impose totalitarian ideological controls. That is how the state capitalist intellectuals describe the fact that their near-total control of ideology was very briefly brought into question. (LR, 9–13)

Nicaragua

We shall now draw together the main themes of this chapter and the previous one by reviewing US policy towards Nicaragua. Both the realities of this policy and the way it has been presented in the United States illustrate very clearly how the official line distorts and conceals the truth.

The reality

US involvement in Nicaragua goes back to the early years of this century:

> The Marines landed in 1909 in support of a US–British inspired revolution . . . and from 1912 to 1933 the country was under US military occupation (apart from one year), leading to the murder of the nationalist leader Sandino and the establishment of the Somoza dictatorship after a brutal counterinsurgency campaign. Little concern was voiced here as he robbed and tortured, employing the US-trained National Guard to control the captive population, which was reduced to misery. (TTT, 127)

The extent of US penetration of the country is indicated by the establishment of the National Bank of Nicaragua not long after the marine landing. All the directors except one were from the Brown Brothers Bank of New York, which held majority ownership; board meetings were held in New York (TTT, 4). A 1977 advertisement in the *Wall Street Journal* promised US investors in Nicaragua 'a country where foreign capital is nurtured', 'a good investment climate', 'stability, peace and a prosperous economy', and so on (WCTWF, 283). Eventually Somoza's brutality and corruption alienated even the business classes, and the Sandinista guerillas fought their way to power.

> Carter supported Somoza virtually to the end of his bloody rule, with Israel taking over the main burden at the end – surely with tacit US approval, despite official denials . . . some 40–50,000 people were killed and the society was reduced to ruins, devastated and bankrupt.
> With the failure of its attempt to maintain the basic structure of the terrorist regime, the US government, along with articulate opinion, became passionately concerned over repression and democracy in Nicaragua. In a less-indoctrinated society than ours, this sudden conversion would be dismissed with the contempt it richly merits. (TTT, 128)

> The crimes of the Sandinistas were soon demonstrated by remarkable improvements in health, literacy, nutritional levels and social welfare. In January 1983 the Inter-American Development Bank, summarizing developments since 1979, concluded that 'Nicaragua has made noteworthy progress in the social sector, which is laying a solid foundation for long-term socio-economic development', including health, literacy, community organizing for the population, and so on. (OPI, 83–4)

President Reagan's response to the new regime followed the usual pattern: 'international terrorism, embargo, pressures on international institutions and allies to withhold aid, a huge campaign of propaganda and disinformation, threatening military manoeuvres and overflights . . . and other hostile measures available to a powerful and violent state' (OPI, 84). He also sent in the CIA, who organized a guerrilla campaign to attack Nicaragua from bases in El Salvador and Honduras. Reagan hoped that the 'contra' guerillas would bring down the Sandinista government, but had to settle for more limited aims. Chomsky cites former CIA analyst David MacMichael:

the principal actions to be undertaken were paramilitary which hopefully would provoke cross-border attacks by Nicaraguan forces and thus serve to demonstrate Nicaragua's aggressive nature . . . it was hoped that the Nicaraguan government would clamp down on civil liberties within Nicaragua itself, arresting its opposition, demonstrating its inherently totalitarian nature and thus increase domestic dissent within the country. (OPI, 85)

The contras were basically a band of thugs and mercenaries, with no coherent political programme and little support in the country. Unable to pose a serious military threat despite massive supplies of equipment from the US, their main targets are economic installations and civilians. (TTT, 134–5).

Chomsky notes the panic reaction in Washington when Nicaragua agreed to the 1984 Contadora peace plan for the region, which was drawn up by a group of Central American countries 'shortly after Ronald Reagan had informed Congress that the purpose of the contra war was to compel Nicaragua to accept the treaty' (OPI, 84). Elections held in Nicaragua the same year were described as remarkably open and fair by international observers, but ignored or dismissed as rigged in the United States. In 1985 Reagan declared that Nicaragua posed 'an unusual and extraordinary threat to the national security and foreign policy of the United States' and announced a trade embargo. Support for the contras continues as I write (mid-1989), despite the Irangate scandal and widespread protest within the United States.

The lack of an 'official line'

We now take up in turn some of the components of the official line that we have highlighted in the last two chapters, as they apply to Nicaragua. Firstly, there has been fierce debate about Nicaragua in US media and scholarship, creating the impression that there is no uniform line about US involvement. As in the earlier case of Indochina, though, the mainstream debate is a narrow one, focusing on tactical questions and not questioning the right of the United States to intervene as it chooses in other countries. For example, the *New York*

Times argued in 1983 that there were 'holes in the Administration's case' on Nicaragua, but these were only 'practical' while the 'moral argument is more compelling' (TTT, 125). The mainstream press assumes without argument that Reagan is genuinely concerned to 'advance human rights and democratic politics' in Nicaragua (CT, 119). The administration was angered by moves in Congress to reduce military support for the contras, but the objections were pragmatic rather than principled: support for the contras waned as it became clear that their prospects were hopeless even with massive US support.

The 'nation'

As ever, the US elite claims to act in the interest of the nation – witness Reagan's declaration, cited above – obscuring its real aim of maintaining the fifth freedom in Central America. To conceal its real aims the State Department set up an 'Office of Public Diplomacy', with the task of leaking 'intelligence reports' to the media which would show Nicaragua in a bad light (CT, 200). A senior US official refers to this operation (and similar ones about Libya and international terrorism) as 'a huge psychological operation of the kind the military conducts to influence a population in denied or enemy territory'; Chomsky adds that this is exactly how the US elite regards the American public – as enemy territory (CT, 201).

The real concerns of US foreign policy are often clear from the internal record, as we saw in the case of the Middle East. For Central America, Chomsky quotes a National Security Council memorandum of 1954 which argues that 'it is essential to arrest the drift in the area toward radical and nationalist regimes'. The document emphasizes the need for 'adequate production in Latin America of, and access by the United States to, raw materials essential to U.S. security'. To this end the United States should 'seek ultimate military standardization, along U.S. lines, of the organization, training, doctrine and equipment of Latin American armed forces, countering trends toward the establishment of European military missions in Latin America' (OPI, 19–21). As usual, such documents tend to be ignored in mainstream discussions of the area.

The well-meaning, blundering giant

The contras' tactics involve intimidation, rape, murder of civilians, destruction of property, kidnapping, and horrific torture. One of the contra leaders said, 'There is no line at all, not even a fine line, between a civilian farm owned by the government and a Sandinista military outpost' – so killing civilians is legitimate in their eyes (TTT, 11). Chomsky comments:

> These matters are considered of scant interest by US journalists in Nicaragua or Honduras, who do not seek out or publish such testimony, though it is permissible to concede that some unpleasant things may have happened in the past while reporting that the contras now 'vow to end rights abuses . . . after reports that the insurgents in Nicaragua have been executing Government soldiers, officials, and village militiamen' – not exactly the content of the testimony that has largely been suppressed in the field. (TTT, 11–12)

As we saw before, things are always 'improving' as far as human rights abuses by US allies are concerned. The mainstream media continues to assume that the US aim of 'containing Nicaragua' is justified: the contras may be an 'imperfect instrument' for this purpose, but the purpose itself is taken for granted. The doveish *Washington Post* opposes aid to the contras, but agrees with the government that we must turn 'Nicaragua back towards democracy' (CT, 251). By keeping the criticism in the domain of errors and blunders, rather than challenging fundamental assumptions, the media obscures the direct link between US aims and the brutality that results from them.

The appeal to expertise

We turn now to an area where things have changed somewhat. During the Indochina war, many US intellectuals could be counted on to provide 'scientific' justification for government policy, in a misuse of the prestige of science that Chomsky bitterly condemned. Some of the principled criticism of the war had an effect, however, despite the attempts to restore imperial ideology after 1975. Opposition to US intervention in

Central America took shape much more quickly in the 1980s than the earlier protests against the Vietnam war in the 1960s. Chomsky comments:

> One can see the change in general consciousness and culture, for example, by comparing the reaction when Kennedy sent U.S. forces to attack South Vietnam in 1962 to the reaction when Reagan made moves toward direct military intervention in Central America a few weeks after coming to office . . . [In the former case] the public reaction was virtually nil . . . Even when a huge American expeditionary force was sent to invade South Vietnam and the United States expanded its war to the North and to Laos, protest was very limited. We sometimes forget that as late as 1966 it was impossible to have an outdoor public meeting in Boston – probably the most liberal city in the United States – to protest the war, because it would be broken up with considerable violence . . . Compare all this with what happened in 1981, when Ronald Reagan moved to escalate Carter's war of torture and massacre in El Salvador with measures that threatened to lead to the direct use of U.S. military forces. . . . there was a spontaneous popular reaction, unanticipated by people who had assumed that the Vietnam syndrome had been laid to rest by the ideological campaigns of the seventies. (CR, 52–3)

Chomsky notes that the media have found it correspondingly harder to call on 'experts' who will support the official line:

> It is intriguing, for example, to see how rarely professional Latin Americanists are called upon for comment, in striking contrast to other regions and other topics, where the academic profession can be relied upon to provide the desired opinions, thus protecting the fabled 'objectivity' of the press. To select one example, it is a staple of Operation Truth that the 1984 elections in Nicaragua were a hopeless fraud while those in El Salvador at the same time were a dramatic victory for democracy. Therefore, it is necessary to suppress the official report of the Latin American Studies Association (LASA) on the Nicaraguan elections, along with corroborative

reports by a balanced Irish parliamentary delegation and others, because it simply drew the wrong conclusions after a careful enquiry by American academic experts on Nicaragua. (CT, 204–5)

One should not exaggerate these changes: on 'other topics', US intellectuals still tend to toe the line. Nevertheless, the level of US intervention in Central America, while destructive enough, has not reached the scale it did in Indochina, a fact worth recognizing.

Forces outside our control

The official line pretends that the contras are a spontaneous uprising by the anti-Sandinista opposition in Nicaragua, protesting against the undemocratic left-wing tyrants who have taken over their country. This is a convenient fiction: the US government can disclaim responsibilities for contra atrocities, and point to any real or imaginary repressive measures taken by the Sandinistas in response to the guerrilla war as proof of their totalitarian tendencies.

In reality, the contras were insignificant without US support:

'When the agency [CIA] was pulled out of this program, these guys didn't know how to buy a Band-Aid,' according to the government official in charge, later identified as Marine Lt.-Col. Oliver North. The extent of CIA control has been detailed by former contra leader Edgar Chamorro, who describes the FDN as a 'front organization' for the CIA. After the mining of harbors, for example, he was given a press release to read taking credit for the mining in the name of the FDN, who 'of course' had no role in the mining carried out by CIA Latin American agents. He describes how every detail of the FDN operations, including propaganda, was stage-managed by the CIA. (TTT, 131)

Once again, the 'Free Press' prefers not to highlight these facts.

'Communism'

It was evident from the first days of the Reagan administration that its policies were designed to ensure that 'Nicaragua will sooner or later become a Soviet client, as the U.S. imposes a stranglehold on its reconstruction and development, rebuffs efforts to maintain decent relations, and supports harassment and intervention' (TNCW, 51), the standard policy adopted in the case of an enemy the US undertakes to subvert or destroy. Chomsky writes:

> To attain the second of these goals, the U.S. rejected a Sandinista request for arms and training, and pressured its allies to do the same, thereby ensuring that Nicaragua, lacking any other source, would become entirely dependent on Soviet arms; the U.S. blocked aid from international lending institutions to the same end. When the U.S. embargo was declared in May 1985, Nicaraguan trade with the Soviet bloc was about 20%, roughly the same as the U.S. and far less than Europe and the Third World, an intolerable situation that must be overcome so as to allow apologists for U.S. international terrorism to justify it as defense against Soviet imperialism. The same U.S. policies, with their predictable effects, enable the Free Press to refer to 'the Moscow-backed Government in Nicaragua,' a phrase with appropriately ominous overtones and one that is literally correct, given the success of the Reagan administration in ensuring that Nicaragua must turn to the Soviet Union for defense against U.S. international terrorism. (CT, 27–8)

As always, it is an *independent* Nicaragua that the US elite fears most. If a country can take control of its own resources and develop progressive economic and social programmes, their example may inspire other countries of the 'Free World' to do the same. The attack on Nicaragua, and the deliberate attempt to force it into the Soviet camp, is designed to deter other countries from following this path. The East–West confrontation is used to camouflage the more important conflict: between the people of the 'Free World' and their US masters.

'Terrorism'

We need not spend much time on this issue here. The 'terrorists' in Nicaragua are the contras and their US paymasters, as the evidence amply demonstrates. No credible evidence of Nicaraguan support for terrorism in other countries has been produced.

Refugees

Here again, we need not linger long. The number of refugees from post-1980 Nicaragua is now considerable, though smaller than the number who fled the previous Somoza dictatorship. No one doubts that most of them are fleeing from the economic catastrophe that was created largely by the US economic war against the country (supported enthusiastically by Britain and the other Western allies) and by the deliberate economic sabotage of the contras. Even larger numbers of people have been made homeless by US aggression elsewhere in Central America, notably El Salvador and Guatemala. Naturally, the relatively small numbers who left Cuba in the early 1980s were given much more prominence in the United States than the far greater numbers who were not fleeing from an official enemy.

The left propaganda machine

We have seen how the mainstream media uniformly support the official line over Nicaragua, with criticism and debate confined within narrow limits. None the less, the view is often put forward that the sneaky communists in Managua have dominated the debate with the help of their left-wing friends in the US press:

> Thus in a cover story of the *Los Angeles Times Magazine*, Arturo Cruz, Jr. informs us that 'the contras, so charismatic in Nicaragua, were always terrible at public relations in America' where the Sandinistas 'won the [Madison Avenue] war handily.' . . . The problem faced by the contras, he explains in the *New Republic*, is that they are 'unable to speak the very special language necessary to communicate with

American journalists', offering responses that are considered 'too pedestrian and tacky to be truly revolutionary' by the ultraleftists who dominate the U.S. press . . . Similarly, U.S. supporters of the contras complain that 'Left-wing opponents of contra aid have thrashed the administration in the propaganda battle on campuses, in churches, *and in the press*' (Morton Kondracke). (CT, 209–10)

As we saw with Nixon's complaints about the press, any deviation from total loyalty to the official line, even within the usual very narrow boundaries, is regarded as dangerous. Chomsky's comment on these fantasies is that they 'can only be understood as a reflection of the fear that if heresy is granted even a tiny opening, then all is lost'. (TTT, 229)

We have seen that the usual patterns have appeared in the case of Nicaragua, both in US actions and in the way they are presented by the official line. Things have improved slightly, as we noted, but the standard policies are still pursued while the intellectuals still assume that the United States is engaged in a selfless struggle to defend freedom and democracy. In the next chapter we shall look at why US intellectuals remain so subservient to the state propaganda system. We shall then look at what Chomsky thinks can be done to change things.

Appendix, mainly for British readers: Ireland

The discussion of US foreign policy in the last two chapters may seem a bit remote for British readers. To bring the issues closer to home, this appendix sketches an account of current events in Ireland, particularly Northern Ireland, in the spirit of Chomsky's political work.[6]

We must start with some general remarks about British imperialism. For several centuries the British Empire was the largest in the world. Huge profits were made by companies importing food and raw materials from the colonies. Rebellions were put down with appalling barbarity: some of the largest massacres were in Tasmania and in India. The brutality with which British armed forces overran large sections of the globe is not always appreciated in this country. As one book puts it:

Britain has one of the most violent and uncivilised histories of any European country, yet the orthodox view is that the English are both non-violent and civilised, and that it is the people whom Britain has oppressed who are violent and uncivilised.

A gigantic exercise in self-delusion has helped to preserve English pride and self-regard down the centuries. Actions taken for reasons of political and economic expediency have been presented as if altruism were the sole motive. Atrocities of all kinds – from Cromwell's massacre at Drogheda, to the slave-trade, to the appropriation of vast tracts of other people's countries – have been justified by claims of religious, cultural and racial superiority. As a result, many English people are unable to see themselves as others see them: to recognise why in other parts of the world the Union Jack has been described as 'the butcher's apron', and the empire as 'the place where the sun never sets and the blood never dries'.[7]

The important point here is that the US brutalities we have documented above are by no means unique in history. Many of the techniques of repression, and the ways of camouflaging them, were invented by the British and only later adopted by the United States.

We turn now specifically to Ireland. The first British attempt to colonize Ireland was in the twelfth century. The Irish put up fierce resistance, and it was not until the early seventeenth century that the Tudor monarchs were able to subjugate the whole country. The British colonialists were brutal in the extreme: in 1574, for example, soldiers under the Earl of Essex slaughtered the entire population of Rathlin Island, some 600 people. When the Irish rebelled once more in the 1640s, Oliver Cromwell's army moved in to quell the uprising, leaving 616,000 people dead and transporting 100,000 to other colonies in the 'New World' as slaves, with the result that the population of the country was halved in a few years.

Further resistance to colonialism was treated in similar ways until 1922, when Ireland was partitioned. The twenty-six counties of the south became the Republic of Ireland, while the six counties of the north remained part of the United Kingdom. The majority of people in the six counties are Protestants, descendants of settlers and landowners from England and Scotland, many of whose families had lived in Ireland for hundreds of years. In the country as a whole, such people are a minority, and they consistently opposed independence for Ireland. The British reluctance to part with the six counties of the north was also linked to the fact that most of Ireland's industry was concentrated around Belfast and Londonderry. Since independence, the Republic of Ireland has to had to build up an industrial base virtually from nothing, and is still one of the poorest countries of Europe.

Until the mid-1960s the Protestant Unionists controlled Northern Ireland with a grip of iron. The best jobs and houses were kept for Protestants. Voting districts were gerrymandered so that the Catholic nationalist minority were not democratically represented. Catholics were murdered by Protestant paramilitary groups. The 'B-Specials', exclusively Protestant part-time auxiliary policemen, intimidated the Catholic community; their assaults on peaceful civil rights marches in 1968 and 1969 were instrumental in initiating the wave of violence that has persisted since then. The Irish Republican Army (IRA), moribund for many years, then came back to life. The British Army was deployed in the six counties in 1969. Since then what are usually called the 'troubles' in Northern Ireland have rarely been out of the headlines in Britain. By mid-1987 a total of 2,587 people had died in the violence, 804 of them military personnel.

Let's now follow the pattern of these two chapters and contrast the official British line on Northern Ireland with an alternative view. The official line maintains that British policy in the North is a selfless attempt to help. The Irish are all emotional extremists, their fanaticism whipped up by religious and political differences. Our brave boys are there to keep the two warring communities from tearing each other apart. Political solutions put forward by successive governments in the traditional British spirit of reasonableness and decency have been scuppered by extremists on one side or the other. The extremists on the nationalist side, notably the terrorists of the IRA and the Irish National Liberation Army (INLA), are by far the worst: their irrational hatred of Britain and their ruthlessness know no bounds. They are unfortunately supplied with money and arms by lunatics in Libya and misinformed Irish people in North America. As long as a majority of people in Northern Ireland wish to remain part of the United Kingdom, we must respect their wishes.

The alternative view claims that the problems in Northern Ireland are the direct result of centuries of British imperialism. Religious and political divisions in Ireland have been deliberately created and exacerbated by the British in the classic divide-and-rule strategy used by oppressors since time immemorial. The violence of nationalists in Ireland pales into insignificance compared to centuries of British atrocities in the country; the current violence results from the persistent failure of loyalists and British governments to respond to non-violent methods of protest. The main reason for the continued British presence in Ireland is a military one: the Republic is not a member of NATO, and the British ruling elite don't want a neutral country so close by. British troops, responsible for many atrocities and a huge drain on taxpayers' money, should be withdrawn from Ireland, and a timetable should be set for the relinquishing of British sovereignty over the North and the reunification of Ireland.

Continuing along Chomskyan lines, we turn now to some of the ways in which supporters of the official line in the media and scholarship distort the truth and confuse the public in the service of state propaganda. Let's start with 'terrorism'. We noted above that this term is typically reserved for 'retail violence' by official enemies, while the wholesale violence of repressive regimes is played down. Nowhere is this ploy clearer than in the official line on Northern Ireland. Firstly, few people in Britain are aware of the history of atrocities committed by the British in Ireland over the centuries. The IRA violence over the last twenty years is presented as the work of a few ruthless fanatics, whose hatred of Britain is emotional and virulent.

In 1980 the government minister responsible for Northern Ireland, Humphrey Atkins, accused loyalist assassins of playing into the hands of 'the terrorists'. The selective use of the term 'terrorism' in the official line is clear in this remark. In general, violence by republicans is treated quite differently in the media from violence by loyalists. Loyalists have been responsible for about a third of the deaths in the current troubles, most of them civilian, but the term 'terrorist' tends to be reserved for republican violence. When Maire Drumm, former vice-president of the republican party Sinn Fein, was murdered in a Belfast hospital in 1976, the *Daily Mirror* headline was 'HATE GRANNY SHOT DEAD'. The report showed no condemnation of the murderers, who were described as an 'execution squad' and 'cool killers'. When Unionist MP Robert Bradford was killed by the IRA in November 1981, the reaction was quite different. 'Ulster was plunged into fury yesterday by the terrorist killing of preacher MP Robert Bradford', wrote the *News of the World*. The killing was condemned by politicians and the media. Bradford had been active in loyalist paramilitary circles and had repeatedly stirred up hatred against Catholics. Liz Curtiss writes: 'Yet neither before, nor after, his death was Bradford dubbed "Daddy of Hate", and the coverage focussed on the iniquity of the killers rather than the victim. Bradford's death, unlike Maire Drumm's, was not portrayed as "the wages of extremism".'[8]

Republicans seldom appear on the radio or television in Britain. On the rare occasions when a republican supporter is allowed to state his or her views, there is a massive outcry in the press and parliament, with the broadcasting companies being accused of treachery. Loyalists, including members of paramilitary groups, appear much more frequently, and there is no outcry on these occasions. The police and the press are often quick to blame the IRA for terrorist acts which later turn out to have been the work of loyalists. In 1981 the Labour politician Ken Livingstone said that treating terrorists as 'criminals and psychopaths' was stupid, and would do nothing to end the violence. His remarks were distorted into support for the IRA, provoking widespread denunciation by newspapers and politicians.

Another key component of the official line is that the British government is only trying to do good in Northern Ireland. In 1981, shortly before Bobby Sands MP died on hunger strike, Peregrine Worsthorne wrote in the *Sunday Telegraph*: 'The English have every reason to feel proud of their country's recent record in Northern Ireland, since it sets the whole world a uniquely impressive example of altruistic service in the cause of peace. Nothing done by any other country in modern times so richly deserves the Nobel prize.'[9]

Murders by British soldiers are typically presented as 'errors' and 'blunders' or as an understandable response to extreme provocation. A book about Northern Ireland intended for schools and colleges describes internment without trial, introduced in 1971, as 'both a political and security disaster', because it was based on out-of-date information and 'the provisionals were hardly touched'. The authors do not criticize internment as fundamentally inhuman and unjust, simply as a failure which 'caused great resentment in the nationalist community'.[10] The similarity with historian Guenter Lewy's account of the Phoenix Program in Vietnam is striking.

The picture of Britain as well-intentioned, and the Irish as ungrateful children, goes back a long way. The philosopher David Hume wrote in his influential *History of England*, published around 1750, that the Irish had always been 'buried in the most profound barbarism and ignorance', that their 'rudeness and ignorance . . . were extreme', and that the British task was 'the subduing and civilising of that country'.[11] There is a direct line from attitudes like this to the patronizing, racist attitudes towards Irish people which are widespread in Britain today, which are fanned by comedians and cartoonists and which, unlike the expression of republican views, are not censored by the broadcasting authorities.

We saw above how official enemies are often accused of having powerful and skilful propaganda machines. Claims of this kind are often made about the IRA:

> As Bobby Sands approached death, [the British media] repeatedly invoked 'IRA propaganda' as a means of explaining – or explaining away – the extensive international interest and sympathy. In the weeks leading to his death, for instance, half of the news reports on the subject broadcast by the London commercial radio station LBC used the phrase 'IRA propaganda war' or variations on it.[12]

The reality is that the British Army in Northern Ireland, the Royal Ulster Constabulary, and the Northern Ireland Office all spend a lot of time and money on propaganda against republicanism. Press releases from these sources are often used verbatim by journalists. Fake news stories and 'black propaganda' are fed to the press by army intelligence agents. Censorship by senior broadcasting staff is widespread: Liz Curtiss lists forty-eight television programmes on Northern Ireland which were banned, curtailed or delayed between 1959 and 1979.

Much more could be said here about how the British public is kept confused and ignorant about Northern Ireland. We have looked at three similarities between the US official line and the British one: the focus on 'terrorism', the assumption that the government is well-meaning and occasionally commits 'mistakes' but never 'crimes', and the myth of the huge propaganda machine used by the official enemy. Oppressors throughout history have used these and similar devices, ably assisted by willing writers, sages, academics and other intellectuals. Anyone who wants to understand what is really going on in the world would do well to bear this point in mind.

8
The Way Forward

The last two chapters have shown Chomsky on the attack, criticizing US foreign policy and the intellectuals who misrepresent it. Assuming that Chomsky's analysis is correct, the next question is what can be done about it. This chapter outlines Chomsky's account of why intellectuals behave the way they do, and his views about how society should be changed to end the cynical abuses of power that he documents so well.

The role of intellectuals

Chomsky's analysis of the part that intellectuals play in society is summed up in these words: 'In every society there will emerge a caste of propagandists who labor to disguise the obvious, to conceal the actual workings of power, and to spin a web of mythical goals and purposes, utterly benign, that allegedly guide national policy' (TNCW, 86). This is a harsh judgement, and it runs counter to the widely held view that intellectuals tend to be more subversive and critical of authority than the public in general. The stereotype of the 'academic Marxist' is quite widespread. Chomsky refers to an organization called 'Accuracy in Academia', one of the new breed of right-wing pressure groups which have sprouted vigorously in Reagan's America:

> [Accuracy in Academia] alleges that there are 10,000 Marxist professors on campus (where 'Marxist', in their terms, includes people who would be regarded as mainstream moderates in European industrial democracies) out of a total number of 600,000 professors. To combat this threat, they propose to monitor these dangerous creatures, using student spies, the aim being 'to promote greater balance', according

to director Laslo Csorba. The idea that an advantage of 60 to 1 does not suffice for 'balance' captures well the totalitarian mentality of these elements. (TTT, 229)

Similarly, Chomsky quotes a respected liberal historian who says that Marxism 'has come close to being the dominant ideology in the academic world'. He comments: 'The concept is so remote from reality as to defy rational discussion' (TTT, 229). Elsewhere he tells a personal anecdote to illustrate the point:

In the spring of 1969 a small group of students in economics here in Cambridge wanted to initiate a discussion of the nature of economics as a field of study. In order to open this discussion, they tried to organize a debate in which the two main speakers would be Paul Samuelson, the eminent Keynesian economist at MIT (today a Nobel laureate) and a Marxist economist. But for this latter role they were not able to find anyone in the Boston area, no one who was willing to question the neo-classical position from the point of view of Marxist political economy. Finally I was asked to take on the task, though I have no particular knowledge of economics, and no commitment to Marxism. (LR, 18)

The idea of universities as hotbeds of subversion has always been an absurd exaggeration. Even in the 1960s, politically active students and academics were in a minority. As we saw in the last chapter, meetings in Boston in the mid-1960s to protest against the war in Vietnam were routinely broken up by violent mobs. The idea that large numbers of intellectuals are left-wing extremists is part of the myth of the huge left propaganda machine that we discussed in Chapter 7. Any small success by the left is presented as a victory by a huge monolithic force which threatens our fundamental freedoms. The reality is that left-wing intellectuals are few in number and spend a lot of time arguing with each other, partly because this sort of behaviour is common among frightened minority groups, and partly because of infiltration by the political police who are experts at stirring up dissension.

The majority of intellectuals support the present economic and political system, and believe the official line about American policy being benign and selfless. Chomsky gives some further evidence that this is so:

> An indication of the real facts was given by an in-depth study of attitudes of 'the American intellectual elite' undertaken in the spring of 1970, at the height of opposition to the war after the U.S. invasion of Cambodia, with universities shut down after student protests and popular dissidence reaching proportions that were quite frightening to elite groups. The results showed that virtually all were opposed to the war and would have been classified as doves. But when we turn to the reasons, we find that the overwhelming majority were opposed on 'pragmatic grounds' – the war would not succeed in its aims – while a minority were opposed because the war was becoming too bloody (what the study called 'moral grounds': a certain amount of killing, maiming and torture is legitimate, but too much may offend delicate souls. Principled opposition to the war was so negligible as to be barely detectable. Perhaps 1 percent of the sample opposed the war on the grounds that aggression is wrong, even if undertaken by the United States . . .
>
> In contrast, much of the general population opposed the war on grounds of principle. As late as the 1980's, after a decade of dedicated efforts to overcome the 'Vietnam syndrome', over 70% of the population regard the war as 'fundamentally wrong and immoral', not merely a 'mistake' as the official doves maintain. (OPI, 129)

In the Soviet Union the price paid by an intellectual who challenges the system can be severe. In the United States the likely consequences are far less frightening. Why, then, do intellectuals in the United States typically submit to the system? Why, if the survey above is accurate, do they believe the official line which they help to promulgate? Why are there so few intellectuals like Chomsky?

There are a number of reasons. Firstly, there is a large incentive to conform:

> Journalists and columnists have the choice of conforming or being excluded, and in a wealthy society, the rewards for

conformity can be substantial. Those who choose to conform, hence to remain within the system, will soon find that they internalize the beliefs and attitudes that they express and that shape their work: it is a very rare individual who can believe one thing and say another on a regular basis . . . The point is not that the journalists or commentators are dishonest; rather, unless they happen to conform to the institutional requirements, they will find no place in the corporate media . . . With some variations, much the same is true in the schools and universities, for similar reasons. (OPI, 125–6)

Access to promotion and publishers, sponsorship, contacts with influential people, and lucrative research contracts, all tend to go along with conformity. People who raise fundamental questions of principle are often seen as an embarrassment: the top jobs are reserved for good boys (and girls occasionally). Intellectuals who are willing to address conferences of business leaders can get free trips to pleasant parts of the world and stay in exclusive hotels. Not many are willing, as Chomsky is, to go to places like Nicaragua or North Vietnam while the United States is attempting to subdue these countries. Huge amounts of money are available to intellectuals who carry out research for the military; doing research into disarmament, or non-nuclear defence, is not a way to get rich.

Many intellectuals are well paid compared to manual workers. Their work is usually less stultifying and exhausting than manual work. There is often greater flexibility in working arrangements and fewer industrial hazards. Intellectual work carries greater prestige than manual work. Intellectuals who conform have the prospect of a relatively privileged existence. Those who don't face the prospect of money worries, housing problems, boring or unpleasant work, and the intense feeling of having 'failed' which the majority of ordinary people have to live with. The need to look after your children, so that your decisions crucially affect their lives and not just your own, intensifies the problem. Given this choice, it isn't surprising that so many intellectuals choose to conform.

A second reason why intellectuals conform is that the institutions in which they work are an integral part of the power structure. This is obviously true of the media:

> The media represent the same interests that control the state and private economy, and it is therefore not very surprising to discover that they generally act to confine public discussion and understanding to the needs of the powerful and privileged. The media are, in the first place, private corporations. Their primary market is business (advertisers), and like other corporations they must bend to the needs of the community of investors. In the unlikely event that they might seek to pursue an independent path, they would quickly be called to account, and could not survive. Their top management (editors, etc.) is drawn from the ranks of wealthy professionals who tend naturally to share the perceptions of the privileged and powerful . . . Thus it is only to be expected that the framework of interpretation, selection of what counts as 'news,' permitted opinion, etc., will fall well within the range that conforms to the needs of the nexus of state–private power that controls the economy and the political system. (OPI, 125)

The same is true of universities. Speaking in 1969, Chomsky noted that the chairman of the political science department at his own institution, MIT, held a research contract worth three quarters of million dollars per year on 'pacification and counter-insurgency', while his equivalent at nearby Harvard was the chairman of the Vietnam study group of the State Department (RP, 199). The idea of an ivory tower university where reason and disinterested study reign supreme bears little relation to reality. Interestingly, the student movement of the 1960s was accused of trying to 'politicize' the universities by supporters of the official line. The reality is that the student movement 'tried to open up the universities and free them from outside control'; Chomsky comments: 'to be sure, from the point of view of those who had subverted the universities and converted them to a significant extent into instruments of government policy and official ideology this effort appeared to be an illegitimate form of "politicization"' (LR, 14).

A third factor which enforces conformity is simply the pervasiveness of the official line. Intellectuals tend to move in limited circles and to find opinions like those of Chomsky unthinkable:

> On the rare occasions in which I have an opportunity to discuss [political] issues, whether in print or in person, with people in the media or the academic professions, I often find not so much disagreement as an inability to hear. I have found all sorts of strange illusions about what, say, my attitude was toward the Vietnam War, because elite intellectuals often simply cannot perceive that one could have the opinions that I do hold. For example, my basic attitude toward the American war in Vietnam was based on the principle that aggression is wrong, including the aggression of the United States against South Vietnam. There's only a small number of people in American academic circles who could even hear those words. (CR, 18)

Opinions that fall outside the permitted narrow range are unthinkable: a person who expresses them is likely to be regarded as a freak or a lunatic. It takes unusual strength of character to survive this kind of treatment. Chomsky remarks that the relative openness of US society means that even information which the mass media ignore is 'accessible, but only for *fanatics*' (LR, 30; emphasis in original). The price that such 'fanatics' pay – apart from the lack of access to the rewards described above – is isolation:

> Part of the genius of American democracy has been to ensure that isolated individuals face concentrated state and private power alone, without the support of an organizational structure that can assist them in thinking for themselves or entering into meaningful political action, and with few avenues for public expression of fact or analysis that might challenge approved doctrine. (CT, 21)

It takes a rare combination of qualities – courage, passion, tenacity and self-confidence – for a US intellectual to challenge the official line publicly and consistently. While this underlines

Chomsky's achievement, the forces pressuring people to conform cast a grim shadow over the question we turn to now:
what can be done to change things?

A just society

A programme for social change has to include two things: a
model of a just society, and a strategy for bringing it about.
Chomsky's idea of what a just society would be like derives in
large part from a political current called *libertarian socialism* or
(equivalently) *anarchism*.[1]

The best way to understand libertarian socialism is perhaps to
contrast it with two other currents that come under the heading
of socialism. Socialists aim to create a society in which economic
and political decisions are taken by the majority of working
people rather than a small elite group of rich and powerful
people. The *social democratic* type of socialism, illustrated by
the Labour Party in Britain or the French Socialist Party, is
committed to gradual reform of the capitalist system by legis-
lation and persuasion. The other main kind is *Leninist* socialism,
typified by the Soviet Communist Party. Leninists do not believe
that the social democratic method is workable: ruling elites will
not tolerate reform which threatens their power and privileges,
Leninists argue, so social democratic parties will be tolerated
within capitalism as long as they do not aim for fundamental
change. Leninist socialists therefore advocate the revolutionary
overthrow of capitalism, not hesitating to use violent means to
defend the revolution if this proves necessary.

Libertarian socialists argue that the social democratic approach
is unlikely to create real socialism. As we have seen, Chomsky
shows in great detail how countries in the 'Free World' which try
to move towards socialism in this way face massive repression
by the current master of the 'Free World', the United States,
and by the local elites in different countries which support it.
This interference is not confined to the Third World. When the
United States Army defeated the fascists in Italy during the
Second World War, they quickly dispersed the Italian resistance
– which had liberated most of northern Italy on its own – and
restored the rule of fascist collaborators. The resistance fighters

were predominantly socialists, and the US did not want post-war Italy to move towards a socialist society:

> From 1948, the CIA undertook large-scale clandestine intervention in Italian politics, labor and social life, spending over $65 million in such projects (which continued at least until 1975) by 1968, part of a more general European program in which US labor leadership also played a significant role, contributing effectively to the weakening of the labor movements. (TTT, 195)

Thus libertarians agree with many of the Leninist arguments against social democracy. At the same time, Chomsky criticizes Leninism because this type of socialism in his view is nothing other than tyranny or rule by a privileged bureaucracy, and is in fact diametrically opposed to socialism. The anarchist Mikhail Bakunin warned in the nineteenth century that socialists of this type would 'concentrate the reins of government in a strong hand, because [they believed that] the ignorant people require an exceedingly firm guardianship' and that ordinary people would be 'under the direct command of the state engineers, who will constitute a new privileged scientific-political estate' (cited in CR, 84). Chomsky believes that history has confirmed the rightness of Bakunin's predictions: we looked at Chomsky's criticisms of the Soviet Union in the last chapter. In short, then, libertarian socialists criticize social democracy for not being *socialist* and Leninism for its lack of *liberty*.

Chomsky gives an outline of the kind of society that libertarian socialists like Bakunin and Kropotkin wanted to see:

> They had in mind a highly organized form of society, but a society that was organized on the basis of organic units, organic communities. And generally they meant by that the workplace and the neighbourhood, and from those two basic units there could derive through federal arrangements a highly integrated kind of social organization, which might be national or even international in scope . . .
>
> Representative democracy, as in, say, the United States or Great Britain, would be criticized by an anarchist of this school on two grounds. First of all because there is a monopoly of

> power centralized in the State, and secondly – and critically
> – because representative democracy is limited to the political
> sphere and in no serious way encroaches on the economic
> sphere. Anarchists of this tradition have always held that
> democratic control of one's productive life is at the core of
> any serious human liberation, or, for that matter, of any
> significant democratic practice. That is, as long as individuals
> are compelled to rent themselves on the market to those who
> are willing to hire them, as long as their role in production is
> simply that of ancillary tools, then there are striking elements
> of coercion and oppression that make talk of democracy very
> limited, if even meaningful. (RP, 245–6)

Libertarian socialists want political and economic power to
be decentralized as much as possible. They want industry and
agriculture to be self-managed by the people who work there.
They distrust political parties which claim to act in the name of
the people and which try to 'lead' the masses towards socialism.
They believe strongly that ordinary people have the capacity
to organize and control their own lives given the opportunity.
Social structures which are imposed from the top do more harm
than good, they argue, both in direct repression by the state and
in the stifling of individual intelligence, creativity and initiative
which 'top-down' organizations cause.

Examples of societies which have run along these lines are
few. Chomsky cites the early Jewish communal settlements
in Israel, the kibbutzim, although he says that more recent
developments have led to their libertarian socialist character
being lost to some extent (RP, 246). He also refers to Spain
during the civil war:

> A good example of a really large-scale anarchist revolution –
> in fact the best example to my knowledge – is the Spanish
> revolution in 1936, in which over most of Republican Spain
> there was a quite inspiring anarchist revolution that involved
> both industry and agriculture over substantial areas . . . [it]
> was, by both human measures and indeed anyone's eco-
> nomic measures, quite successful. That is, production con-
> tinued effectively; workers in farms and factories proved
> quite capable of managing their affairs without coercion from

above . . . That anarchist revolution was simply destroyed by force, but during the period in which it was alive I think it was a highly successful and, as I say, in many ways a very inspiring testimony to the ability of poor working people to organize and manage their own affairs, extremely successfully, without coercion and control. (RP, 246–7)

At this point we should say something about the term 'anarchism'. In the official line, 'anarchists' are treated as virtually the same as 'terrorists': the popular picture of an anarchist is of a man with a bomb in his hand, ready to cause chaos and violence and the destruction of civilized values. There have been a few individuals of this kind, but the popular stereotype is basically a device to prevent anarchist or libertarian socialist ideas from being taken seriously (we should also bear in mind that the damage brought about by such individuals is incomparably less than the wholesale death and destruction caused by governments – recall what we said about 'terrorism' in the last chapter). Since the term 'libertarian socialism' pushes fewer irrational buttons, I have tended to use it here rather than 'anarchism', but it is important to note that for Chomsky the two terms are virtually interchangeable.

Chomsky sees libertarian socialism as the modern answer to the questions raised by the classic liberal thinkers such as Jean-Jacques Rousseau, Wilhelm von Humboldt, and John Stuart Mill. These thinkers were concerned to protect individual freedom from the ever-increasing power of the state. What they did not understand, in Chomsky's view, is that capitalist economic relations were basically unfree, especially now that huge multinational companies wield huge power (RS, 180–1). Reducing state power over the individual is now not enough: we must also 'dissolve the authoritarian control over production and resources which . . . drastically limits human freedom' (IC, 192; also cited in RP, 31). Political and economic freedom are inseparable, in Chomsky's view, and it is only within a libertarian socialist framework that both can be achieved.

Even people who are sympathetic to libertarian socialism sometimes find it hard to concede that the kind of social organization which Chomsky advocates is relevant to an advanced industrialized society. Such people may agree that co-operation,

self-management and decentralized decision-making could work
in small agricultural villages, but they point out that the large
and complex economies and political systems that we find in
countries like the United States require a degree of centralized
planning and control. Chomsky disagrees:

> is it necessary that anarchist concepts belong to the pre-
> industrial phase of human society, or is anarchism the
> rational mode of organization for a highly advanced industrial
> society? Well, I myself believe the latter, that is, I think
> that industrialization and the advance of technology raise
> possibilities for self-management over a broad scale that
> simply didn't exist in an earlier period. And that in fact this
> is precisely the rational mode for an advanced and complex
> industrial society, one in which workers can very well become
> masters of their own immediate affairs, that is, in direction and
> control of the shop, but also can be in a position to make the
> major substantive decisions concerning the structure of the
> economy, concerning social institutions, concerning planning
> regionally and beyond. At present, institutions do not permit
> them to have control over the requisite information, and the
> relevant training to understand these matters. A good deal
> could be automated. Much of the necessary work that is
> required to keep a decent level of social life going can be
> consigned to machines – at least in principle – which means
> humans can be free to undertake the kind of creative work
> which may not have been possible, objectively, in the earlier
> stages of the industrial revolution. (RP, 248–9)

Ideas of this kind tend to be dismissed as romantic idealism
by tough-minded establishment intellectuals, but this sort of
criticism misses the point. Chomsky is raising the question
of what a society would look like which took as its central
purpose 'the vital concrete possibility for every human being
to bring to full development all the powers, capacities, and
talents with which nature has endowed him, and turn them to
social account' (Daniel Guérin, cited in RS, 151). Societies which
exist now are based on oppression and exploitation, rationalized
by the view that most human beings are too stupid or selfish
to control their own lives, and that private profit is the only

basis for an economic system. The institutions of these societies reflect the oppression and the mean-spirited assumptions about human beings which underlie them. Asking how anarchists would manage these institutions is senseless: anarchists want to help build other institutions, based on different assumptions about what people are like.

A similar argument often used against libertarian socialism (and socialism in general) is that it flies in the face of the fact that some people are cleverer, harder working, and higher achievers than others. Given that people differ in natural endowment, it is said, they should be rewarded differently. Chomsky comments:

> I am personally quite convinced that no matter what training or education I might have received, I could never have run a four-minute mile, discovered Gödel's theorems, composed a Beethoven quartet, or risen to any of innumerable other heights of human achievement. I feel in no way demeaned by these inadequacies . . . Human talents vary considerably, within a fixed framework that is characteristic of the species and that permits ample scope for creative work. This should be a matter for delight rather than a condition to be abhorred. Those who assume otherwise must be adopting the tacit premise that people's rights or social reward are somehow contingent on their abilities . . . But insofar as this is true, it is simply a social malady to be overcome much as slavery had to be eliminated at an earlier stage of human history. (CR, 198–9)

Capitalism rewards certain attributes in people. But to argue that this is the only conceivable way to organize things is pure dogmatism:

> One might suppose that some mixture of avarice, selfishness, lack of concern for others, aggressiveness, and similar characteristics play a part in getting ahead and 'making it' in a competitive society based on capitalist principles . . . All that follows, so far as I can see, is a comment on our particular social and economic arrangements . . . The obvious question, of course, is whether other social arrangements might be

brought into being that would not encourage these tendencies but would rather be conducive to the flourishing of other traits that are no less part of our common nature: solidarity, concern, sympathy, and kindness, for example. (CR, 190)

As these passages show, libertarian socialism rests ultimately on beliefs about human nature. We shall return to these beliefs and the scientific basis for them in the final chapter, when we consider the relation between Chomsky's linguistics and his politics.

Strategies for the left

When it comes to the question of how to achieve the kind of society he would like, Chomsky is careful to emphasize that he does not claim to speak with authority. 'I don't have any faith in my own judgement about tactics. I've been wrong much more often than I have been right. Therefore, you shouldn't have any special faith in my judgments in this respect' (RP, 205). None the less, there are certain general principles which Chomsky thinks are crucial.[2]

Assessment of the likely consequences

Speaking to a college audience in 1969, Chomsky makes this important point:

I think the primary principle, especially for people like us, who are, for the most part, among the privileged in society, should be the principle that we keep clearly in mind who we are responsible to. I suggest that we are responsible to the people of Vietnam, to the people of Guatemala, to the people of Harlem. In undertaking some form of action, we must ask ourselves what the consequences will be for the people who are at the wrong end of the guns, for the people who can't escape. That's a consideration of overwhelming importance. Even a very well intentioned act, if it strengthens the forces of repression, is no gift whatsoever to those whose fate we, in some sense, bear in our hands. This is a simple and elementary fact, and I think it should be ever present in one's mind. (RP, 205–6)

Intellectuals in the United States, and in other western democracies, are in a privileged position where we can do a lot of good or a lot of harm. Compared to the peasants of Guatemala or of Vietnam in the days of the US client regimes we do not run a great risk of imprisonment or torture or a visit from a death squad if we speak out against injustice and oppression. If we are serious about wanting social change, it is up to us to use the privileges we have on behalf of those who are considerably less privileged. Obviously it is hard to be sure about the results of our actions. We need to think carefully about the likely consequences, listening where possible to the most reliable voices coming from the ranks of the poor and the oppressed.

Building a mass movement

Any strategy for social change depends crucially on building a strong mass movement which is united behind a clear programme. In the absence of such a movement, only small and limited gains can be made:

> What we don't have and should have is mass popular organization. Then critical discussion and analysis, and serious thought about social issues, can become significant . . . The appropriate role for intellectuals, I guess, is to try to contribute to the work of mass, popular, democratic libertarian movements. But right now they barely exist. (CR, 51)

Without mass organizations committed to change, the most that libertarian socialists can hope to achieve is a small reduction in the scale of repression:

> Sometimes there is a detectable effect, even in the absence of such popular organization. Well, take the Timor case. There weren't more than half a dozen people in the United States

who were devoting real effort and energy to trying to lift the curtain of silence on the topic during the worst period of the slaughter. But there were a few, and after several years they actually did succeed in breaking through to the point where a few people in Congress became quite upset about the issue, there were occasional articles and editorials, and some limited news-reporting. Well, you might say that's a pretty small achievement after a hundred thousand people have been massacred, maybe more. But it is certainly better than nothing. And there was an effect. The Red Cross was finally allowed in sporadically and some aid flowed to the victims. Tens of thousands of lives were saved. That's not a small achievement for a small group of mainly young people. (CR, 51)

Only a mass movement has any chance of changing or removing the powerful social institutions and structures which stand in the way of genuine freedom and democracy. Until these institutions and structures change the most that people like Chomsky can do is a certain amount of damage limitation, along with continuing the effort to understand and explain what is going on and to expose the lies and distortions of the official line.

Chomsky discusses the actual achievements of two movements which gained something like mass support in the United States: the anti-war movement of the 1960s and early 1970s, and the nuclear freeze campaign of the early 1980s. He argues firstly that the anti-war movement was certainly not 'a triumph of American democracy'. The movement did not become really big until very late on, after 'perhaps a million Vietnamese had already been killed in almost two decades of US-organized terror and violence', and when half a million US troops were deployed in Indochina. The war left 'three countries utterly in ruins and many millions dead, hardly an occasion for great self-congratulation'. In addition, 'the successes of the peace movement were largely achieved outside of the system of formal political democracy, by direct action, which raised the cost of aggression' (TTT, 247–8). On the other hand, there was 'a notable improvement in the moral and intellectual climate' as a result of the peace movement (CR, 52). As we noted in our discussion of Central America in Chapter 7, the differences between 1965 and 1980 limited the ability of the Reagan administration to intervene in Nicaragua on the same scale. The extent to which the improvement to which Chomsky refers threatened the US elite can be judged by the huge scale of the subsequent ideological onslaught on the 'Vietnam syndrome', which he ironically describes as 'a dread disease that spread over much of the population with such symptoms as distaste for torture and massacre and sympathy for its victims' (CR, 52).

The nuclear freeze is another interesting case. Chomsky describes the campaign as 'perhaps the most successful organizing campaign ever carried out in the US peace movement – and the one which has had, perhaps, the most meagre results'. The organizers managed 'to convince an overwhelming majority of the population to support a proposal that could have had a major effect on limiting the arms race and thereby enhancing American security, a proposal that was furthermore feasible, supported by the superpower enemy and by world opinion fairly generally'. None the less, the campaign had 'essentially zero impact on American politics' (TTT, 177).

In Chomsky's view, the reason for this lack of impact is that the development of new weapons systems – which the freeze, if successful, would have prevented – has nothing to do with the security of the country. The underlying cause is the need to regenerate profits when the United States economy runs into crisis:

> In a modern industrial society, there is one primary idea as to how to deal with this problem: state intervention to stimulate the economy . . . For a variety of reasons, the device that best serves the needs of existing power and privilege is what is sometimes called 'military Keynesianism': the creation of a state-guaranteed market for high technology rapidly-obsolescing waste production, meaning armaments . . .
>
> There are surely more efficient and less dangerous techniques of economic management than military spending. Why, then, the regular recourse to this device? The basic reason is that the theoretical alternatives do not serve to enhance existing privilege and power as does the creation of a state-guaranteed market for high-technology production –

that is, the military system – which is why the latter measures regularly elicit business support. (TTT, 208–9)

So without changing the institutional structure of power and privilege, which is committed to military expenditure irrespective of the risks, the nuclear freeze option is simply out of the question in the United States. Despite the fact that three-quarters of the population supported the freeze, it was largely ignored by the political establishment and their obedient supporters in the mainstream media. This is not to say that the campaign was a waste of time: it did not achieve its primary goal of halting the arms race, but it educated a lot of people in the right general direction. Perhaps one day the nuclear freeze campaign will be seen as part of the groundwork for a movement which successfully challenges the institutional structure underlying the arms race and other evils.

Non-violence

Chomsky has long been an advocate of non-violent tactics aimed at social change. Writing in 1967 shortly after he was arrested at an anti-war demonstration near the Pentagon, he commented:

> The argument that resistance to the war should remain strictly non-violent seems to me overwhelming. As a tactic, violence is absurd. No one can compete with the government in this arena, and the resort to violence, which will surely fail, will simply frighten and alienate some who can be reached, and will further encourage the ideologists and administrators of forceful repression. What is more, one hopes that participants in non-violent resistance will themselves become human beings of a more admirable sort. No one can fail to be impressed by the personal qualities of those who have grown to maturity in the civil rights movement . . . Perhaps a programme of principled, non-violent resistance can do the same for many others, in the particular circumstances that we face today. (APNM, 297)

Chomsky is not a pacifist. His objection to violent tactics in this passage is mainly pragmatic – he doesn't think they are likely to succeed in those particular circumstances. Advocating non-violence to a Vietnamese peasant whose village is being obliterated by the US air force would be stupid and insulting. The point is to use the space for non-violent protest when it is available. For many Americans this space is quite large:

> by international standards the state is limited at home in its power to coerce. Hence those who enjoy a measure of wealth and privilege are free to act in many ways, without undue fear of state terror, to bring about crucial changes in policy and even more fundamental institutional changes. We are fortunate, perhaps uniquely so, in the range of opportunities we enjoy for free inquiry and effective action. The significance of these facts can hardly be exaggerated. (TTT, 1)

Civil disobedience

In the late 1960s the question of whether to obey the law was an urgent one for many people active in the anti-war movement. Young men, including Chomsky's own students, were being called up for compulsory military service in Vietnam. Those of them who opposed the war had to decide whether to obey the letters they received calling them up, or face imprisonment for refusing. Many left the country rather than serve in a war they thought was unjust. People like Chomsky, who were approached for advice and help, had to consider whether they should support these and other non-violent but illegal forms of protest.

Chomsky supported draft resisters and sympathised strongly with the difficult choice facing them. Speaking after the war was over, he defended their actions:

> It is quite generally claimed now that the American resistance had as its cause the young men's fear of being drafted; that's a very convenient belief for the intellectuals who confined themselves to 'pragmatic' opposition to the war. But it's an enormous lie. For most of those who were in the resistance from its origins, nothing would have been easier than to escape the draft, with its class bias, as many others actually did. In fact, many of the activists already had deferments.

Many of the deserters too chose a difficult and painful course for reasons of principle. But for those who supported the war initially, and who only raised their whisper of protest when the costs became too great, it is impossible to admit the existence of a courageous and principled resistance, largely on the part of youth, to atrocities which they themselves had tolerated. (LR, 31)

In 1971, Chomsky considered whether the destruction of draft files by anti-war activists was a legitimate form of protest. Some people might argue that this type of civil disobedience is not justifiable in a democracy. Chomsky rejects this view: even if – contrary to the facts – the United States were a perfect democracy, he writes, 'there is no principle that supports the conclusion that the people of Indochina must be subjected to a criminal attack if the American people so determine by exercise of their democratic rights' (RS, 77). In fact, the majority of Americans voted in 1964 for Lyndon Johnson, who promised to end the war; once elected, he immediately extended the war massively, putting into effect policies 'which, it appears, had been proposed unanimously by the president's advisers even prior to the election, though the electorate was never so informed' (RS, 77–8).

On the question of whether civil disobedience is likely to help end the war, Chomsky is deliberately diffident:

Judgements about the impact of dissent . . . can only be tentative and impressionistic . . . The real question, however, is: What would public attitudes be if the war in Vietnam were not continually forced to consciousness by such actions . . . My own impression, based largely on extensive speaking to quite a wide variety of audiences over the years, is that mass demonstrations have been a major factor in bringing the war to public attention, and that resistance, particularly draft resistance, has had an appreciable effect in bringing many people to examine their own complicity and to draw them to the kinds of actions that have influenced policy makers. (RS, 79)

The issue of civil disobedience is a difficult and uncomfortable one. It forces each individual to make hard choices which affect their personal lives. Those who condemn civil disobedience often do so out of unworthy motives. On the other hand, Chomsky has no time for useless heroics, the kind of crass activism which aims for confrontation without thinking of the consequences:

> It seems to me that the search for confrontations, aside from revealing a kind of intellectual bankruptcy, a failure to have found effective politics, may also become a manipulative and coercive tactic. I think it often does. It becomes the kind of tactic which attempts to bring people to a certain degree of commitment, not by having it grow out of their own understanding and experience in the realities of the world, but, as the result of a situation which often does not reflect the realities of society. That is manipulative and coercive, and I think also dangerous. I think it is the proper kind of tactic only for a movement of an elitist and authoritarian sort. (RP, 204)

Similarly, Chomsky is suspicious of people who advocate confrontation in order to prove themselves politically:

> When people start concentrating on the character of the tactics, and regarding them as an index of political character, then they are taking an ultimately self-destructive approach. Without impugning anyone's motives, I think that that is the kind of thing that a well-placed police spy would introduce into the movement if he were intent on destroying it. (RP, 205)

The key thing is to weigh up the likely outcomes of any tactics, particularly for the poor and oppressed to whom we are ultimately responsible. Grief and anger about the awful results of US imperialism are quite right – but your choice of tactics to change things for the better has to be based on a dispassionate analysis of benefits and costs.

The task for intellectuals

How can intellectuals, in particular, help in the struggle for social change? Here we can learn from Chomsky's actions as well as his words. Intellectuals who choose not to conform have the resources to seek out the truth, to expose lies and distortions, to ask the dangerous questions which are so often avoided, and to raise the wider issues which often get left aside because of day-to-day pressures. Chomsky writes:

> I think that the main task for intellectuals, aside from resistance to repression and violence, is to try to articulate goals, to try to assess, to try to understand, to try to persuade, to try to organize.
>
> I think that further tasks for intellectuals are to develop an objective scholarship, and also to act collectively and individually to confront repressive institutions when that is the effective politics of the moment rather than merely an exciting thing to do. (RP, 205)

He speaks approvingly of attempts to form groups of radical scholars. Given that real change will only come about when there is a mass movement calling for it, the emphasis now must be on sowing the seeds of such a movement by informing people and explaining what is going on:

> The groundwork for great social movements of the past was laid through many years of searching, intellectual interchange, social experimentation and collective action, organization and struggle. The same will be true of the coming stages of social change . . .
>
> There are no magic answers, no miraculous methods to overcome the problems we face, just the familiar ones: honest search for understanding, education, organization, action that raises the cost of state violence for its perpetrators or that lays the basis for institutional change – and the kind of commitment that will persist despite the temptations of disillusionment, despite many failures and only limited successes, inspired by the hope of a brighter future. (TTT, 253)

When this brighter future comes, the insight and inspiration that many people have derived from the work of Noam Chomsky will have played its part in bringing it about.

9

Connections

So far in this book we have looked at Chomsky's linguistics and his politics separately. This chapter looks at the connections between the two sides of Chomsky's work, and tries to assess his achievements as a whole.

Need there be any connections?

No one should assume that there have to be important links between the two sides of Chomsky's work. It is perfectly conceivable that there are no interesting connections, and that the best way to regard Chomsky is as a linguist who happens to be involved in political activity in his spare time. If Chomsky's field were molecular biology or computer programming, this is probably how he would be seen and commentators would not feel obliged to look for parallels and links. Because he studies language, many people assume that there must be a connection between his academic work and his political activism.

In fact, there are good reasons to play down the connections. Chomsky's linguistics is part of a specialized technical field, one where considerable skill and training are needed. If this were also true of his political writings, then only 'experts' in political analysis would have the ability and the right to discuss the foreign policy issues he deals with. But as we saw in pages 139–40, Chomsky explicitly rejects the idea that special expertise is needed to understand politics. He sees this as misuse of the prestige of science by supporters of the official line. So emphasizing links between linguistics and politics could give quite the wrong impression. Chomsky is aware of this danger, and warns against it:

> one must be careful not to give the impression, which in any event is false, that only intellectuals equipped with special

training are capable of [social and political analysis]. In fact
that is just what the intelligentsia would often like us to think:
they pretend to be engaged in an esoteric enterprise, inacces-
sible to simple people. But that's nonsense. The social sciences
generally, and above all the analysis of contemporary affairs,
are quite accessible to anyone who wants to take an interest in
these matters. The alleged complexity, depth, and obscurity
of these questions is part of the illusion propagated by the
system of ideological control, which aims to make the issues
seem remote from the general population and to persuade
them of their incapacity to organize their own affairs or to
understand the social world in which they live without the
tutelage of intermediaries. For that reason alone one should
be careful not to link the analysis of social issues with scientific
topics which, for their part, do require special training and
techniques, and thus a special intellectual frame of reference,
before they can be seriously investigated. (LR, 4–5)

It is sometimes thought that an analysis of language is vital in
the kind of ideological criticism which runs through Chomsky's
political thinking. Certain words and expressions play a key part
in the official line: words like 'terrorism' are used selectively,
for instance, as we saw in Chapter 7. To take another example,
journalists routinely say 'Britain believes . . . ' or 'The United
States position is . . . ' as a shorthand for 'The British government believes . . . ' and 'The position of the United States
administration is . . . '. This device blurs the distinction between
a country and its government, reinforcing the official line and
making it hard to remember that the government generally acts
in the interests of the business elite. Chomsky's political writings occasionally touch on linguistic matters of this kind, but,
surprisingly perhaps, Chomsky does not think that language
is central here: he refers to 'the widespread belief, which I
personally share only in part, that misuse or control of language
is a central feature of the problem [of the abuse of power and
privilege]' (KL, xxviii–xxix). It may be that here too he wants to
head off the misconception that an understanding of linguistics
is crucial for political analysis.

A further reason to play down the connections between the

two sides of Chomsky's work is that even if language does play a part in the abuse of power and privilege, the kind of linguistics that Chomsky spends his time on explicitly puts this kind of issue on one side. As we saw in pages 57–62, he proposes to idealize the subject matter of linguistics so that it assumes 'an ideal speaker-listener in a completely homogeneous speech community'. The ways in which language is used in society, and the ways that social class distinctions and other oppressive structures are encoded and reproduced by language, are not matters that Chomsky's linguistics concentrates on. So even if linguistics can be connected with politics, there are good reasons not to look for close parallels between *Chomsky's* linguistics and his politics.

On several occasions when he has been asked about the connections, Chomsky is cautious. Here is one example:

> If there is a connection, it is on a rather abstract level. I don't have access to any unusual methods of analysis, and what special knowledge I have concerning language has no immediate bearing on social and political issues. Everything I have written on these topics could have been written by someone else. There is no very direct connection between my political activities, . . . and the work bearing on language structure, though in some measure they perhaps derive from certain common assumptions and attitudes with regard to basic aspects of human nature. Critical analysis in the ideological arena seems to me to be a fairly straightforward matter as compared to an approach that requires a degree of conceptual abstraction. For the analysis of ideology, which occupies me very much, a bit of open-mindedness, normal intelligence, and healthy skepticism will generally suffice. (LR, 3)

We should therefore be careful in looking for direct connections. On the other hand, Chomsky refers in this passage to 'certain common assumptions and attitudes with regard to basic aspects of human nature'. Looking at what he means will help to bring each side of his work into clearer focus.

Human nature and human freedom

We noted in the last chapter that Chomsky's libertarian socialist views about what a just society would be like rest on his views about human nature. Political views have to start with some conception of what the essential qualities of human beings are: given that people have certain needs and capacities, you can then outline what a society would be like in which the needs of all can be met and the capacities of each person can be encouraged to flourish to their fullest extent.

An essential part of human nature, in Chomsky's view, is freedom. Free will, the ability to create new and original things, and the ability to make rational choices are what distinguish human beings from animals and, indeed, from everything else we know about. In developing these ideas, Chomsky often turns to the social and political views of the eighteenth century, 'an earlier period when archaic social institutions were subjected to critical analysis and sustained attack' (RS, 169). Thus he quotes Jean-Jacques Rousseau, whose book *Discourse on Inequality* criticizes the repressive society of his day on the grounds that people are 'intelligent, free . . . the sole animal endowed with reason' while animals are 'devoid of intellect and freedom' (RS, 170). In a similar vein, Chomsky refers to Humboldt's concept of human nature:

> The true end of Man, or that which is prescribed by the eternal and immutable dictates of reason, and not suggested by vague and transient desires, is the highest and most harmonious development of his powers to a complete and consistent whole. Freedom is the first and indispensable condition which the possibility of such a development presupposes. (RS, 177)

This view of human nature leads directly to Chomsky's libertarian socialism in its concern for 'the opportunity for meaningful creative work under the control of the worker' (LPK, 195). If human beings have an inherent need freely to develop their capacities, then 'productive and creative work (including intellectual work) under one's own control' (LPK, 195) is the way that this need can best be fulfilled. Hence capitalism, in which people hire themselves out to do boring or unpleasant

work for others, is not in keeping with human nature. Workers' control and self-management, long advocated by libertarian
socialists, fit much better with the essential nature of human
beings.

The connection with linguistics is that language is something
else which fundamentally distinguishes humans from animals,
so that understanding of language can also give us insights into
what is distinctively human. And once again, central properties
of language are freedom and creativity. Indeed, for many of the
classical thinkers that Chomsky discusses,

> the only sure sign that another organism has a mind, and
> hence also lies beyond the bounds of mechanical explanation,
> is its use of language in the normal, creative human fashion,
> free from control by identifiable stimuli, novel and innovative,
> appropriate to situations, coherent, and engendering in our
> minds new thoughts and ideas. (RS, 173–4)

We saw on page 58 that a generative grammar must be capable
of generating an infinite number of sentences using a finite set of
rules. Most of the sentences that are spoken or written are novel:
the words in them may be familiar, but the particular combination of words may never have been produced before in the history of the world. This open-endedness is an essential feature of
language: it is the key thing that distinguishes human language
from animal communication systems. The open-endedness is
not random, however: it is constrained by the rules of the
language. If there is one phrase which encapsulates Chomsky's
view of human nature, it is *rule-governed freedom*. The system
of rules gives us the freedom to create infinitely many new
sentences, but each sentence must conform to the rules of the
language.

When we turn from the nature of this system of rules to the
way it is used, we likewise see freedom – the use of language
is 'free from control by identifiable stimuli' as we just noted,
and as Chomsky argues at length in his review of Skinner's
Verbal Behaviour. Linguistics therefore provides powerful arguments that freedom is an essential part of human nature. What's
more, these arguments can claim scientific status, a rare thing in
arguments about human nature. Chomsky writes:

> In the realm of social thought we don't really have good
> evidence for anything, so our conceptions are more an expres-
> sion of our hopes and our intuitive judgments and our per-
> sonal experience and the ways we understand history than
> they are the product of any substantial scientific understand-
> ing. (LPK, 195)

It is different with linguistics:

> A crucial part of language is the creative aspect of language
> use and the elements of human nature which make it essential
> to our intellectual lives. Now that is a conclusion of science,
> we have good evidence about that. (LPK, 195)

We thus have a more reliable notion of rule-governed freedom from linguistics, which can be extended to other areas.
In particular, this notion calls into question one of the most
common criticisms of libertarian socialism: the assertion that
human freedom has to be restricted to a greater or lesser extent
by coercion and laws and repressive structures, because otherwise, 'human nature being what it is', we would have total chaos
as people do whatever they feel like. If Chomsky is right, our
essential human nature puts limits on our freedom, and there
is no basic need for coercive social structures to limit it further.
Certainly, people who have long been deprived of freedom may
commit all kinds of excesses when they get their first taste of
it: for instance, in the months after France was liberated from
Nazi occupation in the Second World War, between thirty and
forty thousand collaborators were killed in reprisals (AC, 38). A
Nazi sympathizer could point to this slaughter and argue that
the occupation of France was necessary to restrain the brutal
impulses of ordinary French people. Clearly, though, it was the
occupation which brutalized many French men and women so
that they acted in this way once they got the chance. It wasn't
freedom that was to blame for the massacres, but precisely the
prolonged *lack* of it under the Nazis. Furthermore, the violence
of the reprisals, even on this scale, was small when compared
to the violence of the occupation.

We thus do find an interesting connection between Chomsky's
linguistics and his politics, albeit at a rather abstract level. A child

whose basic material and social needs are satisfied will acquire a language spontaneously because it is in the nature of human beings to do so. No explicit teaching or other institutionalized structures are needed: this part of human nature will flourish very well if it is given the freedom it needs. In general human beings do not, in Chomsky's view, need coercive or manipulative structures for their true, creative natures to flourish. All they need is for their basic material and social needs to be met and the freedom for everyone to develop their capacities and talents. The link between these two areas is not compelling – not all linguists would generalize from language acquisition to social structures in this way – but it is certainly suggestive.

Rationalism and empiricism: political implications

Let's now return as promised earlier to empiricism and rationalism (cf. pages 81–3) and consider their political significance. Empiricism has often been presented as a progressive point of view, one that is more attractive than rationalism for people committed to social change. There are probably two main reasons for this. Firstly, empiricism developed in part 'as a reaction to the speculative character of earlier work, its lack of firm empirical foundation' (RL, 126–7). The rise of modern physics in the seventeenth century led to a scorn for old dogmas and beliefs. The empiricists wanted to sweep away antiquated superstitions and start again from scratch, only admitting what could be justified scientifically. The idea of the mind as a blank sheet at birth was part of this spirit of radical questioning and experimenting with new ideas.

The second reason is the way that the notion of 'human nature' was (and still is) used to justify oppression and exploitation:

> Why this link between progressive social thought and empiricist doctrine? Perhaps because empiricism seemed to have – and in a certain way did have – progressive social implications in contrast to reactionary and determinist doctrines, according to which the existing social structures, slavery, autocracy, the feudal hierarchy, the role of women, were founded on unchanging human nature. Against that doctrine, the idea

that human nature is a historical product had a progressive content, as it also did, one might argue, throughout the early period of capitalist industrialization.

The determinist doctrines in question maintained that certain people were born to be slaves, by their very nature. Or consider the oppression of woman, which was also founded on such concepts. Or wage labor: willingness to rent oneself through the market is considered one of the fundamental and immutable human properties, in a version of the 'human essence' characteristic of early capitalism.

In the face of such doctrines as these, it is natural for advocates of social change to adopt the extreme position that 'human nature' is a myth, nothing but the product of history. But that position is incorrect. Human nature exists, immutable except for biological changes in the species. (LR, 91)

Chomsky believes that the doctrines of the classical rationalists can also be interpreted in a progressive way. We saw in Chapter 7, in fact, that the empiricist David Hume held backward and oppressive views about Ireland. The more important issue, however, concerns the political implications of modern, rather than historical, empiricist and rationalist views.[1] Now that the two positions can be formulated as empirical hypotheses about, for example, language acquisition, the first reason for treating empiricism as more progressive no longer holds. As for the second reason, there is a crucial difference between Chomsky's view of human nature and the reactionary ideas he mentions. Chomsky's account of human nature applies to *all* human beings, irrespective of class, gender, race and other differences between people. We all have abstract linguistic rules and principles genetically encoded in our brains, and we all have the same basic need for freedom. Far from justifying divisions between people, Chomsky's concept of human nature stresses the basic unity of humankind. The poorest Vietnamese peasant and the President of the United States both share a rich and sophisticated genetic endowment. There is no reason nowadays to treat rationalism as a reactionary viewpoint.

Indeed, Chomsky believes that it is now empiricism which is a brake on progress, in the human sciences at least. As we saw in Chapter 4, he regards behaviourism as an unscientific dogma which prevents meaningful work from being done in psychology. Rationalism treats the mind/brain in the same way as other biological systems, looking at its inherent structure and the way this structure shapes and is shaped by its environment. By refusing to consider the mind/brain in this way, behaviourism in fact leaves the territory free for fanciful speculation by non-scientists – exactly what the classical empiricists wanted to prevent.

We turn now to the wider question of why empiricism has been so popular, despite the complete lack of evidence that might support it. Chomsky suggests that the answer may lie in the role of intellectuals in modern society:

> Perhaps, then, some sociological factor might explain in a natural way why [empiricism] has been so widely adopted. We can ask ourselves, who accepts and disseminates these doctrines? Essentially, the intelligentsia, including scientists and non-scientists. What is the social role of the intelligentsia? As I have said, it has been quite characteristically manipulation and social control in all its varied forms . . . And in order to justify such practices, it is very useful to believe that human beings are empty organisms, malleable, controllable, easy to govern, and so on, with no essential need to struggle to find their own way and to determine their own fate. For that, empiricism is quite suitable. (LR, 89–90)

Chomsky argues that intellectuals in modern capitalist societies like the United States, and also in Leninist societies like the Soviet Union, are a privileged elite who tend to regard the masses of ordinary people as empty vessels which they can fill with ideas as they please. By formulating a view of human nature which goes against this attitude, Chomsky is standing up for ordinary people: he calls for 'continual struggle against authoritarian social forms that impose restrictions beyond those set by "the laws of our own nature", as has long been advocated by authentic revolutionary thinkers and activists' (RL, 133). Libertarian socialism, then, reflects a belief that social structures can and should be developed to allow the maximum freedom for each individual, because such a society will allow our essential human nature to flourish.

Behaviourism, IQ and society

Chomsky develops these ideas further in a review of a book by B. F. Skinner, his *Beyond Freedom and Dignity*.[2] In the book Skinner extends his behaviourist assumptions and terminology a step further away from his laboratory experiments with animals and into the realm of political and social issues. He argues that it is an illusion to speak of freedom and dignity, and that 'the science of behaviour and a related technology provide the rationale and the means for control of behaviour' (RS, 105–6). The world can, he believes, be designed so that 'behaviour likely to be punished seldom or never occurs'; to this end, 'control of the population as a whole must be delegated to specialists – to police, priests, owners, teachers, therapists, and so on' (RS, 127–8). Designing such a world is for Skinner an engineering problem: the task is to 'make the social environment as free as possible of aversive stimuli' and thus 'to release for more reinforcing activities the time and energy consumed in the avoidance of punishment' (RS, 116).

Skinner's views were attacked as totalitarian in some circles and praised for their stress on science and rationality in others. Chomsky argues, however, that they are 'quite vacuous' and 'devoid of scientific content'. The basic criticisms are similar to those that Chomsky set out in his review of *Verbal Behaviour*. Skinner, he says, is simply taking terms like 'reinforcement' out of the laboratory, where they have a specific meaning, and into areas where they can only be used as vague replacements for everyday words. Skinner's insistence on explaining away free will is sheer dogmatism: 'The task of scientific analysis is not – as Skinner believes – to demonstrate that the conditions to which he restricts his attention fully determine human behaviour, but rather to discover whether in fact they do (or whether they are at all significant), a very different matter' (RS, 108).

Chomsky argues that Skinner's framework fails to get to grips with straightforward instances of rational behaviour such as persuading other people to change their minds by producing powerful arguments, sticking to your principles despite pressure to abandon them, or pretending to agree with someone to avoid unpleasant consequences. He concludes that there is no 'science of behaviour' of the sort Skinner claims exists. In view of the prestige of science and technology it is vital, in Chomsky's opinion, that psychologists explain to the public the limits of what is known scientifically about human behaviour, rather than making extravagant claims with no supporting evidence.

There are strong parallels between Chomsky's rejection of behaviourism in linguistics and his critique of the social and political consequences of behaviourism. The most important point for our purposes has to do with the assumptions about human nature which he thinks underlie Skinner's work:

> Running through [Skinner's] discussion is a vague background assumption that unless 'reinforcements' are provided, individuals will vegetate. That there may be an intrinsic human need to find productive work, that a free person may, given the opportunity, seek such work and pursue it with energy, is a possibility that is never faced – though of course the vacuous system of Skinnerian translation would permit us to say that such work is 'reinforcing' (and undertaken for this reason), if we happen to enjoy tautologies. (RS, 132)

Chomsky finds similar assumptions in work by the psychologist Richard Herrnstein,[3] which he discusses at length alongside his criticism of Skinner's book.[4] Herrnstein claimed that economic inequality was inevitable. Firstly, differences in intelligence, as measured in IQ tests, appear to be inherited. Secondly, more intelligent people tend to succeed more in terms of money and prestige, and to marry high-achievers like themselves. As society gets more egalitarian, in the sense that everyone has the same opportunity to achieve, then the more intelligent people will tend to form a 'hereditary meritocratic elite' (RS, 133). Attempts to redistribute wealth, and to create a society where there is no big disparity between rich and poor, are therefore, Herrnstein argued, doomed to failure.

Herrnstein's views were widely discussed in the early 1970s: any intellectual who produces arguments that justify capitalism or oppression in general is virtually guaranteed extensive coverage in Western media. Chomsky's discussion centres on a crucial assumption in Herrnstein's work – the assumption that 'people labour only for gain, and that the satisfaction in interesting or socially beneficial work or in work well done or in the respect shown to such activities is not a sufficient "gain" to induce anyone to work' (RS, 137). If this is not true, then Herrnstein's case falls apart: his argument depends on the claim that money and prestige – especially money – are the only things which motivate people to work hard and 'succeed'.

The crucial assumption – found in both Skinner and Herrnstein, as Chomsky notes – is such a basic part of capitalist ideology that it is rarely justified explicitly. Chomsky points out that many people choose work because it is of benefit to society rather than for material gain. Others choose work which interests them: even if Herrnstein could earn more as a garbage collector, Chomsky doubts that he would choose to give up his teaching and research job (RS, 139). The idea that humans are basically selfish and greedy and only accidentally unselfish and co-operative is common in right-wing thought, but there is no reason to accept it. It is true that capitalist economic and social structures reward greed, but nothing says that society must be organized in this way.

The idea that there is such a thing as 'intelligence' and that it is reliably measured by IQ tests has been criticized by many socialists. Interestingly, Chomsky does not criticize Herrnstein in this way. He notes that Herrnstein's ideas 'will surely be exploited by racists to justify discrimination, much as Herrnstein may personally deplore this fact' (RS, 143). He argues, however, that even if IQ is heritable, so that some people or social groups are born more intelligent than others, this only matters on the assumption that people who are more intelligent deserve more money, better houses, and better rewards in general. This again depends on the idea that people only work for material rewards, which we do not have to accept. Nor is the question of the relation between race and IQ of scientific interest, quite apart from its social implications:

> inquiry into such questions as race and IQ appears to be of virtually no scientific interest. Conceivably, there might be some interest in correlations between partially heritable traits, but if someone were interested in this question, he would surely not select such characteristics as race and IQ, each an obscure amalgam of complex properties. Rather, he

would ask whether there is a correlation between measurable and significant traits, say, eye color and length of the big toe. (CR, 200)

As we have seen, Chomsky does not claim that the view of human nature which he subscribes to is definitely correct: we are dealing here with 'our hopes and our intuitive judgments and our personal experience and the ways we understand history' rather than 'substantial scientific understanding' (LPK, 195). None the less, many people will find his view of human nature plausible, and a stimulating guide to social action as we try to build a just society. With due allowance made for caution in relating this picture of human nature to Chomsky's work in linguistics, it is interesting that this view of human nature finds some support from the scientific study of language. Negative and demeaning ideas of human nature have a long history, as do oppressive social structures. Challenging the former can play a significant part in ending the latter.

Science and society

There is another plausible connection between Chomsky's linguistics and his politics, though he would probably not accept it in its entirety. A strong case can be made that libertarian socialism is the best way that society could be organized for science to progress. The mixture of freedom – the freedom to study, experiment, learn from each other, follow hunches, and so on that scientists need – and government by inherent rather than externally imposed rule – the rule that nothing is accepted without evidence, that theories are always regarded as tentative, and the other agreements that scientists make – is exactly what characterizes a scientific community at its best. Authority in such a community derives from the power of rational argument rather than economic privilege.

Because of their need for freedom, scientists have provided many examples of cooperation despite deep divisions in the world at large. During the Second World War, for example, astronomers in Germany and German-occupied countries continued to exchange scientific papers with their colleagues in

Britain and the United States, using scientists in neutral countries as intermediaries. In principle, at least, the usual things
that divide people – race, class, gender, nationality, and so on
– count for nothing within the community of scientists. What
counts instead is the mixture of freedom and co-operation that
libertarian socialists advocate for the whole of society.

An examination of the periods in history when science has
advanced supports this view. In his monumental *Science in History*, J. D. Bernal shows that the progress of science has been
uneven, with periods of rapid progress and other periods of
stagnation.[5] He argues that:

> the where and when of scientific activity are anything but
> accidental. Its flourishing periods are found to coincide with
> economic activity and technical advance. The track science
> has followed – from Egypt and Mesopotamia to Greece, from
> Islamic Spain to Renaissance Italy, thence to the Low Coun-
> tries and France, and then to Scotland and England of the
> Industrial Revolution – is the same as that of commerce and
> industry . . .
>
> Between the bursts of activity there have been quiet times,
> sometimes periods of degeneration such as that of the later
> Egyptian dynasties, or of late classical times, or of the early
> eighteenth century. These, we shall see, coincide with periods
> when the organisation of society was stagnant and decadent,
> so that production followed traditional lines and concern for
> it was considered to be debasing for a man of learning . . .
>
> When the productive relations are changing rapidly, as
> when a new class is rising into a position of power, there is
> a particular incentive to improvements in production which
> will enhance the wealth and power of this class, and science
> is at a premium. Once such a class is established and is still
> strong enough to prevent the rise of a new rival, there is an
> interest in keeping things as they are – techniques become
> traditional and science is at a discount.

Bernal goes on to argue that 'the most important and fruitful
periods of scientific advance were those in which the class
barrier was at least partially broken down and the practical
and the learned men mixed on equal terms'. These were times

of rapid economic and technological development, which led to enormous social upheavals. At such times, not only is the money available to pay for scientific research, but the climate tends to be right for new ideas as old dogmas are challenged. Technological change is itself a driving factor in science: the need to regulate the calendar in early agricultural societies gave rise to astronomy; the need for reliable navigation in the early period of colonial expansion was a key factor in Galilean/Newtonian physics; the needs of the new textile industry in the nineteenth century gave rise to modern chemistry. Once the powerful elite are secure, however, there is less need for technological advance, and the result is that science stagnates for a time. The conditions most favourable for scientific progress, then, are where technologists and scientists – Bernal's 'practical and learned' people – work together, for the benefit of all rather than just to make profits for the ruling elite. To ensure a permanent era of scientific progress, rather than just the temporary stages of the past, class barriers need to be broken down completely and irretrievably.

To what extent does Chomsky's linguistics move in this sort of direction? What kind of scientific community has developed around Chomsky's ideas? Certainly, a case can be made that generative grammarians in many respects form an admirable scientific community. Chomsky's insistence on the need to move beyond description to explanation has led to incisive and vigorous theorizing, discussion and progress. Scholars in many countries have contributed to a common enterprise, especially during the last ten years as research into parametric variation has become increasingly important. The considerable progress that has been made – in particular the more powerful depth and breadth of explanation that Chomsky and his colleagues have achieved – testify to a field that is very much alive and growing.

On the other hand, it is arguable that Chomsky's influence has widened, rather than narrowed, the gap between scientific linguistics and those people whose interest in language is practical. We looked at the links in Chapter 4 and found that there were some, but that they were rather limited. We made a distinction there between scientific knowledge and technical knowledge about language. If Bernal is right, generative grammar would benefit by trying to build more links between the two. Chomsky is rather sceptical about this idea. Asked about the usefulness of his work for language teachers or translators, he says:

> the capacity to carry out practical activities without much awareness of what you're doing is usually far more advanced than scientific knowledge. The history of the physical sciences is interesting in this respect. Engineers knew how to do all sorts of complicated and amazing things for hundreds of years. It wasn't until the mid-nineteenth century that physics began to catch up and to provide some understanding that was actually useful for engineers. Now physics in the nineteenth century was vastly more advanced than our understanding of languages today, and building bridges is much less complex than what is actually taking place in the teaching of languages or translating. So I think the answer to your question is, I don't think modern linguistics can tell you very much of practical utility. (LPK, 180)

None the less, if the lesson of history is that strong links between theoretical research and practical applications are a key factor in scientific progress, the effort to bring the two together is crucial for the future of linguistics.

Conclusion

We have looked at Chomsky's ideas, his impact on linguistics and other fields, and some of the reactions – positive and negative – to his views. How can we sum up the scope and importance of his work?

One thing that stands out in Chomsky's life is his tenacity, the way he has stuck firmly to his basic beliefs throughout his working life. Looking at the whole span of his writings, two of these beliefs stand out: in linguistics, the belief that explaining things is more important than just describing them, and in politics, the belief that intellectuals have a duty to expose lies and deceit. On the basis of these two beliefs, Chomsky has pursued a complex and often lonely path, reaching conclusions about language and about US society which challenge widely accepted dogmas.

His tenacity, combined with the brilliant way in which he has argued for his views, has inevitably brought strong support from some people along with hostility from many others. As we saw in Chapter 8, many intellectuals have been 'unable to hear' Chomsky's political views, so strong is the grip of the official line. The same is true of his linguistics, where misunderstanding has been rife. Many linguists have regarded generative grammar as just another descriptive technique, failing to see that its aims are completely different from those of traditional linguistics. It takes a lot of inner strength to deal with such widespread incomprehension and hostility.

Chomsky has always refused to stay within the narrow specialized boundaries that divide the academic world. He has constantly drawn links between linguistics, mathematics, philosophy and psychology, in particular. He takes the view that a person's lack of formal training in, say, mathematics, is not important; what counts is what a person has to say, and whether his or her ideas are interesting. This attitude is not as common as it should be in the intellectual community, for reasons that reflect the role of intellectuals in capitalist society, in Chomsky's opinion. And of course, Chomsky's willingness to take an active role in grassroots political activity has not endeared him to many academics who find this kind of thing distasteful.

As an intellectual, Chomsky is in many ways exemplary. His readiness to ask bold, challenging, fundamental and often uncomfortable questions is one obvious quality. It is worth pointing out another one: many scholars of his stature would have been content to rest on their laurels after achieving the enormous fame and recognition that came Chomsky's way early in his career. Many academics are only too ready to let their research students and junior colleagues carry on doing the work while they take the credit. Chomsky has never done this. He has stayed at the forefront of research in his field, bringing forward new theories and moving in new directions. Amazingly, Chomsky has been criticized for his continuing willingness to innovate: 'he is hard to keep up with, because his ideas keep changing' goes the complaint. But living fields of study change all the time – think how rapidly medical knowledge has gone out of date in recent years. If a scholar has asked important and productive questions, obviously the answers will change and evolve in the light of new research. It is to Chomsky's credit that he not only formulated the questions but also continues to take part in the search for answers.

A further exemplary quality is Chomsky's kindness towards his students and colleagues. Many of his former students have recorded how helpful and constructive he is as a teacher. Many people, including the present writer, have written to Chomsky with questions or comments and have been pleasantly surprised by the speed of his response and the care and effort that went into it. If he disagrees with something Chomsky does not mince his words, but that is how a scientist ought to behave. On the other hand, we have seen many occasions where he puts forward his views with the appropriate caution, and where he stresses the responsibility of intellectuals to make it clear how little is known in certain areas.

I don't know whether Chomsky's linguistics will grow or diminish in importance in the future. I believe, however, that Chomsky's resolve to stand firm in his scientific and political views offers an inspiring model that any thinking person can learn from. In a recent interview, Chomsky looks back over his life:

> I faced a serious and uncomfortable decision . . . in 1964 – much too late, I think. I was deeply immersed in the work I was doing. It was intellectually exciting, and all sorts of fascinating avenues of research were opening up. Furthermore, I was pretty well settled then into a comfortable academic life, with very satisfying work, security, young kids growing up, everything that one could ask from a personal standpoint. The question I had to face was whether to become actively engaged in protest against the war, that is, engaged beyond signing petitions, sending money, and other peripheral contributions. I knew very well that once I set forth along that path, there would be no end. For better or worse, that is what I decided to do, with considerable reluctance . . . I had to give up many things, personal and professional, that I very much wanted to do, and to take on many obligations that I often found far from pleasant.
>
> On the other hand, there are numerous compensations, even apart from the fact that it is possible to look at oneself

in the mirror without too much shame . . . I met wonderful people whom I would never have come to know, and experienced aspects of life here and abroad that I would never have seen directly. And while I expect that any worthwhile cause will achieve at best very limited success, and will quite probably largely fail, nevertheless there are accomplishments that give much satisfaction, however small they may be in the face of what one would like to see. (CR, 54–5)

For anyone who likewise wants to be able to look at himself or herself in the mirror without too much shame, the intellectual and moral commitment of Noam Chomsky is worth serious consideration.

Notes

Where Chomsky is quoted in the text I give the source immediately after the quote. You will find below the source of significant quotes in the text by other people, and suggestions for further reading.

1 Basics

1 The book by Chomsky's father, William Chomsky, is *Hebrew, the Eternal Language* (Philadelphia: Jewish Publication Society of America, 1958).

2 John Searle, 'Chomsky's revolution in linguistics', in G. Harman (ed.), *On Noam Chomsky* (Amherst, Mass.: University of Massachusetts Press, 1982), pp. 2–33.

3 Good general introductions to linguistics include V. Fromkin and R. Rodman, *An Introduction to Language*, 4th edition (New York: Holt, Rinehart & Winston, 1988) and R. Hudson, *Invitation to Linguistics* (Oxford: Robertson, 1984). A good sample of pre-Chomskyan American linguistics can be found in M. Joos (ed.), *Readings in Linguistics* (Washington, DC: American Council of Learned Societies, 1958).

4 Z. Harris, *Methods in Structural Linguistics* (Chicago: University of Chicago Press, 1951).

5 For the history of science, J. D. Bernal's four-volume *Science in History* (Harmondsworth: Penguin, 1969) is essential reading. A good introduction to the philosophy of science is A. Chalmers, *What Is This Thing Called Science?*, 2nd edition (Milton Keynes: Open University Press, 1982).

6 A good non-technical account of first language acquisition is D. Crystal, *Listen to Your Child: A Parent's Guide to Children's Language* (Harmondsworth: Penguin, 1986). For a more thorough treatment, see A. Elliot, *Child Language* (Cambridge: Cambridge University Press, 1981).

7 'Completely bankrupt': C. Hockett, *The State of the Art* (The Hague: Mouton, 1968), p. 3

8 'Unmitigated nonsense': C. Hockett, *The View from Language* (Atlanta: University of Georgia Press, 1977), p. 255.

9   'An intellectual embarrassment': Y. Wilks, 'Bad metaphors: Chomsky and artificial intelligence', in S. Modgil and C. Modgil (eds), *Noam Chomsky: Consensus and Controversy* (Barcombe: Falmer Press, 1987), pp. 197–206; quote is on p. 205.

10   'Catastrophic': B. Derwing, *Transformational Grammar as a Theory of Language Acquisition* (Cambridge: Cambridge University Press, 1973), p. 42.

11   'An intellectual fraud': B. Gray, 'Now you see it, now you don't: Chomsky's *Reflections*, *Forum Linguisticum*, vol. 2, 1977/78, pp. 65–74.

12   'A rubbish heap': R. A. Hall Jr, Review of F. Newmeyer, *Linguistic Theory in America: the First Quarter Century of Transformational Grammar* (New York: Academic Press, 1980), *Forum Linguisticum*, vol. 6, 1981/82, pp. 177–88. Reprinted in R. A. Hall, *Linguistics and Pseudo-linguistics: Selected Essays 1965–1985* (Amsterdam: John Benjamins, 1987), pp. 103–12. The quote is on p. 112 of the reprint.

13   Even the remark in the *New York Times* about Chomsky being 'arguably the most important intellectual alive' had a sting in its tail. The sentence read: 'arguably the most important intellectual alive, how can he write such nonsense about international affairs and foreign policy?'

2   Achievements

1   Straightforward introductions to grammar are D. Crystal, *Rediscover Grammar* (London: Longman, 1988) and M. Newby, *The Structure of English* (Cambridge: Cambridge University Press, 1987).

2   This chapter simplifies drastically a very complex area. Many of the 'details are open to challenge, as is natural in a living, developing field. In particular, my insistence that an antecedent must *precede* an anaphor, and that movement to the right is impossible, need to be heavily qualified. For a less sketchy account of this area, try G. Horrocks, *Generative Grammar* (London: Longman, 1987), pp. 94–162; for a discussion by Chomsky, see Chapter 3 of KL. An earlier version of some of the material in this chapter appears in my 'Core grammar and periphery', in S. Modgil and C. Modgil (eds), *Noam Chomsky: Consensus and Controversy* (Barcombe: Lewes, Falmer Press, 1987), pp. 109–17.

3   R. Quirk, S. Greenbaum, G. M. Leech and J. Svartvik, *A Comprehensive Grammar of the English Language* (London: Longman, 1985).

4   CGEL does say that 'the basic reflexive pronoun always corefers to the subject of its own clause' (p. 357), a stipulation which would rule out (14), although this is a separate rule from the one which covers (5'). Showing in detail that Chomsky's account is superior would take more space than is available here.

5 Informed readers will notice that a more thorough treatment of example (16) would have *herself* governed by the modal *would*, which instantiates the INFL node. We would then say that the subordinate clause is the governing sentence of *herself*, and that it has no antecedent within this sentence, violating the Binding Principle.

6 On the Structure Preserving Hypothesis, see J. Emonds, *A Transformational Approach to English Syntax* (London: Academic Press, 1976).

7 Japanese anaphors are discussed by D. Sportiche in 'Zibun', *Linguistic Inquiry*, vol. 17, 1986, pp. 369–74. A more general discussion of anaphors in languages other than English is A. Giorgi, 'Toward a theory of long distance anaphors: a GB approach', *The Linguistic Review*, vol. 3, 1983–4, pp. 307–61. For a detailed study of parametric variation, see M. Rita Manzini and K. Wexler, 'Parameters, binding theory and variability', *Linguistic Inquiry*, vol. 18, 1987, pp. 413–44.

8 For a brief summary of work on first language acquisition inspired by Chomsky's ideas, see T. Roeper, 'Grammatical principles of first language acquisition: theory and evidence', in *Cambridge Survey*, vol. 2, pp. 35–52. Solan's research is presented in his *Pronominal Reference, Child Language and the Theory of Grammar* (Dordrecht: D. Reidel, 1983). Hyams's study is *Language Acquisition and the Theory of Parameters* (Dordrecht: D. Reidel, 1986).

3 Costs

1 The terms 'I-language' and 'E-language' are introduced and discussed in Chapter 2 of KL.

2 Instantaneous acquisition: RL, 15 spells out the assumption; RL 119–22 and KL 52–4 are Chomsky's main attempts to defend it.

3 See D. Hymes, 'On communicative competence', in J. Pride and J. Holmes (eds), *Sociolinguistics* (Harmondsworth: Penguin, 1972), pp. 269–93.

4 G. Scheurweghs, *Present Day English Syntax* (London: Longman, 1959), p. 124.

5 D. Gil, 'Reply to Salkie', in Sohan Modgil and Celia Modgil (eds), *Noam Chomsky: Consensus and Controversy* (Barcombe: Lewes, Falmer Press, 1987), pp. 143–5.

6 See *Collins COBUILD English Language Dictionary* (London: Collins, 1987).

7 Any book on generative grammar will explain phrase-structure rules and transformations in much more detail than I have done here. For the shift from systems of rules to systems of principles, see Chapter 3 of KL.

4 Implications

1 Books which illustrate Chomsky's influence in diverse fields are:
  Music Theory: J. Sloboda, *The Musical Mind: the Cognitive Psychology of Music* (Oxford: Clarendon Press, 1985).
  Computer Science: A. V. Aho and J. D. Ullman, *The Theory of Parsing, Translating and Compiling: Vol. 1, Parsing* (Englewood Cliffs, NJ: Prentice-Hall, 1972).
  Literary Criticism: A. Banfield, *Unspeakable Sentences: Narration and Representation in the Language of Fiction* (London: Routledge and Kegan Paul, 1982).

2 Fred D'Agostino, *Chomsky's System of Ideas* (Oxford: Clarendon Press, 1986), p. 11.

3 Similarities between Chomsky and Kant are suggested by Bryan Magee in his interview with Chomsky (see writings by Chomsky below, page 227). An excellent introduction to Kant's philosophy is S. Korner, *Kant* (Harmondsworth: Penguin, 1955).

4 The 'prediction and control' quote from Skinner is on p. 12 of *Verbal Behaviour* (Englewood Cliffs, NJ: Prentice Hall, 1957). The longer quote is on pp. 5–6.

5 J. Fodor, *Modularity of Mind* (Cambridge, Mass.: MIT Press, 1983). Chomsky is not, of course, responsible for Fodor's views.

6 The quote by Caplan is on page 251 of his paper 'The biological basis for language', in *Cambridge Survey*, vol. 3, pp. 237–55.

7 The material in this section is partly based on Suzanne Flynn, 'Second language acquisition and linguistic theory', in *Cambridge Survey*, vol. 2, pp. 53–73 and Ellen Broselow, 'Second language acquisition', in *Cambridge Survey*, vol. 3, pp. 194–209. Flynn's work is presented in full in *A Parameter-Setting Model of L2 Acquisition* (Dordrecht: D. Reidel, 1987). The proposal by O'Neil is in the preface to Flynn's book.

8 Susan Curtiss, 'Abnormal language acquisition and the modularity of language', in *Cambridge Survey*, vol. 2, pp. 96–116.

9 D. Crystal, P. Fletcher and M. Garman, *The Grammatical Analysis of Language Disability* (London: Edward Arnold, 1976).

10 R. Quirk, S. Greenbaum, G. M. Leech and J. Svartvik, *A Grammar of Contemporary English* (London: Longman, 1972). This book has now been superseded by *A Comprehensive Grammar of the English Language* (see Ch. 2, note 3 above).

5 Challenges

1 W. V. Quine, *Word and Object* (Cambridge, Mass.: MIT Press, 1960); 'Methodological reflections on current linguistic theory', in G. Harman (ed.), *On Noam Chomsky*, 2nd edition (Amherst,

Mass.: University of Massachusetts Press, 1982), pp. 104–7 (the quote is on p. 110); and 'Reply to Chomsky', in D. Davidson and J. Hintikka (eds), *Words and Objections: Essays on the Work of W. V. Quine* (Dordrecht: D. Reidel, 1969). A good introduction to Quine's philosophy is C. Hookway, *Quine* (Cambridge: Polity, 1988).

2   S. Kripke, *Wittgenstein on Rules and Private Language* (Oxford: Basil Blackwell, 1982).

3   L. Wittgenstein, *Philosophical Investigations* (Oxford: Basil Blackwell, 1953).

4   For a clear introduction to Wittgenstein's philosophy see D. Pears, *Wittgenstein* (London: Fontana, 1971).

5   C. Hockett, *The State of the Art* (The Hague: Mouton, 1968).

6   T. Moore and C. Carling, *Understanding Language: Towards a Post-Chomskyan Linguistics* (London: Macmillan, 1982).

7   J. Searle, 'Chomsky's revolution in linguistics', in G. Harman (ed.), *On Noam Chomsky* (Amherst, Mass.: University of Massachusetts Press, 1982), pp. 2–33.

8   Newmeyer's argument is on pages 5–6 of his article 'Extensions and implications of linguistic theory: an overview', in *Cambridge Survey*, vol. 2, pp. 1–14.

9   Two books by AI researchers sympathetic to Chomsky's work are M. Marcus, *A Theory of Syntactic Recognition for Natural Language* (Cambridge, Mass.: MIT Press, 1980) and R. Berwick, *The Acquisition of Syntactic Knowledge* (Cambridge, Mass.: MIT Press, 1985).

10 Winograd's views are taken from page 187 of his book *Language as a Cognitive Process. Vol. 1, Syntax* (Reading, Mass.: Addison-Wesley, 1983). A series of articles in the journal *Cognition* debated some of the disagreements between AI researchers and generative grammarians:

   a. B. Dresher and N. Hornstein, 'On some supposed contributions of artificial intelligence to the scientific study of language', vol. 4, 1976, pp. 321–98.

   b. R. Schank and R. Wilensky, 'Response to Dresher and Hornstein', vol. 5, 1977, pp. 133–46.

   c. B. Dresher and N. Hornstein, 'Reply to Schank and Wilensky', vol. 5, 1977, pp. 147–50.

   d. T. Winograd, 'On some contested suppositions of generative linguistics about the scientific study of language', vol. 5, 1977, pp. 151–79.

   e. B. Dresher and N. Hornstein, 'Reply to Winograd', vol. 5, 1977, pp. 377–92.

11 Halvorsen's paper is called 'Computer applications of linguistic theory' and can be found in *Cambridge Survey*, vol. 2, pp. 198–219. The extract is on pp. 201–2.

12 Robinson's criticisms are contained in his book *The New Grammarians' Funeral: A Critique of Noam Chomsky's Linguistics* (Cambridge: Cambridge University Press, 1975).

13 On generative semantics, see Chapters 4 and 5 of Newmeyer's *Linguistic Theory in America*, on which this section is partly based.

14 J. R. Ross, 'On declarative sentences', in R. Jacobs and P. Rosenbaum (eds), *Readings in English Transformational Grammar* (Waltham, Mass.: Ginn, 1970), pp. 222–72.
15 G. Lakoff, 'On generative semantics' in D. Steinberg and L. Jakobovits, *Semantics*, (Cambridge: Cambridge University Press, 1971), pp. 232–96.
16 The Republican insults are discussed in G. Lakoff, 'The role of deduction in grammar', in C. Fillmore and D. T. Langendoen (eds), *Studies in Linguistic Semantics* (New York: Holt, Rinehart & Winston, 1971), pp. 63–72.
17 The fullest account of GPSG is G. Gazdar, E. Klein, G. Pullum and I. Sag, *Generalized Phrase Structure Grammar* (Oxford: Basil Blackwell, 1985). For a brief overview, see Chapter 3 of G. Horrocks, *Generative Grammar*. A short introduction to GPSG by Gerald Gazdar, with comments by Chomsky and a reply by Gazdar, can be found in H. C. Longuet-Higgins, J. Lyons and D. E. Broadbent (eds), *The Psychological Mechanisms of Language* (London: Royal Society and British Academy, 1981), pp. 53–69.

6   The 'Free World'

1 The statistics about American Indians are from Thomas H. Brewer, 'Disease and social class', in M. Brown (ed.), *The Social Responsibility of the Scientist* (New York: Free Press, 1971), pp. 152–3.
2 The attack on the Pennsylvania miners is described in R. Boyer and H. Morais, *Labor's Untold Story* (New York: United Electrical, Radio and Machine Workers of America, 1955), pp. 43–56.
3 Richard Nixon, *No More Vietnams* (London: Comet, 1986), p. 236.
4 The US intelligence officer is quoted in the *New Statesman*, 25 September 1972.
5 Guenter Lewy, *America in Vietnam* (Oxford: Oxford University Press, 1978). The 'intelligent and reasonable' quote is on pp. 440–1; the Phoenix quotes on p. 281.
6 Nixon, op. cit,. p. 167.

7   Outside the 'Free World'

1 Richard Nixon, *No More Vietnams* (London: Comet, 1986), p.16.
2 The discussion of Cuba is highly simplified. For more details see Rius, *Cuba for Beginners* (London: Writers and Readers, 1975) or Hugh Thomas, *Cuba: the Pursuit of Freedom* (New York: Harper and Row, 1971) – a very thorough study.
3 Nixon, op. cit., p. 209.
4 Guenter Lewy, *America in Vietnam* (Oxford: Oxford University Press, 1978), pp. 433–5.

5 Nixon, op. cit., pp. 161–2.
6 This section draws heavily on two books:
   a. Liz Curtiss, *Ireland, the Propaganda War: The British Media and the Battle for Hearts and Minds* (London: Pluto Press, 1984).
   b. *Nothing but the Same Old Story: the Roots of Anti-Irish Racism* (London: Information on Ireland, 1984).
7 *Nothing but the Same Old Story*, p. 96.
8 Curtiss, op. cit., p. 100.
9 *Nothing but the Same Old Story*, p. 79.
10 The book about Northern Ireland aimed at schools is P. Arthur and K. Jeffery, *Northern Ireland since 1968* (Oxford: Basil Blackwell, 1988). The comments on internment are on p. 73.
11 *Nothing but the Same Old Story*, p. 36.
12 Curtiss, op. cit., p. 203.

8 The Way Forward

1 Anarchism is not exactly the same as libertarian socialism: there are anarchists who are not socialists. Chomsky's anarchism is clearly of the socialist variety, however. For a good collection of essays on anarchism see H. Ehrlich, C. Ehrlich, D. De Leon and G. Morris (eds), *Reinventing Anarchy: What are Anarchists Thinking These Days?* (London: Routledge and Kegan Paul, 1979).
2 A book which discusses strategies for social change from a libertarian socialist perspective, and which is endorsed by Chomsky on the back cover as 'a serious contribution to the reconstruction of an effective movement of the left in the United States', is M. Albert, *What Is to Be Undone?* (Boston, Mass.: Porter Sargent, 1974).

9 Connections

1 For a useful discussion of the political implications of empiricism and rationalism see H. Bracken, *Mind and Language: Essays on Descartes and Chomsky* (Dordrecht: Foris, 1984).
2 B. F. Skinner, *Beyond Freedom and Dignity* (Harmondsworth: Penguin, 1973).
3 R. Herrnstein, 'I.Q.', *Atlantic Monthly*, September 1971.
4 Chomsky's review is entitled 'Psychology and ideology' and appears in RS, 104–50.
5 J. D. Bernal, *Science in History*, vol. 1, pp. 47–8, 50.

Guide to Further Reading

Where publication details are not given, they can be found in the list of abbreviations of books by Chomsky at the front of the book.

Works by Chomsky

Chomsky's books and papers on linguistics are often hard for the beginner; like any specialized technical writing, they are not intended as light entertainment but are an attempt to explore difficult problems.

There are three bibliographies of Chomsky's writings: K. Koerner and M. Tajima, with the collaboration of C.P. Otero, *Noam Chomsky: a personal bibliography, 1951–1986* (Amsterdam: J. Benjamins, 1986); S.C. Sgroi, *Noam Chomsky: Bibliographia 1949–1981* (Padova: CLESP, 1983); and L.S. Ramaiah and T.V. Prafulla Chandra, *Noam Chomsky: a bibliography*, (Gurgaon, Haryana: Indian Documentation Service, 1984).

For the reader who wants to get an idea of the main aims and assumptions of Chomsky's linguistics, the best place to start is with transcripts of interviews. There are two complete books of interviews with Chomsky, *Language and Responsibility* (1979) and *The Generative Enterprise* (1982). A shorter interview can be found in Bryan Magee, *Men of Ideas* (Oxford: Oxford University Press, 1982), pp. 173–92).

For a recent summary by Chomsky of his work in linguistics, aimed at a non-specialist audience, the best book is *Language and Problems of Knowledge* (1988). The book contains five lectures which Chomsky gave in Managua in 1986. The style is relatively informal, and Chomsky answers questions from the audience.

Other general surveys by Chomsky of his linguistic ideas are the first chapter of *Aspects of the Theory of Syntax* (1965), *Language and Mind* (1968, enlarged edition 1972), *Reflections on Language* (1975), *Rules and Representations* (1980) and *Knowledge of Language* (1986). *Lectures on Government and Binding* (Dordrecht: Foris, 1981) is the most detailed statement of the main issues in Chomsky's recent work. References in these books will orientate you towards other more technical papers and books by Chomsky.

Chomsky's most extended criticism of descriptive linguistics is *Current Issues in Linguistic Theory* (The Hague: Mouton, 1964; also in J. Fodor and J. Katz [eds], *The Structure of Language* [Englewood Cliffs,

NJ: Prentice-Hall, 1964], pp. 50–118). For a discussion of seventeenth and eighteenth-century work in linguistics and philosophy, see his *Cartesian Linguistics* (New York: Harper & Row, 1966).

This book has concentrated on syntax. Anyone interested in Chomsky's work on phonology should look at Chomsky and Morris Halle, *The Sound Pattern of English* (New York: Harper & Row, 1968). *Studies on Semantics in Generative Grammar* (The Hague: Mouton, 1972) deals with the relation between syntax and semantics.

There are various collections of political writings by Chomsky, all worth reading. The best recent summary of his political views is *On Power and Ideology* (1987); like *Language and Problems of Knowledge*, this book is based on transcripts of lectures in Managua. His first political book *American Power and the New Mandarins* appeared in 1969 at the height of the anti-war movement, and it reflects some of the immediate issues (and passions) of the time. It contains a long and important essay called 'Objectivity and liberal scholarship', as well as other material on the role of intellectuals.

Later books of particular importance include:

For Reasons of State (1973). Includes the review of Skinner's *Beyond Freedom and Dignity*, a paper on anarchism, and a paper called 'Language and freedom' in which Chomsky tries to relate his linguistic and political views.

The Washington Connection and Third World Fascism and *After the Cataclysm* (1979), co-authored with Edward Herman, make up a two-volume work collectively called *The Political Economy of Human Rights*. They are a comprehensive indictment of US foreign policy in many countries of the 'Free World', and the way this policy is represented by intellectuals. *After the Cataclysm* contains a long and important chapter on post-1975 Cambodia.

Towards a New Cold War (1982) includes a crucial essay 'Intellectuals and the state', and other papers on a variety of themes, among them a devastating review of Henry Kissinger's memoirs. *The Fateful Triangle* (1983) looks at US policy in the Middle East, particularly in the light of the Israeli invasion of Lebanon in 1982 and its aftermath. *Turning the Tide* (1985) and *The Culture of Terrorism* (1988) both concentrate mainly on US aggression in Central America, but also survey the political scene in the United States in the Reagan years. *Necessary Illusions* (London: Pluto Press, 1989) concentrates on the role of the media in purveying what we have called the 'official line'.

An earlier book which contains a lecture on linguistics and one on politics is *Problems of Knowledge and Freedom* (1972).

There are two collections of Chomsky's political writings edited by other people. *Radical Priorities*, edited by Carlos Otero, deliberately picks short pieces which are not found in any of Chomsky's other books. Otero is a linguist as well as a political activist, and his introductory essay, 'Introduction to Chomsky's social theory', is worth reading. *The Chomsky Reader*, edited by James Peck, contains a good selection of important papers from the books listed above, as well as a several interesting pieces such as 'The manufacture of consent' and 'Equality: language development, human intelligence, and social organisation' which are not found in other collections of Chomsky's writings, and an interview with Chomsky.

Books about Chomsky

The best-known book is *Noam Chomsky* by John Lyons (2nd edition, London: Fontana, 1978). The book is particularly lucid and approachable, but it is somewhat out of date now and does not try to cover Chomsky's politics.

A more useful up-to-date book is Vivien Cook's *Chomsky's Universal Grammar: an Introduction* (Oxford: Basil Blackwell, 1988). The book goes into the details of recent work in generative grammar in greater detail than I have attempted here, and explores the implications for first language acquisition and second language learning and teaching. Once again there is no attempt to cover Chomsky's politics.

David Lightfoot's *The Language Lottery* (Cambridge, Mass.: MIT Press, 1982) is a good account of the aims of generative grammar by a close colleague of Chomsky's. Another useful book is Neil Smith and Deirdre Wilson's *Modern Linguistics; the Results of Chomsky's Revolution* (Harmondsworth: Penguin, 1979) (but see my review of this book in *Linguistics* [no. 18, 1980, pp. 311–34] for some critical comments).

There are three books of essays on Chomsky's work: Gilbert Harman (ed.), *On Noam Chomsky* (Amherst, Mass.: University of Massachusetts Press, 1982), includes in particular a useful survey essay by John Searle, and an interesting review of Lyons's book by Dell Hymes. Sohan Modgil and Celia Modgil (eds), *Noam Chomsky: Consensus and Controversy* (Barcombe: Lewes, Falmer Press, 1987) covers a wide range of issues arising from Chomsky's work. Most contributions are in 'pairs', one person writing from a position mostly in agreement with Chomsky, and one person writing from a mainly critical standpoint. Alexander George (ed.), *Reflections on Chomsky* (Oxford: Basil Blackwell, 1989), contains essays mainly by philosophers. At the time of writing, Asa Kasher (ed.) *The Chomskyan Turn* (Oxford: Basil Blackwell, 1990) has not yet appeared: it looks as if the book will contain two useful papers by Chomsky and various discussions of his ideas by philosophers.

Fred d'Agostino's *Chomsky's System of Ideas* (Oxford: Clarendon Press, 1986) is a reconstruction of some of Chomsky's assumptions by a philosopher, and is worth reading by anyone interested in the philosophical implications of generative grammar. See however the review of this book by C. P. Otero in *Mind and Language* no. 3, 1988, pp. 306–19.

For extended critiques of Chomsky's linguistics, try any of these: Charles Hockett, *The State of the Art* (The Hague: Mouton, 1967); Ian Robinson, *The New Grammarians' Funeral: A Critique of Noam*

Chomsky's Linguistics (Cambridge: Cambridge University Press, 1975); Peter Matthews, *Generative Grammar and Linguistic Competence* (London: Allen & Unwin, 1979); Terence Moore and Christine Carling, *Understanding Language: Towards a Post-Chomskyan Linguistics* (London: Macmillan, 1982).

Introductions to generative grammar

There are many books on this subject, some of them extremely good.

Andrew Radford, *Transformational Grammar* (Cambridge: Cambridge University Press, 1988) is an approachable textbook based on Chomsky's recent work. For some critical comments see the review by Bob Friedin in *Journal of Linguistics* no. 25, 1989, pp. 509–18.

Geoffrey Horrocks, *Generative Grammar* (London: Longman, 1987), compares Chomsky's work with Generalized Phrase Structure Grammar and Lexical-Functional Grammar.

Frederick Newmeyer, *Linguistic Theory in America*, 2nd edition (London: Academic Press, 1986) is a lively and informative history of generative grammar.

For an excellent collection of essays on generative grammar and related work in linguistics, see Frederick Newmeyer (ed.), *Linguistics: The Cambridge Survey*, 4 vols (Cambridge: Cambridge University Press, 1988) (referred to as *Cambridge Survey*).

Index